Petticoats
in the
Pulpit

The Story of
Early Nineteenth-Century
Methodist Women Preachers
in Upper Canada

Elizabeth Gillan Muir

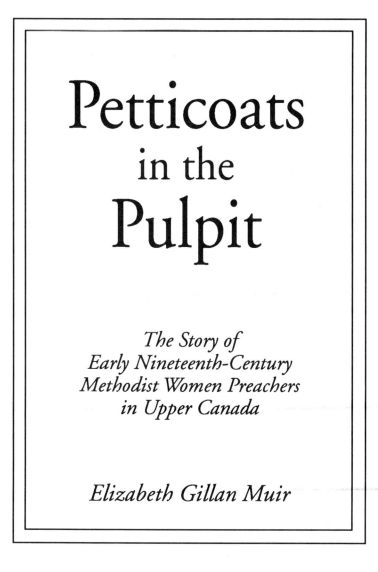

Petticoats
in the
Pulpit

*The Story of
Early Nineteenth-Century
Methodist Women Preachers
in Upper Canada*

Elizabeth Gillan Muir

THE UNITED CHURCH PUBLISHING HOUSE

Canadian Cataloguing in Publication Data

Muir, Elizabeth Gillan
    Petticoats in the Pulpit

Includes bibliographical references and index.
ISNB 0-919000-78-9

1. Methodist Church - Ontario - Clergy - History -
19th century. 2. Women clergy - Ontario - History -
19th century. 3. Methodist Church - Ontario -
History - 19th century. 4. Clergy - Ontario -
History - 19th century. I. Title.

BX8345.7.M85 1991   287'.082 C91-094848-8

The United Church Publishing House
85 St. Clair Avenue East
Toronto, Ont.
M4T 1M8

Publisher: R.L. Naylor
Editor-in-Chief: Peter Gordon White
Editorial Assistant: Elizabeth Phinney
Cover Design: Nina Price
Production: Graphics and Print Production
Printed in Canada by: Gagné Printing Ltd.

5 4 3 2 1 91 92 93 94 95

To Deirdre Kathleen Muir
and
James Gillan Muir

CONTENTS

List of Illustrations

PREFACE

A few years ago, I began a search for Methodist women preachers. Studies in the history of the Christian church led me to believe that in religious movements that were charismatic and placed a major emphasis on the free and generous bestowal of gifts from the Holy Spirit, women often held preaching and other leadership roles. Since Methodism fit this category, this suggested that women might have been preaching in that denomination.

Although at that time little had been written about women preachers, finding Methodist women preaching in Great Britain was not difficult. My research led me to Leslie F. Church's works, which in turn referred me to Zechariah Taft's writings and other early accounts. The earliest histories and biographies were the most rewarding. Recently, however, two excellent studies by Deborah Valenze and Julia Stewart Werner, mainly on British Primitive Methodist women, have been published.

Canadian Methodist women preachers proved much more elusive, but extensive archival research has been productive. As with the British women, the oldest accounts have been the richest sources, although the paucity of Canadian women's autobiographical material that has survived is both disappointing and frustrating.

In the last few years, a number of essays and monographs on American women preachers, particularly in the evangelical tradition, have appeared. Although Methodist women have figured prominently in these accounts and analyses, a singular lack of attention has been paid to the work of Primitive Methodist women.

Perhaps the most interesting question raised by this quest, and one I have attempted to answer, is why Canadian

Methodist women lost so much ground by the second half of the nineteenth century that they had virtually given up preaching, while their American counterparts struggled and won ordination before the turn of the century.

Traditional answers which have been used to explain diminished roles for women in other situations – such as industrialization, the introduction of ordination, the acceptance of the Victorian stereotype of women, and the church-sect typology, which suggests that women often hold major roles in the sect phase of a religious movement and lose these positions in later church development – are inadequate in this instance. These phenomena were common to both countries. It was necessary, therefore, to find another explanation, and I have turned to the different religious and political climates in Canada and the United States to provide the rationale.

The staff at a number of libraries and archives have assisted me in my research. Among these are The United Church of Canada Archives, the Ontario Archives, the McGill University Archives, the John Rylands University Library of Manchester, the City of Brampton Public Library and Art Gallery (Chinguacousy Branch), the Newcastle Public Library Board (Bowmanville Branch Library), the Regional Municipality of Peel Archives, the University of Prince Edward Island Robertson Library, the London Public Libraries, the Peterborough Public Library, the Congregational Library of the American Congregational Association, the United Methodist Church General Commission on Archives and History, and the staff at St. Paul's United Church, Orillia. I am especially grateful, however, to Norma Johnston and Jennifer Wheeler of the Faculty of Religious Studies Library at McGill University for their interest and support and whose assistance has been invaluable in tracking down obscure source material.

Several people have either provided useful information or suggested possible sources. At the risk of omitting men and women who have been helpful, I would like to thank Phyllis Airhart, Edna Barrowclough, Virginia Coleman, Dorothy Graham, Howard Harris, William Lamb, Donald Smith, George Rawlyk, Wendell Sedgwick, Robert Shaw, Deborah Valenze, and Betty Ward. John Moir assisted by editing much of the material in chapter 4, parts of which initially appeared as a chapter in *Canadian Protestant and Catholic Missions, 1820s-1960s*. David Braide helped me enter the computer age, making the writing of this book possible. Countless other friends have encouraged me in this endeavour. Finally, I express my appreciation to Ed Furcha and George Johnston at McGill University, and to my co-worker Marilyn Whiteley, for their careful reading and editorial suggestions. Stylistic errors that remain, however, must be attributed to the author.

I.
INTRODUCTION

*Of late I've been requested in silence for to
keep,
Because I've grieved the Pastor and likewise
his dear sheep;
But if my Savior calls me to speak in his dear
name,
I can't obey the Pastor, although a man of
fame.*

Polly M. Stevens
L.I. Sweet, *The Minister's Wife*, p.107

F rom its eighteenth-century beginning, English
Methodism attracted a large number of women,
and it was not long before they held leadership
positions. Many of them became effective and popular
preachers travelling and preaching throughout England and
Ireland. Convinced that they had been called by the Holy
Spirit, some of them engaged in intentional undisguised
preaching of the gospel from a pulpit or a similar position.
Other women prayed in public, exhorted, and testified.[1] At
the beginning of the nineteenth century, however, the English

and Irish Conferences placed severe restrictions on their preaching activity because "there were enough preachers without them." Still they surfaced and were warmly welcomed by women and men in local areas. Indeed, they did the same work as effectively as male preachers, although even before the legislation in 1802 and 1803 that prohibited their preaching, they had not generally been accorded similar official status. In 1835, the London Conference again expressed its disapproval of women preaching, and eventually women disappeared from the "pulpits" of the British Wesleyan denomination.

Scores of other women kept up the tradition as local and itinerant preachers in Great Britain and beyond, mainly in the more radical Bible Christian and Primitive Methodist movements. Some of these women, often as part of a clergy couple, came to North America where they preached to overflowing congregations, rode circuits through field and forest, and endured the hardships of the new land. In the United States, although they faced opposition and psychological abuse, Methodist women inched their way to ordination well before the turn of the century. In Canada, they met with greater resistance, and by mid-century, many of them had given up preaching.

In her recent study of five upper-middle class British women who emigrated or travelled to Upper Canada in the nineteenth century, the Canadian biographer Marian Fowler traces their development from dependent wives nurtured in the Church of England tradition, to strong, assertive, independent pioneer women:

> *These women had been programmed to be delicate and passive, to cling like sea anemones to their conjugal rocks. On the Canadian*

2

frontier, if they wished to survive, they had to
be brave, aggressive, resourceful. Fragile silk
was gradually replaced by strong canvas.[2]

By contrast, the Methodist women who responded to the early nineteenth-century challenge of the New World as missionary preachers were not "fragile silk," but "strong canvas." Many of them had been raised in poverty and hardship. Convinced that they had been called to preach "the gospel," most of them had learned to be assertive, to overcome obstacles, and to rely on their religious faith for guidance and support. Nevertheless, within a few decades in Canada only a handful of women remained who were preaching in the various Methodist denominations. Uneasy about the propriety of their preaching in the first place, some of the women apparently came to accept the conventional view that women were not suitable for this kind of activity and left the pulpit to their male co-workers. Others succumbed to a variety of pressures to stop preaching. By the late nineteenth century, their "cloth" had taken on a more delicate texture.

There are a number of reasons why this devolution took place in Canada. The increasing urbanization and industrialization of society, the institutionalization of the church, and the professionalization of the ministry were all factors, as was the social pressure placed upon women to fit into a more acceptable mould. These phenomena, however, were common to both Canada and the United States, and do not explain why Canadian Methodist women followed an essentially different path from their American counterparts. Much more decisive for Canadian women was the reactionary political climate in Upper Canada, and the increasing conservatism which permeated Canadian Methodism after the

3

union with the British Wesleyans in 1833. In the late 1820s and early 1830s, the church leaders of the Canadian Methodist Episcopal body deliberately dissociated their denomination from the United States and affiliated themselves with the more traditional and conservative Wesleyan Methodists from Great Britain. As the denomination adopted the more restrictive policies of the British group rather than the progressive attitudes of the United States, women were no longer tolerated as preachers in the largest Methodist body. Women continued to be accepted on the preaching plans of the smaller and more radical Bible Christian and Primitive Methodist Societies for two or three more decades, until these denominations, too, became permeated with Upper Canadian conservatism.

It is difficult to estimate how many women preached in Upper Canada in the early nineteenth century. There is very little material available from the women themselves. Some of Elizabeth Dart Eynon's journals and letters were reproduced in Bible Christian periodicals and newspapers; a snippet remains from Eliza Barnes Case's diary; Elizabeth Peters' account of her family's sea voyage to Canada has been preserved; and Ann Copp Gordon's story was recorded by her daughter. But in the main, the letters, journals, and autobiographies in archival collections are those of husbands who quite often make no mention of their active wives or do so in an anonymous fashion.

Records of early American women preachers are somewhat more plentiful. A few of their diaries and theological reflections have been published, and we can read first hand about the experiences and struggles of preachers such as Jarena Lee, Dorothy Ripley, Phoebe Worrall Palmer, and Margaret Newton Van Cott. Excerpts from both Ann Wearing and Ruth Watkins' journals were reproduced in their denomination's magazine and a letter from Watkins is available. Sections from the William and H.M. Knowles journal are signed by both husband and wife. On the whole, however, both in Canada and in the United States, we have to rely on brief references to these women found in magazine and newspaper accounts, other biographies, church records and early histories, and on archaeological evidence such as tombstones and memorial plaques, and piece together their lives as well as possible.

The problem of reconstructing their activity is compounded by the fact that much of the available material is unreliable. It has been written that "we don't know who discovered water but we're sure it wasn't fish," with the comment that we are all in relation to our own environment "in the same state of unawareness."[3] Methodist histories and early newspapers are riddled with this same contextual blindness. Most Methodist historians have been unaware that women were preaching in both their own and other denominations. Apparently they have been influenced by the proliferation of statements that denied that women were preaching when in fact the evidence quite clearly indicated otherwise. Indeed, recent studies have shown that prescriptions against women preaching are most plentiful during periods in history when women are most active in that arena; and, as is often the case, these prescriptions have later been interpreted as descriptions. Many earlier historians have made the erroneous assumption that the norm for women in their particular epoch of society has always been the norm. As a result, the reality of women's lives was often in direct contradiction to the myths that developed and were recorded as history.

In some instances, the facts have been obscured. Biographies, obituaries, and memorials often acknowledge only part of the women's work, leaving out or playing down any reference to the women's preaching activity. Euphemistic phrases, such as "she was very useful in the work," commonly referred to women (and men) who were active in the work of the church. Sometimes the phrase described women who went beyond the bounds of acceptable behaviour for women in the writers' context, and the "useful" designation was very often used in connection with women who preached. This was true both for women who were contemporaries of the writers and for women who had been preaching at an earlier time.

Not only is it difficult to recover the existence and the work of these women, but it is even harder to discover much about their actual experiences, their feelings, and their expectations, since so much of the information has been refracted through a Methodist hagiography. Accounts often inform us only of their piety and of their enthusiasm in doing the "work of the Lord." Conversely, a negative picture of the women's personalities sometimes emerges, depending on the writers' biases. One historian who believed that John Wesley had been treated badly by Grace Norman described her as "vain, selfish and supercilious" and subject to "hypocondriacal and hysterical fits," whereas in other accounts it is said that she had "quick energy, natural tact, popular usefulness and devotion to the work of God" and was "attractive" and "capable."[4]

Given these limitations in source material, it is important to assess very carefully what has previously been written about women, and to treat much of it with suspicion. In setting contemporary standards for writing about women in history, Gerda Lerner has pointed out that it is not enough simply to reinstate women by slotting them into the gaps where they have been missing in our history. It is also essential, she notes, to reassess our traditional sources in light of other information that has been recovered more recently.[5] For example, in considering Methodist history, it is necessary to re-evaluate the numerous dissenting Methodist denominations such as the Primitive Methodist and Bible Christian movements. Traditionally, these smaller Methodist groups, which were formed in protest against the institutionalization of the parent body, have been treated as less valid expressions of Methodism, as aberrations beyond the fringe of the mainstream church, and have been given little notice in Methodist histories. Yet all these movements are part of Methodist history and may be truer expressions of the ideals of Methodism than what has been considered the principal denomination. In Canada, it is primarily, though not totally, in these protest denominations that women were allowed to exercise their talents in leadership roles.

The following chapters recover the stories of a number of women who were preaching in different Methodist denominations in Canada, examine their religious heritage in Great Britain, compare their experiences with sister preachers in the United States, and explore the reasons for their discontinuance.

Chapter 2 examines the evolution of Methodist women preachers in John Wesley's Britain, tracing their rise and enormous popularity, and illustrating the continual resistance to them. Although there is little new empirical data in this section, an analysis of their British heritage helps explain their appearance in North America and sheds light on their eventual decline in Canada.

Chapters 3, 4, and 5 examine in some detail the work of Canadian women preachers in the Bible Christian, Primitive Methodist, and Methodist Episcopalian churches. At the risk of being repetitious, I have deliberately dealt with each of these denominations separately and at some length for three reasons. First, because much of the resource material is fragmentary, it seemed necessary to include as much evidence as possible in order to indicate the extent of the women's work and the number of women who took part in preaching activity. Most of the information in these chapters is new data and is not available in any other known secondary source material. Second, separating the different traditions in Canada allows comparison with similar traditions in the United States. And third, although there are common elements in the women's stories in the different denominations in Canada, there are also important differences. Whereas many of the Methodist Episcopal women preachers spilled over into Canada from the United States, the majority of the Bible Christian and the Primitive Methodist women emigrated as part of a clergy couple from Great Britain. Most women's preaching activity in the Methodist Episcopal tradition ceased abruptly in 1830, whereas in the other two denominations, women's activity gradually shifted over a few decades from an active itineracy to guest appearances in the pulpit.

Methodist women preachers virtually disappeared in Canada, but in the United States, they eventually achieved licensing and ordination after a lengthy and painful struggle. Chapter 6 tells the stories of many of these American women, indicating both similarities to and differences from their Canadian counterparts. Since there are already a number of excellent studies on American women preachers, I have concentrated on women whose stories have been omitted in most histories, such as the Primitive Methodist women and Dorothy Ripley.

Chapter 7 focuses on Barbara Heck, perhaps the best-known Methodist woman in North America. It is not the purpose of this section to discredit Heck, but rather to show the nineteenth-century paradigm shift in normative behaviour for women in mainstream Methodism in Canada and the United States. The subject is not Heck as much as the evolving understanding and handing down of her story.

There are a number of reasons for the disappearance of women preachers in Canada in the nineteenth century, making a single explanation difficult. Many of the phenomena that affected women's lives were occurring in both Canada and the United States during virtually the same decades. These are explored in chapter 8. In the United States, however, Methodist women achieved significantly more success in gaining leadership status. In an attempt to explain this difference, I have elaborated on the political climate in Canada, and this country's reaction to Methodists and Methodism.

II.

THE EVOLUTION OF WOMEN PREACHERS: THEIR BRITISH HERITAGE

Sir, a woman's preaching is like a dog's walking on his hind legs. It is not done well; but you are surprised to find it done at all.

Boswell, *Life of Dr. Johnson*, 31 July 1763

It should not be surprising that Methodist women preached in Canada in the early nineteenth century. As early as the 1760s, women had been accepted as preachers in the British Methodist movement – a religious movement which began in England in 1739 when John Wesley experienced a profound spiritual conversion. Large numbers of women were attracted to Wesley's first classes, and the doctrines and church organization of the Wesleyan movement soon assured a preaching role for many of them.

Women have usually been more numerous than men in religious revivals, and Methodism was no exception. In 1745, 68 per cent of all of the Methodist Society members who met at the Foundry, the first official worship centre in London, were women – 352 out of a total of 516. This was also the case among the class leaders in the "Select Society" meeting

10

there the year before. Again women accounted for 68 per cent of the total membership, 53 out of 78 members. Describing the Society at Newcastle that same year, William Briggs wrote Wesley that he had had conversations with 36 women and 9 men who had found "freedom from all outward sin" and wanted to be "delivered entirely from sin." The fact that Briggs spoke with four times as many women as men suggests that considerably more women were involved in the Methodist movement there as well.[1]

The burial list at City Road Chapel, the first recognized Methodist headquarters in London, contains the names of 4,452 men and women buried there between 1780 and 1858. Of these, 62 per cent were women. Five per cent of all the members on the burial list lived to be over 80 years old. Seventy-eight per cent of these were women, as were the only 2 people who lived to be 100 years old.[2]

Evidence suggests that the situation was similar in the United States and in Canada. In New York City, at least 35 of the 250 original subscribers for the first John Street Preaching House were women, surely a large number of financial donors for 1786. Recent analyses of the Second Great Awakening in the early nineteenth century in New York State indicate that between 52 and 72 per cent of all the converts at that time were women. John McKillicam, a Sunday school agent, noted in his *Annual Report* of 1862 that in most places, religion was left entirely to women. His meetings were made up almost entirely of married women and a few young girls, he wrote, while the men sat outside "waiting to *escort* the young females home."[3]

Although women are predominant in revivalistic movements, other factors attracted women to Methodism. Wesley's social assistance programmes, directed mainly towards women, were advanced for his time. In the 1740s, he organized a medical dispensary for the poor, provided housing for a limited number of women, and opened schools for orphans. He created employment opportunities for unemployed women, hiring them to knit woolen goods; the final products were delivered to the poor. These opportunities would have been especially appealing to women facing poverty and the desperate conditions of industrialized England. As well, Wesley demanded exacting moral standards of all his class members; this would have helped make women's lives more bearable. In 1743, he expelled one-eighth of all the members in his fledgling Society for violations of his strict behavioural code, including idleness and wife-beating.[4]

Large numbers of women in Methodism in its early days, however, would not in itself ensure a preaching role for them. But this factor, coupled with Methodist polity and doctrine, resulted in scores of women assuming public leadership positions. Very quickly these leadership opportunities evolved into preaching roles.

At the heart of the organization of the Methodist church was the small class meeting and the even smaller band. Wesley had seized upon the idea of the class meeting in 1742 as a result of trying to discharge a Society debt in Bristol. He had asked his helpers to visit a number of followers and collect a penny from each person. But on finding how negligent some of the men and women were in their spiritual devotions and moral behaviour, he resolved to make the visitation a weekly exercise. This proved to be too time-consuming for his assistants and, determined to bring the people to the visitors, he set up small classes at regular meeting times and places. The arrangement was similar to the small group model used by the Moravians, a denomination Wesley greatly admired. Although the small class meetings became an opportunity for fellowship, initially they were designed as a vehicle to check up on the morality and spiritual progress of the men and women. Each class had approximately six or seven members with a designated leader. Smaller groups called bands, of no more than four people, were organized for prayer and spiritual growth.[5]

In this system the main element that worked in women's favour was the restriction of classes to either men or women, especially at the beginning of the Methodist movement. Wesley was convinced that segregation of the sexes – another custom he adopted from the Moravians – had been the practice in the early church. Thus, we find large numbers of women immediately thrust into positions of leadership as leaders of women's classes. In April 1742, there were forty-seven women who were class leaders at the Foundry, compared with only nineteen men.[6]

Men and women were separated not only in classes but at church services as well, although later records indicate resistance to this seating arrangement. In 1770, the Methodist *Minutes* recorded the question: Is there any exception to the rule, "Let the men and women sit apart"? The answer was that in those galleries where they had already been sitting together, men and women could continue to do so. Everywhere else, the rule had to be observed. Ten years later, still trying to enforce this policy, the Conference asked an additional question: "But how can we secure their sitting apart?" In 1786, firm direction was given to societies to segregate sexes during public worship or risk losing the privilege of being able to collect money for new buildings.[7]

Wesley had initiated the policy of segregation, but he favoured flexibility. Classes were not always segregated. In a letter to "Miss B.," he asked if she would be willing to lead a small class at Bath where there had been a Society for thirty years. There were about thirty Methodists there, and half of them at least would meet with Joseph Harris. But, wrote Wesley, "I had rather that the single women in both Classes who desire it, should meet with you."[8]

Later Canadian and American Societies adopted segregation, but whether or not the classes were mixed was often dictated by circumstances and leadership availability. The Canadian *Book of Doctrines and Discipline of the Wesleyan Methodist Church* of 1836 included the rule of segregation in church but not in classes, and early classes were often made up of men and women. The original Stanstead, Quebec class of 1803 consisted of a male leader, four women, and four other men. The rule book stipulated, however, that bands must consist only of men or women, and more specifically, only of single or married people.[9]

Although class segregation was not always enforced or adhered to in the early Methodist movement, it provided not only an opportunity for women to assume leadership roles, but an obligation to do so. Idleness, Wesley pointed out, was a sin. All Methodists, and especially preachers, were required to be diligent, never to be unemployed and never to be "triflingly employed." Talents, Wesley stressed, had been given by God to be used. "I fear you are too idle," he wrote Elizabeth Bennis (1725-1802) in 1773. "Up and be doing!" he challenged. "Do not loiter. See that your talent rust not." The next year, he wrote again with a similar rebuke:

> *You are not sent to Waterford to be useless. Stir up the gift of God which is in you; gather together those that have been scattered abroad, and make up a band, if not a class or two . . .*

He repeated this message to Miss Furly in 1776:

> *Now use all the ability which God giveth, and*
> *he will give more: unto him that hath shall be*
> *given . . . it is the hand of the diligent that*
> *maketh rich.*

By this time, Wesley was encouraging women beyond the sphere of groups confined to women. In replying to one of Miss Furly's questions, he agreed that she could certainly "meet with" a class of men if the leader and the class both wished it. This, he explained, would not assume authority over men but would be an act of "friendship and brotherly love." In leading the group, he continued, she would be acting not as a superior, but as an equal.[10]

Talented women were encouraged to become class leaders, and as class leaders they developed their talents further. They took part in leaders' meetings, becoming skilled in interpersonal relationships and public speaking. Many would have gained a great deal of self-confidence. For most, it was an opportunity not open to them in other aspects of their lives. The early Methodists were from the lower economic strata, many of them unemployed. In 1772, one-third of Wesley's followers were without jobs. However, as the majority of the women's classes were scheduled for the evening, it is likely that most of the women worked outside the home during the day. Probably they were poorly paid. Almost half the women in the first classes were unmarried without family responsibilities, compared to less than one-third of the men. Many of the women in the Society were young, and a number of them began preaching in their late teens.[11]

From class leader, it was a small step for the women to

become preachers. Sometimes the classes were so large that they unwittingly found themselves in the role of public speaker or preacher. Sometimes their talents and spiritual gifts were so obvious that the people pressed them to speak, often because no other preacher was available.

Wesley, however, only gradually accepted women as preachers. The women themselves, partly because of cultural conditioning and partly from a genuine humility, hesitated to assume this role. Their correspondence with Wesley reveals their dilemma. In 1761, he answered Sarah Crosby's questions about whether or not she should speak in public by telling her that she had not overstepped the bounds of propriety. He advised her to tell the people of her difficulty, that Methodists did not allow women preachers, and that she did not wish to become one. Read them notes or sermons, he advised, and just tell them what is in your heart "as other women have done long ago." Eight years later, in 1769, he wrote to her with more advice, pointing out that he had already given this same advice to Grace Walton. First of all, he said, she should pray in public or private as much as she could. Second, she could mix prayers and exhortations, but she should keep away from preaching as much as possible. Never take a text, he advised, and never speak "in continued discourse" without four- or five-minute breaks. In fact, he said somewhat cunningly, tell them you will have other "prayer meetings" at different times and places.[12]

By 1771, however, he had sanctioned her to preach. On June 13, Wesley wrote to Crosby from Londonderry affirming that she had an extraordinary call to preach, as indeed had all his lay preachers. Methodism, he noted, was "an extraordinary dispensation" from God, and extraordinary things were bound to happen within it. He believed that Crosby was an effective preacher; he mentioned her "usefulness" in "exciting believers to go on to perfection" in a later letter to Jane Barton.[13]

In 1787, Wesley "and the Conference" authorized Sarah Mallet Boyce (b.ca.1764) to preach. She was already officially recognized as a preacher on the Norwich Circuit. Two years later, Wesley wrote to give her advice on how to speak effectively. By this time there was no suggestion that the service be disguised as a prayer meeting. He recommended that she limit her worship service to an hour, including singing, prayer, and preaching. "Never scream," he wrote, "never speak above the natural pitch of your voice." He encouraged another woman, Ann Gilbert (d.1790), to "do all the good" she could, and she preached to crowds of up to fourteen hundred people even when she was almost blind. He referred to Elizabeth Reeve's preaching in 1790. She continued to preach until ill health forced her to stop. A bookseller, Miss Newman, refused to stock novels, plays, and romances after she converted to Methodism. Wesley encouraged her to preach and later approved of her marriage to Jonathan Cousins. Alice Cambridge, who was preaching in Ireland, was given Wesley's blessing in 1791. In January of that year, he wrote to her that when God commanded her to speak, she was not permitted to be silent. "If you want books, or anything," he offered, "let me know; I have your happiness much at heart."[14]

Diaries, letters, and journals reveal the remarkable careers of some of the women who were preaching and speaking in the latter part of the eighteenth and early nineteenth centuries. The records of other women are probably lost forever.

Mary Bosanquet Fletcher (1739-1815), Sarah Crosby (1729-1804), and Alice Cambridge (1762-1829) are among the best known. Fletcher often had male ministers in her congregations, and at times, crowds of up to three thousand men and women. She shared a ministry with her husband, John, after they were married in 1781. In one typical year's work, Crosby walked or rode 960 miles, spoke at 220 public meetings, led six hundred classes and bands, wrote many long letters, gave interviews, and visited the sick. Most days of the week, she rose at four in the morning, conducted a service at five, and often held others in the afternoons and evenings. "I hope you will always have your time much filled up," Wesley had written to her in 1777, "for is not the harvest plenteous still?" Cambridge did most of her work in Ireland, preaching even to soldiers in barracks where her message reduced them to tears. Crowds flocked to hear her, and Methodist chapels, Presbyterian meeting-houses and even an Episcopal church were opened for her meetings. Cambridge had broken her engagement to an "unbeliever" in order to devote herself entirely to her itineracy.[15]

Elizabeth Tomlinson Evans (1776-1849) stayed up until two or three in the morning mending lace in order to earn enough money to travel as an itinerant. She is memorialized in George Eliot's novel *Adam Bede* as Dinah Morris. Mary Barritt Taft (1772-1851) travelled more than most of her contemporaries, and wherever she spoke, conversions took place and often revivals broke out. She preached in barns, town halls, dye-houses, and malt-kilns. Taft even attended Conference meetings when they were held in Leeds or Manchester, and one Conference meeting requested that she preach at it. Mary Sewell (ca.1764-1786) from Thurlton was officially listed as a local preacher on the Norwich Circuit in 1785. She began preaching when she was twenty years old, but died after two years of very intense activity. Elizabeth Ritchie Mortimer (1788-1835) had so many appointments that she could barely keep up with her work.[16]

Most of the women preached because they could not help it. At the heart of Methodist doctrine was the experiential knowledge of the forgiveness of sin. When women and men felt the removal of their burden of guilt, sin, and fear, they were filled with a happiness and joy that could not be contained and had to be shared. In the *Dairyman's Daughter*, when Elizabeth Wallbridge was converted, she immediately sped the "good news of Christ's forgiveness" to her elderly parents and the rest of her family and friends. Wallbridge's letters and the story of her life were published at the turn of the century as a pattern for Methodist women to follow.[17]

Indeed, every Methodist was an evangelist in this sense. In 1776, Wesley wrote Elizabeth Bennis (1725-1802) that if God had given her this "light," she must not hide it under a bushel. "It is good to conceal the secrets of a King," he wrote, "but it is good to tell the loving-kindness of the Lord." Everyone, Wesley said, should declare what God had done for them. According to Leonard Sweet, conversion was a "vocational decision." It put women to work for the Kingdom.[18]

Many of the women preachers had outstanding gifts and received much popular acclaim. Indeed, it was not unusual for members of their audiences to judge women preachers superior to male preachers in speaking skills. Those women approved by Wesley had to meet the three Methodist tests for people who thought they had been "moved by the Holy Ghost and called of God to preach." Their theology was "correct," they had obvious talents, and their lives indicated that they had been "well and truly converted."[19]

Many of the women showed organizational ability. Selina Shirley Hastings, the Countess of Huntingdon (1707-1791), prominent in the Calvinist branch of Methodism under George Whitefield, has been called the first "Methodist bishop." Critics named her "Pope Joan." She built chapels, appointed preachers to their circuits, and expelled those who were unfaithful. She established a theological college to train "her" preachers. Hannah Ball (1733-1792) started a Sunday school at High Wycombe in 1769, eleven years before Robert Raikes began his experiment, although it is Raikes who is generally credited with beginning the Sunday school movement in England.[20]

Grace Norman Murray Bennet (1718-1803), a woman Wesley at one time hoped to marry, became one of his chief administrators. In 1743, she was appointed matron of the Orphan-House, the Methodist Centre in Newcastle-upon-Tyne. An extremely talented and spiritual woman, Bennet was soon leading classes and bands. At one time, she held two separate classes for at least one hundred Methodists, and led a different band every day of the week. She visited several Societies in the neighbouring countryside, meeting with the women in the daytime and the whole Society at night, and it was not long before Wesley put her in charge of all of the women's classes throughout England and Ireland. Bennet generally travelled on horseback, often alone. She allowed no man to assist her into the saddle and had trained her horse to kneel down when she touched its shoulder. A colourful figure, Bennet would spring "lightly into the saddle," wave her arm, and speed off so quickly on a journey that "in a moment," she "was out of sight."[21]

Many of these women were well-educated and literate. Wesley required all Methodists to be as well read as possible. Tutored at home by his mother Susanna Annesley (1669-1742), a writer of theological dissertations and expositions, Wesley had developed a keen appetite for learning. He not only encouraged his followers to study constantly, but he placed resources at their disposal. He established Book Rooms where books could be purchased inexpensively; he edited volumes of what he considered to be the best literature and made them readily available. His mother had insisted that girls be taught to read well, before they learned housekeeping skills, and Wesley encouraged women to be as proficient in academic subjects as men. He suggested a reading list for "Miss L.," recommending that she study for about four or five hours a day. The list included books on grammar, arithmetic, geography, logic, ethics, natural philosophy, history, metaphysics, poetry, and divinity. That course of study, he noted, should take her from three to five years, depending on her health and previous education. He set high standards for his preachers, expecting them to read works by Sallust, Caesar, Cicero, Castellio, Terence, Virgil, Horace, Vida, Buchanan, Plato, Epictetus, Ignatius, Homer, Arndt, Boehme, Pascal, and other authors. Wesley insisted that Methodist followers keep diaries; Frances Mortimer Pawson wrote four volumes of hers in flawless French. As Methodism developed, rules required that itinerants and missionaries submit regular reports and journals. Canadian preachers were expected to read at least five hours out of every twenty-four, submitting a list of books they had read every quarter.[22]

In spite of this emphasis on education, however, literate Methodist women could evoke disbelief. George Stevenson described the activities of a Ladies Working Society that met at the City Road Chapel in the early nineteenth century. He was amazed that as they sewed they read essays and held discussions that they recorded, and he was even more in awe that their conversation showed "mature judgement, intellectuality and deep spirituality." Quite clearly, Wesley's educational expectations for women were considerably greater than was usual for well-bred English women at the time. Even young ladies who were given intensive education at home by their parents – such as Elizabeth Gwillim, later the wife of Canada's Governor General John Graves Simcoe – spent far less time on academic subjects. Designed by her father, Gwillim's curriculum consisted of English literature, a little geography, very little arithmetic, and a "smattering" of languages. At least half her time was spent on "accomplishments," such as painting, music, sewing, and deportment. The popular "courtesy books," which women read avidly, recommended "diffidence in voicing an opinion," a "tongue, often silent, and ears, always attentive." Bashfulness was much more highly prized than academic knowledge.[23]

Increasing Opposition

The women who preached received a wide measure of popular acceptance, but as they developed an enthusiastic following, they faced increasing opposition from some of the male preachers and the church administration. All Methodist preachers were subjected to hostility and harassment from many segments of British society, simply for being Methodist. Women, then, faced opposition on two fronts, and it was more than some could withstand. For example, Elizabeth Hurrel had been encouraged by Wesley to travel and preach, and it was her preaching which converted the first Methodist missionary to the West Indies. But in the face of increasing resistance, she gave up her "work," although it is reported that "she repented before her death." The Methodist preacher William Bramwell explained in a sermon that there were not more women preachers because they were "not faithful to their call." Mary Bosanquet Fletcher announced meetings rather than preaching services because she felt that it was less ostentatious and gave her opponents less cause for offence. "I do nothing but what Mr. John Wesley approves," she added, "and as to reproach thrown by some on me, what have I to do with it, but quietly go forward saying, *I will be still more vile*, if my God requires it?"[24]

In 1789, Wesley wrote Sarah Mallet Boyce that he was happy that opposition to her preaching was dying down. Two years later, he advised Alice Cambridge to give as little offence as possible. Never speak close to where a male preacher was preaching, he suggested to her, "lest you draw away his hearers." Ann Cutler (1759-1794), or "Praying Nanny" as she was affectionately known, did not preach formal sermons, but often spoke simply to people of God, sin, and salvation. She was responsible for a number of revivals, and the Society approved her work. Yet she offended some by the "loudness of her voice." Male preachers confessed to being extremely jealous of her success. "Wherever she went there was an amazing power of God attending her prayers," wrote the revivalist William Bramwell in a short account of her work. "This was a very great trial to many of us," he admitted, "to see the Lord make use of such simple means, and our usefulness comparatively but small."[25]

Mary Barritt Taft began speaking before she was seventeen years old, and she was so well received by the people that she drained a neighbouring chapel eight miles away of its members. "It is at the peril of your soul that you meddle with Mary Barritt," one male minister was told by another Methodist. "God is with her – fruit is appearing wherever she goes." She received invitations from far and wide to preach but concentrated her ministry among local families. In 1802 when she was thirty years old, she married the Methodist preacher Zechariah Taft, and that year they worked together in the Dover Circuit as a clergy couple. Barrit attracted such crowds that the Connexion chairman ordered her to stop preaching, but she continued with Taft's support. Her refusal precipitated a nation-wide controversy that resulted in an almost total ban on women preaching.[26]

In July 1802, the Methodist Irish Conference, meeting in Dublin, concluded that it was contrary to both scripture and "prudence" for women to preach or exhort in public. Moreover, any woman who did so was to be immediately expelled from the Society. The London Conference followed suit the next year. Although this Conference did not categorically prohibit women from preaching, legislation made it so complicated that it was virtually impossible for women to obtain official approval. A vast number of people were opposed to women preaching, the Conference noted, and since the Methodists had an ample supply of male preachers who had been "accredited by God," women preachers were unnecessary. If a woman felt that she had an "*extraordinary*" call, then she could speak to her "*own sex,*" the *Minutes* recorded, but only under two conditions. First, in order to preach in the circuit where she resided, she must obtain the approval of the superintendent and of a quarterly meeting. Second, in order to preach in another circuit area, she must receive a "*written*" invitation from that superintendent as well as a note from the superintendent in her own circuit.[27]

Still women continued to preach. By the end of 1803, Mary Bosanquet Fletcher wrote that her breath was short and she confined herself to her own "preaching room." Yet people came there from "near and far," and she led as many as six or seven different meetings a week. In 1804, Elizabeth Tonkin Collett (b.1762) was preaching at a chapel her husband had built at St. Erme. Diana Thomas (b.1750) was authorized in 1809 by the quarterly meeting and by her superintendent to preach around Lyonshall. Elizabeth Tomlinson Evans (1776-1849) preached with her husband Samuel – often in the open air – and kept on until her death. She had encountered a great deal of prejudice against her preaching until she married and her husband opened the way for her. Later, they both withdrew in protest from the Connexion for a time because her name was listed on the circuit with an asterisk instead of her name. Mary Dunnel was offered a pulpit on the Tunstall Circuit in 1807 to keep her from speaking at a camp-meeting. Sarah Mallet Boyce and her husband were still on the preachers' plan in York in 1825. Mary Woodhouse (b.1751) and her husband, George Holder, worked together as itinerants for thirty years. Generally, she exhorted after her husband preached. In his book on women preachers, Zechariah Taft described the careers of a number of them who were still preaching in the 1820s, including his wife, Mary Barritt, who continued her ministry into the 1840s. In fact, he noted, of the eleven new preachers who were received at the Conference in Leeds in 1824, two of them had been converted as a result of women preaching. Taft continued to be an outspoken supporter of women, even calling their opponents "bigots." Whether or not this helped their cause, it is largely through his writings that the activity of many of these women has been preserved.[28]

Alice Cambridge was expelled from the Society in Ireland because she continued to preach. The American preacher Lorenzo Dow was appalled that she had been "turned out" of the Society for no other reason than "because in conscience she could not desist from holding public meetings." Indeed, her great work could not be ignored, and in 1811, the Conference decided to readmit her. She continued to preach until 1830 in every county in Ireland, speaking to crowds of up to one thousand men and women. In some areas, she was given the responsibility of being the only preacher. Ann Lutton began preaching in Ireland before 1802 and was still travelling around the country in 1838. She came from a "good" family and attracted aristocracy to her meetings. Her listeners included both Roman Catholics and Protestants. Apparently she spoke "officially" only to women. A historian writing in the 1820s described Lutton as a "pious, modest, diffident young woman" who spoke only to "her own sex." At one gathering in Tullamore, however, the women sat inside a meeting hall, while the men listened from the outside. The doorkeeper deliberately left the door open so the men could hear.[29]

Most of the women preachers were received enthusiastically by the ordinary men and women who made up the Methodist Societies. In fact, the legislation designed to stop the women's preaching activity barely passed because of popular support for them. Yet official Methodist publications deliberately omitted most references to the women's preaching. The editor of the *Methodist Magazine* refused to print an account of the life of the popular preacher Elizabeth Tonkin Collett, even though it had been written by a male minister and submitted by her son Richard. The editor returned it saying that it might set a "precedent to young females in the Connexion." Her career had been remarkable. The mother of eleven children, eight of whom survived her, she preached regularly with the support of her husband. During her ministry at Roseland, seven societies were founded and seven chapels were built. She set up classes and led at least one revival.[30]

Accounts of the lives of other women were published, yet references to their preaching were omitted. Diana Thomas, who was officially authorized to preach in 1809, travelled thousands of miles on a white pony in Wales and England as an itinerant. Yet in the published memorial to her, no mention is made of this work. Mary Barritt Taft was memorialized at her death with six sentences in the 1851 *Methodist Magazine*, leaving out all reference to her outstanding sixty-two-year career in ministry.[31]

In 1835, the Wesleyan London Conference reiterated its stand on disallowing women to preach, evidently not "for its own sake" but because of certain "concomitants." However, there is no explanation of these special circumstances. The Conference also specified that only male class leaders could attend special circuit meetings. Gradually women either ceased their work or joined other emerging Methodist denominations that were much more liberal and open to women serving as itinerant and local preachers. Martha Williams (b.ca.1790) had travelled throughout England since 1819, but in about 1825, discouraged by the opposition, she and Ann Carr (1783-1841) formed an Independent Methodist Society where they employed local preachers and built two large chapels. Carr had been preaching before the 1803 prohibition with a style peculiarly her own. It is reported that she pointed a finger at each "sinner," one by one, with "excellent results." Carr stood solidly against her opposition. "If God be for me," she is reported to have said, "no matter who is against me . . . It is better to obey God rather than man." Mary Dunnel was soon refused the right to preach in Tunstall and elsewhere, and she became an itinerant for a new Methodist protest movement – the Primitive Methodists. By the mid-nineteenth century, mainstream Wesleyan women were channelling their talents and energies into fundraising activities such as the four-day Orphan-House Wesleyan School's Bazaar, which took thirteen months to plan, was staffed by ninety-six women, and produced a profit of over $7,000.[32]

Table 1 – Methodist Men and Women Buried at City Road Chapel, London, England, 1780-1858

Year of death	Male	Female	Total
1780-1800	14	38 (73%)	52
1801-1820	32	52 (62%)	84
1821-1840	33	48 (59%)	81
1841-1858	23	31 (57%)	54

The percentage of women in the Wesleyan Societies decreased, partly because other Methodist movements were more accepting of women in leadership roles and therefore had more appeal. By the 1840s and 1850s, of those members buried at City Road Chapel, only slightly more than half were women, compared to almost three-quarters in the two decades before the turn of the century. (See Table 1)[33]

The number of women who were class leaders also declined. By 1870 at the City Road Chapel, 34 of the class leaders were male, and only 11 were female. This was not only because there were fewer women, but also because the classes were no longer segregated. Men led 29 mixed classes, 3 all-male classes and 2 all-female classes. Women led only 9 all-female classes and 2 mixed classes.[34]

Biographers and historians either rarely referred to the women's preaching activity or named it differently. Mary Bosanquet Fletcher's journals record that she was preaching from at least 1773 until 1811. Even at the age of seventy-one, she held five meetings a week. Yet the biographer Henry Moore described her preaching as a "daily and hourly conversation." Indeed, he emphasized, she never "meddled with church government nor usurped authority over the man."

Even writers who recognized the contributions women had made were reticent to acknowledge the fact that they had been preachers. Gabriel Disosway wrote in 1861 that Fletcher held "public meetings" and "taught." Abel Stevens explained that John Wesley considered the women not as preachers but as deaconesses and prophetesses, and he referred to Fletcher as a "public speaker." Matthew Simpson's *Cyclopedia* records that she "exercised her talents in publishing salvation in the name of Christ," and describes her in unflattering terms as being small and short, having "protruding eyes" and a "masculine" voice and manner.[35]

There are several reasons for this lack of official recognition. With few exceptions, preaching women had not been part of the Church of England tradition. Wesley's mother had conducted worship services for her family and for at least up to two hundred neighbours. Zechariah Taft was aware of a Mrs. Stevens who was connected to the Church of England and who preached in her own chapel. But these were unusual occurrences. Many nonconformist or dissenting groups relied heavily on the skills of women members. For example, scores of Quaker women were speaking and travelling throughout Great Britain and around the world at that time. But as a Church of England clergyman, Wesley was insistent that Methodism was not a dissenting sect but a spiritual emphasis within the established church. He looked upon the movement not as something new but as a revitalization of an existing denomination.[36]

Yet the Methodist movement did encourage a break with tradition. Conversion, a turning away from the past, was central to its doctrines, and this focus helped make it acceptable in the beginning for women to assume non-traditional roles. The format of the early spontaneous Methodist meetings also turned the tradition upside down. The open air rather than church buildings was the *locus* for worship, and meetings took place at unaccustomed hours. However, as Methodism shifted from a radical group or sect within a church to a church in its own right and developed regular places of worship and more formalized structures, traditional roles for women were re-emphasized. The subversion of the tradition had had a tenuous hold on the denomination.

Since the beginning of the Christian church, charismatic sects such as the Methodist movement have generally evolved into institutionalized denominations following a predictable pattern. As second generation church members are born into the tradition, less emphasis is placed on conversion. The membership of the church broadens and increases, and expediency demands administrative structures, rules, regulations, and consistency of doctrine. Traditionally, ministry becomes more ordered, regulated, and professional. In addition to relying on selection by the Holy Spirit, candidates for ministry are assessed on the basis of education and other tests. The movement becomes a church, it loses its separate identity, and it conforms more closely to its cultural context. The behaviour and dress codes of society, including acceptable roles for women, are adopted as the norm for the denomination.[37]

After Wesley's death in 1791, three factors hastened the inevitable process of the development from a Wesleyan Methodist sect to a church: the insistent demands of the Methodist membership for an autonomous church; the prevailing social and political upheaval in Great Britain; and the ultra-conservatism of Jabez Bunting, the dominant Methodist leader in the early nineteenth century, who was secretary of the Wesleyan Missionary Society for eighteen years, four-time president of Conference, and president of the Wesleyan Theological Institution for twenty-four years. While he was in control, he used his influence to discourage all the "Liberal and Radical elements" in the Society.[38]

The nineteenth century was a time of flux. Society was changing everywhere, although the most concrete and dramatic examples of the destruction of the existing order in the late eighteenth century were the French and American Revolutions. Rebellion was in the air. Thomas Paine's radical book *The Rights of Man* (1791-1792) shook the British establishment, but it reflected the desire for democracy that was "creeping over" a number of countries. Women became vocal, demanded their rights, and insisted on equality. Deploring the status of women, the English educationalist Mary Wollstonecroft cried out for justice in her *Vindication of the Rights of Women* in 1792. Horace Walpole called her a "hyena in petticoats." Mary Hays argued against marriage and in favour of women's sexual freedom in an *Appeal to the Men of Great Britain in Behalf of Women*, and later, in 1803, she compiled a six-volume biography of outstanding women. Mary Radcliffe repeated the challenge in *An Attempt to Recover the Rights of Women From Male Usurpation* in 1799. The Bluestockings, the first literary society in London, encouraged this kind of radical thinking and publication. Across the Channel in France, Olympe de Gouges insisted on greater freedom in her *Declaration of the Rights of Women*.[39]

Dissension was rife within the Methodist ranks. Society members agitated to receive communion in their own chapels instead of only at Church of England worship services. Lay leaders resented what appeared to them as heavy-handed control by some of the more prominent Methodist leaders. Faced with rebellious and sometimes defiant members, Methodist leaders responded with restraining and conservative legislation. Much of British society reacted negatively towards the Methodist followers, and Methodist reactionary policies were in part a response to counteract these negative attitudes.[40]

Ever since John Wesley and George Whitefield had been forced to preach out of doors because Church of England churches were closed to them, Methodists had been harassed. They were subject to taunts, ridicule, some physical violence, and press-gangs. Their services were interrupted by mobs of ruffians with musical instruments, noise-makers, cowbells or other irritating distractions. Preachers were sometimes run out of town. No doubt such treatment was in part a human response to the "other," as well as a defensive reaction on the part of lukewarm church members to the critical statements made by the very presence of more enthusiastic Methodist worshippers. Insisting that their meetings were a legitimate part of Church of England worship, however, Wesley had refused to register his chapels as dissenting meeting places under the Toleration Act. Had he done so, the early Methodists would have been afforded some measure of protection from this kind of abuse.[41]

After Wesley's death, the persecution Methodists faced was less physically violent, but more intimidating to their leaders. Members of the British Parliament feared that the tide of republicanism and democracy that threatened to swamp the English nation had some relationship to the enthusiastic "fanatical" Methodists. Rumours circulated that there would be reprisals in the form of legislation restricting freedom of worship. Pamphlets insinuating Methodist disloyalty were common. The fact that Methodists championed the poor and desired to dissociate themselves from the established church was for many people enough proof of the Society's treasonable intent. In an effort to be politically and socially acceptable, Methodist leaders delivered sermons and wrote articles for official periodicals affirming Wesleyan loyalty to the crown and advising their members to stay clear of reformers. It was a preview of what would take place in Canadian Methodism a few decades later under the leadership of two itinerants, Egerton and John Ryerson. Guided by right-wing leaders such as Jabez Bunting and Thomas Coke, the Irish and English Conferences enacted reactionary legislation which resulted in four major secessions between 1796 and 1815 and a number of other minor conflicts. The Independent Methodists were formed in 1796, the Methodist New Connexion in 1797, the Primitive Methodists in 1811, and the Bible Christians in 1815.[42]

In 1796, Conference introduced legislation forbidding itinerants to publish articles or books without the sanction of a book committee. Four years later, Conference resolved that all meetings were to be conducted with a strict adherence to order and regularity. In 1802, additional rules required preachers to undergo a public examination as to their suitability. That same year, and in 1803, legislation was enacted that attempted to stop women from preaching. In the latter year, as well, permission was required in order to hold "love-feasts" and band meetings. Four years later, Conference prohibited camp-meetings and allowed only accredited preachers in Wesleyan pulpits. By 1818, Wesleyan ministers were using the title of "Reverend," a custom sanctioned by Conference in 1821. In 1836 ordination took place by laying on of hands. Decision-making in the church was shifted almost totally away from the laity to the ordained ministers. Lay readers lost their function. Jabez Bunting explained to Egerton Ryerson in 1840 that it was

> *very well for men to spend their strength in preaching and let others [laymen] read the prayers, when Methodism was only a Society*

> *supplementary to the Church; but having in*
> *the order of Providence grown up into an*
> *independent and separate Church, the preach-*
> *ers were something more than mere preachers*
> *of the Word – they were ministers of the Church,*
> *and ought to read as well as preach.*[43]

Spontaneity was rapidly erased from the heart of Wesleyan Methodism, and brakes were applied to liberalism in order to create a more respectable denomination. This respectability did not include women in the pulpit. "The aristocratic world," wrote Edward Lytton Bulwer in 1833, "does not like either clergymen, or women, to make too much noise."[44]

In 1831, the Canadian itinerant George Ryerson wrote to his brother Egerton that he feared the Wesleyan Conference in England was "an obstacle to the extension of civil and religious liberty." George Ryerson had been sent to England by a group of liberal-minded Canadian citizens to lay their case before the British Parliament. He had time to observe the Methodist church in England and despaired of what he found. The Church had become too "legalized," he wrote. "Every act is a legislative act, even on so trifling a subject as whether a certain chapel shall have an organ." Even the Irish delegates to the British Conference were too "churchified," he noted, and all the clergy were "too well provided for" to consider a posting to a country such as Canada. Many of the preachers' sons were being educated for the Church of England ministry, and a number of the Methodist members who had become wealthy had left the Methodists to join the Established Church. Ryerson sought the reason that the Methodists had not increased in members in the previous year, but the Society was unwilling to discuss this topic with him. He did discover, however, that they were "enormously in debt" because of new chapels. The worship services had become exceedingly formal, he wrote, and the whole morning service of the Church of England was being read in most of the Methodist chapels with as much formality as in the parent body. George Ryerson criticized the Wesleyans' "exalted opinion of themselves," their politics, and "their servile reverence for great men and great names." He went as far as to say that what Alexander Pope had said of "Churchmen" could be literally applied to Wesleyans: "Is he a Churchman, then he's fond of *power*." Family business took George Ryerson to England again the next spring and in another letter home to his brother Egerton, he described the "sneering contempt" with which some of the Wesleyans spoke of the American Methodist Episcopal ordination and the Canadian Methodist *Christian Guardian*. "They have no friendly feeling or designs towards Canadian Methodism," he wrote.[45]

In the same year, the *Wesleyan Protestant Methodist Magazine* published an article on education for women, describing the "reigning mode of education" as the worst curse of the age. It was producing women with "accomplishments," the writer complained, rather than preparing women for the station in society which "Providence" had destined them to occupy – that of wives, mothers, and mistresses of families. Frustrated that Methodist women were still not safely ensconced in the home, in 1835 the Conference again prohibited women from preaching. In the Conference *Minutes* of that year, the list of those who could attend "Special Circuit Meetings, if one shall be convened," included travelling preachers, circuit-stewards, stewards, local preachers, trustees of the Chapel, and specifically mentioned male class-leaders. It was evidently assumed that all the other functions except leading classes would be done only by men.[46]

Although a number of women did manage to continue

preaching in Wesleyan Methodist chapels and on circuits, many of them turned to newly formed secession groups such as the Primitive Methodists and Bible Christians.

The Primitive Methodists

In 1811, the first Primitive Methodist Society tickets were issued in Tunstall to two hundred men and women who gathered to support Hugh Bourne and William Clowes, both expelled from the Wesleyan Methodist Church for holding camp-meetings. The two men had been encouraged in this venture by Lorenzo Dow, the eccentric American itinerant who had just returned from Canada and the United States much impressed by the frontier tent meetings he had witnessed there. Not that Bourne had needed coaching. He had already taken a radical stand in 1808 when he published a defence of women preaching. He had listed the women Jesus Christ had authorized "to preach," including the Old Testament women Miriam and Deborah, and in the New Testament, the Virgin Mary and Mary Magdalene. Bourne's mother had been influential in forming his attitude towards women and their abilities. She had taught him and all her family to read. In 1810, Hugh Bourne, his brother, and an unidentified woman preached at Standly in Staffordshire, resulting in the formation of a small society, later identified as the beginning of the Primitive Methodist denomination.[47]

In 1815, the popular Sarah Kirkland Harrison Bembridge (1794-1880) became the first woman itinerant with this denomination. Two years earlier, when she was nineteen years old, she had been put on the preachers' plan in Derbyshire. Her first convert had been a gypsy, and afterwards whenever she was preaching close by, he acted as a "herald" announcing her presence. Now in 1815, Hugh Bourne paid her salary out of his own pocket to allow her to travel in the Primitive Methodist ministry. Five years later, one-fifth of all the preachers were women, 30 out of 150. Lorenzo Dow, apparently biased in favour of women preachers, recorded in his journal that he had heard one of them and was extremely "satisfied." "She stopped when she had done," he wrote, "whereas a great many men, instead of stopping when they have got through, must spin it out and add to it or have a repetition over and over again."[48]

In her detailed analysis of lower class women preachers in England, Deborah Valenze notes that she found records of more than 200 women preaching in the first half of the century, a great majority of them affiliated with the Primitive Methodist movement. The *Minutes* of Conference in 1832 officially listed at least 13 women preachers. There were likely others, but initials were sometimes used in place of first names, and it is impossible to determine the sex of all the preachers.[49]

Other men in addition to Hugh Bourne and Lorenzo Dow supported women as preachers and argued publicly in their favour. The editor of the *Primitive Methodist Magazine*, an official denominational publication, pointed out in 1821 that the early Christian church had set a precedent for women to preach. He explained that a number of biblical passages referred to women "prophesying," and in his opinion, prophesying included "public prayer, preaching, exhortation, and speaking experience." In another article in the same issue, the biblical scholar Dr. A. Clarke came to the same conclusion, pointing out that many people "have spent much useless labour" trying to prove that women in the New Testament did not preach. But in spite of such backing, the Primitive Methodist women were not granted equal privileges in the preachers' meetings. The *Minutes* in 1824 of the circuit quarterday meeting, a gathering of leaders, stewards, delegates, "and such other persons as the meeting may judge proper," passed a resolution that "none of our females speak or vote unless specially called upon."[50]

The women preachers were listed on official preaching schedules, although some women refused to wait for official sanction. In 1824, three Primitive Methodist men – a travelling preacher, a local preacher, and a steward – published a disclaimer in the denomination's journal. They referred to a woman whom they did not name, but they noted that this woman was "neither a preacher nor a member of our society" and added that they did not authorize her to take preaching appointments at Hull.[51]

Carroll Smith-Rosenberg claims that radical revivalistic sects have the greatest appeal to the socially marginalized, such as adolescents. And indeed the Primitive Methodist women were young, a number of them hardly strong enough to travel around the country as itinerants. Lucy Collison (1813-1834) was a local preacher at Lynn and Snettisham. Unfortunately, she got wet going to one of her appointments and died from a cold and scarlet fever at the age of twenty-one. Hannah Williams had been married for only ten months when she died in 1834, and her husband took over her appointments afterwards. An examination of twenty-eight women who were preaching in the southwest of England between 1827 and 1841 indicates that their median age was nineteen and a half. They were also poor. Over half of another group of one hundred women had been servants or farm labourers living in poverty. Preachers' salaries did not go far in alleviating this situation. In 1820, a woman was paid £8 a year, whereas an unmarried man could earn £15 and a married man up to £37 14s.[52]

One of these preachers, Elizabeth Smith Russell (1805-

1836), had been first a dressmaker and then a household servant before she became a Primitive Methodist itinerant. A good speaker, self-possessed and determined, she attracted crowds wherever she went. At the Conference in 1830, the Brinkworth Circuit reported that Russell was "attentive to discipline; a general family visiter [sic]; very peaceable; her preaching generally acceptable; not addicted to long preaching; preaches a full, free and present salvation; is successful in the conversion of sinners; her general conduct good"; and added that "she has been useful here." At her death at the age of thirty-one, her husband, Thomas, also an itinerant, found a list of thirteen stations that had asked her to come and preach. He estimated that nearly two thousand men and women attended her funeral.[53]

A zealous evangelist, Russell felt compelled to travel and preach throughout England in order to bring salvation to the unconverted. Methodist preachers often expressed their emotions in poetry, and she was no exception. In 1837, she explained her motivation in "The Missionary's Prayer":

> But here our zeal cannot be ended,
> While parts of England desert lie;
> O, let thy arm be downward bended!
> Lord, send to Berks [Berkshire] a rich supply.
> For Hampshire we as suppliants bow,
> Our humble cries besiege thy throne;
> Thy Spirit pour, O, pour it now,
> Answer our anguish'd earnest groan.[54]

Like most of the committed preachers, Elizabeth and Thomas Russell endured extreme hardship for their cause. Their circuits were large and travelling was done on foot. Their custom was to walk through a village singing a hymn and then take a "Ranter stand" to address the people who had collected. One morning when Elizabeth felt so ill she could not eat, her husband offered to fill her evening appointment for her. The appointment was twenty-five miles away. The next year, while she was preaching at Mitcheldever and Winchester, a young man "maliciously strung up a lot of dead rats." After ripping them open, he hung them in a row on a long stick and dangled them before her face. She closed her eyes and kept on with her sermon.[55]

Sometimes the women's presence disarmed their opponents. When Thomas preached at Ramsbury, about twenty young men sang "wicked" songs during his sermon, and men and boys rang hand bells, sheep bells, and horse bells, blew horns, and shouted. Russell warned his wife, who was scheduled to preach next, but she insisted on filling her appointment. Her followers were waiting for the mob with their own arsenal of "stones, eggs and other missiles" in their pockets. But when the ringleader came and found a woman preaching, he crept foolishly away with his gang.[56]

The Primitive Methodist preachers had a large following. In the two decades between 1821 and 1841, it has been estimated that membership increased phenomenally from 16,394 to 75,969 men and women. They built chapels; their publications increased. Gradually, the same institutionalization that had helped foster a conservative Wesleyan church took shape among Primitive Methodism as it shifted from a "cottage" religion to a mainstream denomination. In 1842, Hugh Bourne and William Clowes retired, and with new leadership, a new organization was put into place. The centralized denomination moved its headquarters from "an obscure hamlet" to London in 1843. "Rev." was used extensively as a title for male ministers by 1840, and by 1851, a three-year plan of study had been set up for probationary preachers to read while they were itinerating. By the 1860s, newspapers and magazines contained few biographies of women preachers. Whereas strong-willed independent women had preached confidently in the beginning of the movement, towards the end of the century, not only was it unusual to find a woman preaching, but it was noted that women had even stopped praying in public.[57]

Bible Christians

As in the Primitive Methodist Society, the Bible Christian movement afforded opportunities in the early nineteenth century for women who believed that they had been called to preach. William O'Bryan, the Bible Christian leader, had been convinced after a trial period that women should be included on the preaching plan.

A Wesleyan Methodist lay supply preacher, O'Bryan had sought and been denied full preaching status because he was a married man. The Wesleyan London Conference had decided in 1791 that it was too costly to maintain married men as preachers, and it had ruled that only those married men who produced a signed statement that they had ample financial resources would be accepted on a plan. If men could not support their own families and preach as well, they would have to remain single. Believing that he had received a divine call, however, O'Bryan threw himself into the preaching assignments he had been given as lay supply. He even added extra places where he found there was no preacher or where preaching had been abandoned. Some Sundays he walked thirty or forty miles, preaching three or four times. The Church did not applaud this enthusiasm and independence and instead censured O'Bryan for not adhering to a plan. Because he refused to stop preaching where he felt he was needed, he was formally excluded from the Wesleyan Church, and on October 9, 1815, O'Bryan, his wife, Catherine, and twenty other women and men gathered together in a farm house at Shebbear in Devon to form a new Society. Elizabeth Dart, who later played a prominent role in the Society's work in Canada, was among this first group of Bible Christians.[58]

Another founding member, shopkeeper Johanna Neale Brooks, had felt compelled to speak out during a worship service but had gone to church three times before she was able to summon up enough courage to stand up in public. After she was finished, her husband and a parish officer forced her to leave, even though the congregation followed her outside and pressed her to continue. O'Bryan admitted that when he first heard her, her speaking was "not what is commonly called preaching." But Brooks joined the new Society, and under O'Bryan's tutelage, learned to preach. O'Bryan's wife, Catherine, and Mary Thorne, both married women with families, were preaching by 1816. He had chosen his wife because of her speaking abilities, and she had been assisting him since 1803 when they were married. All of the women preachers proved to be so effective that by 1819 they had received official sanction. At the first Conference held that year, fourteen women out of a total of twenty-nine were listed as itinerants: Elizabeth Dart, Betsey Reed, Elizabeth Gay, Ann Mason, Patience Bickle, Margaret Adams, Susan Furze, Mary Ann Soper, Ann Cory, Catherine Reed, Elizabeth Trick, Grace Mason, Sarah Cory, and Sarah Baulch. At least two of these women – Elizabeth Dart and Elizabeth Trick – later emigrated to Canada. One of the youngest to begin as an itinerant, Patience Bickle had been only fourteen years old when she started working for the Society. Like the Primitive Methodist women preachers, many of the Bible

Christian women were in their teens when they first felt the call to preach. William and Catherine O'Bryan's daughter Mary began speaking in public at age eleven.[59]

The women preached and travelled in spite of ill health, gruelling conditions, and opposition in the communities where they were sent to open new societies. One year, Elizabeth Dart travelled on a twenty-mile circuit, preached three times on Sunday, and usually every evening except Saturday. Sometimes she felt that itinerating was "foolishness," but she believed that her spiritual life would be "imperilled if she refused to testify." She began teaching school during the week to earn extra money but had to give it up because she found it too exhausting. In Cornwall, she was told that the crowds who flocked to hear her only came because she was a woman, and once their curiosity was satisfied, she would have no congregation. "But, blessed be the Lord," she exclaimed, "I found it otherwise." When she arrived at the house where she was to preach in Tavistock, the people were afraid to let her come in because some "great man" had threatened them with punishment if they did. So Dart preached in the doorway. Another man told her that all preaching women should be burnt, she recorded in her journal, but a few days after his "abuse" of her, she heard that his house had been burnt. She preached to a large congregation in Callington where the male local preacher was afraid of the mob. But she spoke out without fear, believing that her audience was "hungering and thirsting after truth." There was "much opposition in some places," she wrote, but she was determined "to cry aloud and spare not."[60]

At the first Conference, the question was raised as to whether or not women should be allowed to preach. There was opposition, with both the opponents and supporters quoting biblical passages to sustain their arguments. Finally the Conference decided that God could enable women as well as men to "speak to edification, and exhortation, and comfort." "The Lord" had already used women "to turn many to righteousness," the Conference pointed out, asking "What but this is the end of all preaching?" Indeed, the Conference delegates decided, it would be "insolent" to "dictate" whom God should use to preach. That year, the preaching plan listed at least one man and one woman in every circuit, except in one instance where a woman, Elizabeth Gay, was the only preacher.[61]

The women did have some restrictions not placed on men. Women were "directed to change preaching places under the direction of the General Superintendent." Men had greater freedom. Dart noted the discrimination in her journal but accepted it. Other women were less compliant. For example, Ann Mason Freeman (1791-1826), chafed under all human authority. In 1819, on her own initiative, she sent an unofficial letter to all those who had attended Conference, urging them to stand fast against Satan. That same year, she only reluctantly agreed to follow the assignments given her, believing that they were not divinely inspired. But she eventually did comply, noting that it was not her own will but only in "obedience to the elders." Catherine O'Bryan expressed her unhappiness with the male domination in a poem entitled "The Female Preachers' Plea":

> . . . By sweet experience now I know,
> That those who knock shall enter in;
> God doth his gifts and grace bestow,
> On Women too, as well as men . . .
>
> The sacred fire doth burn within
> The breasts of either sex the same;

44

The holy soul that's freed from sin,
Desires that all may catch the flame.

This only is the moving cause,
Induc'd us women to proclaim,
"The Lamb of God." For whose applause,
We bear contempt – and suffer pain.

If we had fear'd the frowns of men,
Or thought their observations just,
Long since we had believ'd it vain,
And hid our talent in the dust.

Knowing our labours have been blest,
(However plain our words have been,)
We are determin'd not to rest;
But strive to save poor souls from sin . . .

While men with eloquence and fame,
The silver trumpet manly blow,
A plainer trump we humbly claim,
The saving power of God to show . . .[62]

At the second Annual Meeting, women faced further restrictions. It was decided that if the "sisters" were unable to travel "through indisposition of body," they would receive the same financial support as when they travelled. The women, however, had to "maintain a becoming character" and either remain single or be married to a travelling preacher in order to receive this support. No similar rule existed for men.[63]

In spite of opposition, the women were popular, and drew large crowds. At St. Ervan, where Betsey Reed came to take Elizabeth Dart's place because of the latter's ill health, several hundred gathered in the open air, and at times "her hearers" were too numerous to be counted. After Sarah Willis Stevens (b.1770) and Ann Mason preached indoors and in the streets in Brighton, they received excellent reviews in the *Herald*. One of the women, it was reported, spoke fluently in "correct language" with animation, and her doctrines were compared to those of the Wesleyan denomination. The other woman, the newspaper account noted, had "respectable" connections. Willis and her husband had been Wesleyan preachers, travelling together extensively before her husband's death in 1813. Reed astonished a doctor in her audience who concluded that "she must have been inspired by God."[64]

The little Society expanded rapidly. Mary Ann Werrey (1801-1825) was sent to the Scilly Islands, the first missionary from the new Missionary Society formed in 1821. Multitudes flocked to hear her, sometimes two to three thousand at one meeting. The Conference had insisted that preachers take care of their health, but often there was no accommodation and little food. By 1824, Werrey had worn herself out, and she died the next year. Mary Toms was stopped by a constable from preaching outside a friend's house on the Isle of Wight in 1823, but before a month was up, two more women had been sent out to help her because the converts were so numerous. In 1824, there were 68 itinerant preachers, 47 men and 21 women. In addition, the Society recognized approximately 80 female and numerous male local preachers. In his history of the Bible Christian movement, Frederick W. Bourne refers by name to 42 women who were engaged in a preaching ministry throughout England and Wales. The Conference *Minutes* list 60 women who itinerated for the denomination between 1819 and 1851.[65]

Women continued to be an important part of the Bible Christians' activity, but as the number of travelling preachers increased, the ratio of women to men decreased. In 1827, there were 62 male itinerants and only 27 female. Eleven years later, out of 95, only 11 were women. In less than twenty years, the percentage of women had dropped from 48 per cent in 1819, to 13 per cent in 1838. Even by 1832, such resistance had developed that O'Bryan felt compelled to publish a vindication of women preaching in the *Arminian Magazine*. He described how useful women had been in converting sinners. Answering scriptural objections, he suggested that it was totally inconsistent to allow women to pray, sing, and prophesy and not to preach. Nevertheless, by 1844, at the same time that the itinerant Ann Vickery Robins was experiencing hostility in Upper Canada, there were only 7 women itinerants, but 111 men. And by the end of that decade, the women had virtually disappeared as itinerants.[66]

As in the other Methodist denominations, the salary scale was discriminatory, but that was not unusual for this period in history. In 1837, a single man received from £10 to £14 a year with board and lodging. A single woman earned £7 along with room and board. Married men were given a bonus in order to try to keep their wives preaching: £30, a furnished house, and allowances for each child. Conference had recommended in 1820 that if preachers were to marry, they should choose "wives" from among those women who devoted themselves "wholly to the work." A number of women did itinerate while they were raising their families. Ann Vickery Robins often carried her youngest child to church, handing it to a member of the congregation to care for while she preached.[67]

Like the Primitive Methodist denomination, the Bible Christians evolved into a more regular denomination. By

1830, the denomination was in such financial difficulty that it had to ask its preachers to take a cut in salary. Because of this measure, some of the itinerants emigrated to America; others simply left the Society. Preachers became less rigid in their adherence to discipline, and in 1832, the fourteenth Annual Conference chastised its male preachers for wearing double-breasted coats – "a departure from our former simplicity." The process of institutionalization can also be seen in the changing emphasis in the Society's annual reports. Lists of funds appeared – the book fund, the chapel fund, the preachers' fund, and the children's fund – as the denomination became more established. The number of itinerant preachers and missionaries gradually decreased as the number of teachers and grammar schools increased. In 1851, there were only 65 itinerant preachers, but 2,814 teachers. The number of women preachers continued to decline and by 1853, only one woman itinerant remained on the list of preachers, and she had no posting. Most of the Bible Christian women stopped preaching and fit more closely into the norm expected by mainstream society, nurturers closely confined to the hearth and home. But before this happened, women such as Ann Vickery Robins and Elizabeth Dart Eynon had emigrated to Canada with their husbands, becoming clergy couples in North America.[68]

Elizabeth Ritchie Mortimer (1788-1835), Wesleyan Methodist preacher in England. (Photo: John Rylands University Library of Manchester.)

The Countess of Huntingdon (1707-1791), called the first "Methodist bishop." (Photo: John Rylands University Library of Manchester.)

Mary Barritt Taft (1772-1851), Wesleyan Methodist preacher in England. (Photo: John Rylands University Library of Manchester.)

Grace Norman Murray Bennet (1718-1803) organized the women's classes in Great Britain. (Photo: John Rylands University Library of Manchester.)

PRIMITIVE METHODIST PREACHERS' PLAN.
For the HOME BRANCH of HULL CIRCUIT.—1827.

PLACES AND HOURS.	APRIL.			MAY.			JUNE.			JULY.		PREACHERS.
	15	22	29	6	13	20	27	3	10	17 24	1 8	W. CLOWES, Supernumerary
Mill Street 10½—6	2	3	4	1	2	3	4	1	2	3 4	1 2	1 William Suddards
Mill Street 3		5	13	20	13	23	6	1	12	9 20	21 22	2 Thomas Bletcher
Mill Street 7	18	12	10	21	9	20	5	22	23	6 13	24 21	3 William Dent
Church Street 6	18	12	10	21	9	20	5	22	23	6 13	24 21	4 Mary Burks
Beverley 10½—2		13	1	10	31	9	20	12	4	5	1 20 3	5 Henry Bentley
Beverley 6		2	1	4	3	2	2	4	4	2	1 4 3	6 George Gill
Sutton Bank 2		23		12		18		13		21	33	7 Mary Thornham
Sutton 6	20	33	22	12	10	18	9	13	24	21 22	33 5	8 Benjamin Dorsey
Hessle 6	12	24	5	6	33	17	20	9	18	13 10	23 31	9 William Weston
Cottingham 2	22	2	3	4	32	2	10	4	13	2	5 4 10	10 Thomas Newsom
Cottingham 6	32	20	3	9	32	5	10	24	13	18	3 12 10	11 John Coates
Woodmancy 6	10		60		5		13		22		24 12	12 William Malton
Willerby 6		32		24		22		23		10	6	13 John Wallis & W.L.
Swanland 6		17		13		24		8		33	32	14 Thomas Greasley
Elloughton 10	*	4	28	3	15	1c	26	2	17	4	8 3 7	15 John Smith
South Cave 2	*	4	28		15	1c	26	2	17	4	8 3 7	16 John Lidget
North Cave 6	28	4c	26	31	17	1	28	2	*	4 26	3 15	17 William Anson
Ellerker 10—Brantingham 2	7		*		8		17	28		15	17	18 Robert Wood
Newbald 2	28	15	26	11	17	*	28	7	32	15 26	* 11	19 James Scholefield
Halton 1½		1		25		1c		16		1	27	20 Marmaduke Hirst
Goxhill 6	1	6	2	30	1c	27	3	25	1	20	2 16 4	21 Richard Rispin
Barrow 2	1	6	2	30	4c	12	3	25	1	20	2 16 4	22 J. Lockwood
Barton 10½	1	6	2	2	4c	12	26	3	1	20	2 2 4	23 Elizabeth Jackson
Barton 6	19	1	18	16	25	1	22	27	16	1	19 25 29	24 John Dennison
Ferriby 1½	25	27	18	2	19	16	22	3	16	25	19 2 29	25 Enoch Bell
Ferriby 6				2c				3			2	26 Job Gibson
												* Hannah Johnson
Mill Street..........M	4		3		2		4		4		1	**ON TRIAL.**
Ferriby.............T	4		3c		3T		4		4		1	27 W. A.
Brantingham.......W	4		3c		3T		4		4		1	**EXHORTERS.**
South Cave .... Th	4		3		3T		4		4		1	28 Thomas Pawson
Ellerker.............F	4		3c		3c		4		3		1	29 John Smith
Newbald ....M	4		1c		1c		2		4		3	30 Joseph Faulding
Elloughton ....T	4		3T		1		2		4		3	31 William Slater
Swanland ....W	4		3c		1		2		4		3	32 Charles Ellerington
Hessle ....Th	4		3T		1		2		4		3	33 —K.
Beverley ....T	2		4		1		2		4		3	L. Lovefeast
Sutton ....Th	2		4		1T		1		2		4	C. Collection
Mill Street ....F	2		4		1		2		4		3	T. Tickets
Woodmancy.........M	2		1T		3		1		2		4	The Preparatory Meeting for the Home Branch to be at Hull, on Friday, June 1st, to commence at 6 o'Clock.
Sutton Bank ......Th	2		1T		3		1		2		4	
Barton Water Side ....F	2		1		3		1		2		4	
Goxhill ....M	1		2		1T		3		1		2	The Preachers Meeting to be at Hull, on Tuesday, June 5th, to commence at 9 o'Clock in the Morning, and the Quarter Board at One o'Clock on the same day.
Halton ....T	1		2		1T		3		1		2	
Barrow.............W	1		2		1T		3		1		2	
Ferriby............Th	1		2		1T		3		1		2	
Barton ....F	1		2		1T		3		1		2	☞ Every Preacher is expected to attend his own Appointments, or get them supplied by those whose names are on the Plan—if that be found impracticable, he is requested to give proper Notice to the Committee by the preceding Thursday that they may get them properly attended to.
Cottingham..........T		1	2T		4		3		1		2	
Pottery ....Th		1	2T		4		3		1		2	
Mill Street ....F		1	2		4		3		1		2	
Cottingham..........T	3		1		2T		4		3		2	
Willerby ....W	3		1		2T		4		3		2	
Hessle ....Th	3		1		2T		4		3		2	
Mill Street ....M	3		1		2		4		3		1	
Beverley...........T	3		1c		2		4		3		1	
Tickton ....W	3		1T		2		4		3		1	
Church Street ....Th	3		1		2		4		3		1	

☞ A Home Missionary Meeting will be held in Mill-Street Chapel, Hull, on the Evening of Tuesday the 5th of June; Service to commence at Six o'clock—Also, on the preceding Sunday Evening, a Preparatory Sermon will be preached in the same place by J. NELSON, from Bridlington.

Stations of the Preachers.

Hull.	Driffield.	Scarbro'.	J. Holliday	Redruth.
W. Suddards	T. Webb	R. Woodall	West Gate.	J. Garner
T. Bletcher	J. Oxtoby	W. Sanders	W. Turner	W. Driffield
W. Dent	J. Thompson	Whitehaven.	T. Morris	B. Stranger
M. Birks	Bridlington.	W. Summersides	T. Greaves	St. Austill
Keyingham.	J. Nelson	W. Thackray	Alston Moor.	J. Hewson
W. Brinning	J. Hirst	Barnard Castle.	J. Flesher	W. Teal
S. Priestman	M. Allen	T. Ford	D. Beattie	Plymouth.
		T. Holliday	J. Leakley	R. Abey

Primitive Methodist Preachers' Plan from the Hull Circuit, England, 1827, lists four women preachers. (Photo: The United Church of Canada/Victoria University Archives, Toronto.)

III.
PARTNERS IN MINISTRY:
BIBLE CHRISTIAN WOMEN IN CANADA

*Why do so many men laugh at and ridicule
the idea of women having a voice in the man-
agement of the affairs of her country? Because
laughter and ridicule are the strongest arguments they can bring against it.*

Observer, 16 January 1884

In 1883, on the eve of the union of the Bible Christian
Church with the other Canadian Methodists, the denominational newspaper began a series of articles, "De-
layed But Not Forgotten," excerpts from the diary of Elizabeth Dart. It was an attempt on the part of the editor to
recover the contribution women had made in the Bible
Christian Church – a part of its history that was all but
forgotten. Dart had been the first itinerant for the Bible
Christian Church when it began in 1815 as a protest movement against an increasingly conservative and institutionalized Methodist Church in Great Britain. In fact, some considered her to be the best missionary the Bible Christians ever
had.

The editor apologized for the delay in recognizing her work – first in England and later in Canada. This active yet delicate woman had died twenty-six years earlier, worn out from serving her God, her societies and congregations, walking and riding through the summer heat and the snows of winter, enduring the taunts of men and the rotten eggs thrown by mobs. The editor noted with dismay that, in the late nineteenth century, women's "place" was no longer on the circuit, but at home in front of the hearth, guarding the spiritual values of the nation. "It is often said that woman shapes the destiny of man," he continued. "Perhaps feminine influence in this respect is overestimated." In spite of the accepted thinking at that time, "research and observation" had not convinced him that the mother's influence in the home was "so much more potent" than that of the father. Was not the church guilty of perpetuating the idea that women should be only at home, he asked, by publishing excellent accounts of its male preachers, but none about the "heroic and devout women" who had suffered and accomplished so much in earlier days?[1]

The *Observer* editor was not the only Bible Christian to comment publicly on that denomination's failure to include women's history in official church records. In his account of the Canadian Conference at London, Ontario in 1865, William Hooper reported that the President apologized for leaving the notes for his key address, the Jubilee Sermon, in his study at Charlotte Town [sic]. According to Hooper, the speaker introduced a number of illustrations of church leaders from the beginning of the Christian church up to late nineteenth-century Bible Christians, but he omitted any mention of all of the women "who figured so prominently, and were rendered of God so extensively useful." No doubt, Hooper quipped, "the women were in the papers left behind."[2]

One of the most prominent of these women had been Elizabeth Dart Eynon (1792-1857), an itinerant preacher in Great Britain for almost twenty years, and an itinerant and class leader in Upper Canada for at least thirty. She and her husband, John, were one of the first Methodist ministerial couples to arrive in North America.

In his detailed analysis of ministers' wives from the sixteenth to the nineteenth centuries, Leonard Sweet suggests four stereotypes based on the work these women were allowed and encouraged to do: the companion – a ministering supportive angel; the sacrificer – who asked little and stayed out of the way; the assistant – who shared many pastoral responsibilities; and the partner – who ministered alongside her husband. It is the latter model, the partner, which best describes Dart's activity and that of the numerous other Bible Christian ministerial wives who preached in England and Wales and later in Canada. In Sweet's study, most of the "partner" wives he describes were encouraged to become full partners only after their marriage. Almost without exception, however, the Bible Christian women were undertaking full ministries before their marriages and were enthusiastically encouraged by their husbands to continue afterwards.[3]

Like the early Methodist preachers in England, the women who preached in Canada were motivated by an intense missionary zeal and an inner compulsion to witness to their faith, in spite of hardships and physical handicaps. Dart had never been physically strong. Often when she preached, her body was "racked with pain." But she was prepared to die if she had to, in the course of carrying out her ministry. "My health, or even life itself," she wrote, "did not seem too much of a sacrifice to give for the salvation of souls." Like the other women preachers, she believed she had been called by God and could not disobey. She thought of herself as a soldier whose Captain demanded perfect obedience. Yet sometimes she was tempted to leave the "work" because she felt that there were others who could do it so much better and she might get in their way. At such times, her belief in Christ strengthened her, and she remembered that God had given her talents for her work and obligated her to develop these talents even further. When the doctor ordered her husband, John, to bed for several months in Upper Canada in 1839, she attempted, at forty-seven years of age, to supply his congregations as well as carry on with her own work. "No doubt the rigor of our climate, with the toils and exposures of pioneer missionary life, had the effect of hastening the collapse of her delicate physique," the *Observer* editor wrote in his testimonial to her. But even with recurring illness, including asthma for the last twenty years of her life, she had a lengthy ministry. There are records of her leadership in Canadian churches when she was sixty-two years old.[4]

Born in 1792 into a farming family in the parish of Marhamchurch in Cornwall, England, Dart was given superficial religious training in the Church of England. Her parents were church members, and although she considered them to be "moral in their habits," they were not deeply religious. Her father was more interested in the crops and livestock on his farm, but her invalid mother sometimes talked to her about "spiritual matters." Dart read the Bible and other books considered to be "good" reading for a child.[5]

She was profoundly affected by her reading, at times reflecting so intensely on Christ that she could visualize him hanging on the cross as a sacrifice for sin. But it was not until she was nineteen years old in 1809 that she joined a congregation, the decisive step which established the direction the rest of her life would take. The year before, she had had a burning desire to attend church on Easter Day but her parents believed she was too young to be a communicant. Instead, she was "induced" to visit friends, spending a miserable day surrounded by "people who delighted in all kinds of frolics and sports" and other "Revel Sunday" (parish feast day) activities. A few days later, her elder sister Mary invited her to go on another outing, but she declined, explaining that "to see Time passing, Death coming, and Eternity hastening on" destroyed all her taste for such pastimes. She was drawn to Wesleyan Methodists preaching in her community, and she eagerly discussed religion with them. They confirmed her growing unease that "vital godliness" and "worldly sports" were incompatible.[6]

Dart's diary reveals a spiritual struggle to feel accepted by God. Methodist conversion involved the experiential knowledge of forgiveness for sin, and she strove for some time to reach that inward experience. "Though some of my relatives told me I was good enough, I felt that I was inwardly defiled by sin, and deserved banishment from God," she wrote of her anguish. She prayed and read the scriptures, and in 1811, the year she joined a Methodist class, while walking alone through a field, she experienced the acceptance she sought. She described the event in her diary:

> *The blessed time I never shall forget. My burden of sin and fear of death were gone, and Christ was my all in all. It was my desire and delight to do my Saviour's will.*[7]

Still Dart was not satisfied with her life. The goal of all earnest Methodists was sanctification, perfect love of God. All her work of "self-denial" and "consecration" was not done, she wrote. Her whole desire was to find "perfect holiness in the fear of the Lord." She read the writings by Hester Ann Roe Rogers describing the latter's spiritual journey. Rogers was one of Wesley's most ardent workers, and one of the few people he had described as "perfect in love." Finally, one evening while she was on her way to milk her father's cows, Dart came to believe that she had reached this same level of spirituality. Her words reveal her elation at that moment:

> *God came very near to me, and all His works appeared so glorious. Everything seemed vocal with His praise.*

Despite these experiences, she lived her life in painful awareness of her shortcomings and fought a feeling of despair and unworthiness. Years later, when she was itinerating in Cornwall, she recorded that her one big mistake in life was being too concerned about the results of her actions instead of simply doing what she perceived to be her duty and "leaving all results to God."[8]

On October 9, 1815, Dart was one of the twenty-two men and women who gathered together in a farm house at Shebbear to form the first Bible Christian Society in England. According to her diary, she had been speaking in public a few months before the Society began, even though the Wesleyan Methodists had imposed their first ban on women preaching twelve years earlier. In March, she had led in prayer and had given short exhortations. In June, at Tregoin, where she began dressmaking to earn a living, she held some public meetings and evidently for the first time met some male "opposition." Like most of the women preachers, she began hesitantly and reluctantly. It was hard for her even to lead in prayer. In her diary she admits that she had "a great struggle" before she could decide "to speak for Christ in a public way."[9]

In spite of ill health, frequent spiritual depression, and a genuine belief that others could preach much more successfully, in 1816 Dart became the first Bible Christian itinerant and one of the most effective. Her reputation became so great that in 1825 Zechariah Taft included her in his study of women preachers, although most of the women he portrayed were Wesleyan Methodists. She was partly responsible for a large revival that took place at the close of the fledgling Society's fifth quarterly meeting on January 1, 1817. In a large crowded barn, a "love-feast" had turned into a revival, with scores of "penitents" still on their knees at two o'clock in the morning. Dart and other preachers prayed with them, talked to them, and offered comfort and hope. Adjourning to the farmhouse, they kept on praying until seven, ate a hearty breakfast, and continued until two o'clock that afternoon. About fifty men and women "found peace with God," and several claimed to have experienced sanctification. Dart ministered to the sick; trudged through "storms and opposition, frosts and floods," sometimes with severely blistered feet; preached outdoors; and some weeks, walked forty miles. One day alone, she walked fourteen miles. By 1819, she was listed on the preachers' plan "to travel as her health will permit." Still she continued. She began a Society in Bristol and was responsible for the movement's success in Wales, although she travelled mainly around Devon and Cornwall.[10]

Dart has been described as an effective speaker. It was noted in Canada that as a preacher she was "superior" and "free from ostentation." She was constantly sought after and had great success in winning converts. Her voice was not timid. When she was ministering in Bowmanville, Upper

Canada, the local historian James Fairbairn wrote that her voice could be heard out on the street when she was holding a prayer meeting in her small frame house. The Bible Christians, he noted, "were not afraid of the gospel they believed." She was literate, fond of books, and described as a "woman of strong intellect and sound judgement." Methodists were encouraged to keep diaries, and the excerpts published from hers are well written. Fairbairn states that the Bible Christians who came to Bowmanville at that time were "among the most intelligent" of the population. The English historian F.W. Bourne held her in high regard, explaining that "she added a transparent simplicity of character, a quaintness of manner, and a power of sympathy which increased her personal charm and her public usefulness." A friend said that she never spoke ill of anyone. A Canadian writer remembered her as a "splendid woman."[11]

Almost eighteen years after she began as an itinerant for the Bible Christians, Dart accepted the challenge of working in the Canadian mission. On June 19, 1833, she reached the Port of Quebec on board the brig *Dalusia*. She was one of eight immigrants to Canada on the ship, including her husband of two months, John Hicks Eynon. He had been converted in Wales through her preaching, and in 1826, he had been received on probation as an itinerant minister.[12]

The Bible Christians had begun missionary activity beyond Great Britain in 1831 by sending John Glass to Upper Canada and Francis Metherall and his family to Prince Edward Island. The Metheralls' trek to the New World was not easy. When their ship reached Newfoundland, it sprang a leak, and they put back to Ireland for repairs. The next year they set sail again, this time landing at Bedeque, forty miles from their destination of Charlottetown. Leaving his wife to look after their children in a strange pioneer country, Metherall set off on foot for Charlottetown, blazing a trail to make it easier for his next hike, this time with his family, carrying one of the children most of the way. Nine months after they had left the coast of England the second time, they were settled in their new Canadian home, but as he wrote to the English Society the following year, it was not ideal. "I very much want a better house to live in," he told them. "That which we now occupy is neither *wind* nor *water* proof." But at least the Metheralls did remain. In Upper Canada, John Glass found the work too difficult. Discouraged, he soon returned to England. John Hicks Eynon, still a bachelor, volunteered to replace him.[13]

Eynon was a thickset, determined Cornishman, seemingly well-suited to the rigours of the new climate, the long journeys and the treacherous roads. On a visit to New York, a gentleman whom he met said to him, "Well, sir, you look as if you were a regular John Bull." "I am, sir," Eynon replied, "and I glory in it." Yet he needed all his determination to reach Canada. After setting sail from Liverpool in October, 1832, his ship was tossed about on the seas and blown to the coast of Ireland. There all his possessions were stolen. He returned to England where Dart and he were married the next March, and on the first of May they set sail from Padstow for Canada as a missionary couple. Storms forced them back to port, yet they persevered and set sail again five days later.[14]

Eynon's journals describe the terror of their ocean crossing. Much of Dart's journal of the voyage was not published in the denomination's magazine because, the editor noted, it was similar to her husband's. The *Bible Christian Magazine* did, however, publish a portion of "On Solitude," a poem that she found in one of the books she took with her on her voyage; it expressed the terrible loneliness she felt:

Ye winds! that have made me your sport,
Convey to this desolate shore,
Some cordial endearing report
Of a land I shall visit no more.
My friends! do they now and then send,
A wish or a thought after me?
O tell them, I yet have a friend
Though a friend I am never to see!

For forty-two days they were "tossed up and down upon the raging sea." The ocean "swells like mountains," Eynon wrote. "It looks awful, and yet very grand." At one point in the voyage, the wind carried away the ship's fore-boom and main trisail gaff. Later they learned that ten vessels had been shipwrecked that spring because of ice. Eynon described "Betsy's" loneliness, fear, and nausea, his own headache and sore stomach. At times he could barely hold up his head. They both tired of the salted provisions and longed for fresh fish.[15]

By the time they reached Quebec, Eynon's head was so bad that he was advised to take medicine before going up river where the fever and ague were prevalent. On the afternoon of June 23, they arrived in Montreal where a year earlier the well-known British immigrant, Catherine Parr Traill, also en route to Cobourg, had battled the deadly cholera. Eynon and Dart had passed eleven ships under quarantine. Twenty-nine people had already died on one of the vessels. Immigrants were particularly susceptible to the disease after the fatigue and poor nutrition of a long sea voyage. In 1832 alone, one-twelfth of Canada's population had died from cholera, many of them from among the fifty thousand men, women, and children who had thronged to the pioneer country from across the seas.[16]

By July 7, they had reached their new mission, the booming town of Cobourg. Six years earlier, in 1827, the community had consisted of 350 pioneers. Since then the population had tripled, and Cobourg was regarded as one of the "most brilliant and polished" societies in Upper Canada. A harbour had been built in 1832, and fast sailing steamers were plying Lake Ontario. A railway was planned to Peterborough, although this would not be completed for two decades. The town boasted a new circulating library of 800 volumes and a one-year-old amateur dramatic society. According to Catherine Parr Traill, it was a "neatly built and flourishing village," with "a select society" and containing many good stores, mills, a banking house, and a printing-office. The "handsome and commodious" Anglican church was being improved when Dart and Eynon arrived; the "ladies" had made and arranged new crimson hangings for the pulpit. A visitor to it the previous year, however, had found rows of empty pews on the main floor and three people in the gallery. Tenders were being called for a Presbyterian church to be built of stone. The Methodist Society was holding Temperance meetings, and plans were being made for a Wesleyan Methodist chapel.[17]

It was into this prosperous and fast-paced social and economic centre that Dart and Eynon brought their sober theology and plain dress. But they were not without friends. Many of the settlers in that area had recently emigrated from the West Country in England as well, and they welcomed the missionaries. In fact, the whole area around Cobourg in the early 1830s was ripe for a religious reform movement such as the Bible Christian denomination. Carroll Smith-Rosenberg has suggested that "irregular" or anti-ritualistic charismatic religions prosper at times of social and economic disruption. In Upper Canada at that time, cholera was epidemic, a middle class bourgeoisie was developing, and the country was rapidly changing from an agrarian to an urban society. The social environment was certainly unstable.[18]

Yet even with this fertile ground, the missionaries had to seize every opportunity to push the work forward. As soon as they arrived, they held a local preachers' meeting for the Cobourg station and preached to the people. The work, however, proved to be more taxing than in the home mission. One day that summer Eynon walked more than thirty miles in the blazing sun. "I find I must have a horse," he declared, "or shorter journeys." Between the heat and the "Misquitos," he wrote, "I have scarcely known what to do." Even with a horse, however, travelling was almost impossible. Catherine Parr Traill had written in the fall of 1832 that, although she had heard how bad the roads were in Canada, she was not prepared for what she had to travel on around Cobourg. Another traveller who journeyed from Cobourg to Peterborough described the trip as "thirteen miles of bad road, a lake blotted by weeds and seven miles of barely navigable river." In 1834, Parr remarked that the roads had not yet improved and "a few miles' journey seems an awful undertaking." In some areas, one had to navigate over root, stump, stone, mudhole, and "corduroy" trails.[19]

Dart was expecting her first child but was far from idle. She preached her first sermon a few days after they arrived, and that summer she walked or rode in a one-horse carriage to appointments as far away as Whitby, a distance of forty-five miles. Often she and her husband went their separate ways on a two-hundred-mile circuit, speaking in fields, barns, homes, woods, and schools. At times they conducted services together. She quickly felt at home but found it strange that so many people went without shoes and stockings. In her work, Dart often felt afraid and inadequate but had learned to trust in the "power" of the Lord. "I walked about six miles through the woods; on entering which I was tempted that fear would overcome me; but after I proceeded some distance, I felt not the least fear, and my soul was so filled with heaven and God, that I felt all within was joy and love," she wrote after one journey. She was particularly sensitive to her environment, often recording in her journals the beauty of the woods and the waters. "These things lead me to reflect," she noted "on the power of the Creator, and the valuable purposes they serve."[20]

Dart was ill their first winter in Canada, suffering particularly from chest pains. In January, when she was almost forty-two years old, she lost a daughter in childbirth, her first and only child. Still she kept up a rugged pace. She and her husband held open-air meetings and led revivals and protracted meetings. Dart, herself, was responsible for at least one protracted meeting in Cobourg while her husband was away on other parts of their mission. They ministered to converts in the Upper Canadian towns and villages of Cobourg, Bowman'svale [sic], Darlington, Whitby, Cavan, and Dummer. In March 1837 they opened a chapel in Cobourg, forty-two by sixty feet with an eight-foot-high basement, lit by lamps, and with hot air heating. In 1842, they were both working at Dummer, "witnessing the greatest reformation" they had ever seen in the province. They reported that more than fifty people "obtained salvation" at that time alone.[21]

Eynon found the journeys long, the summer heat intense, the winter cold severe, and the work hard. By 1839, he had been ordered to bed for several months by his doctor, and Dart did as much of his work as she could, along with her own responsibilities. Her faith kept her going and sustained her. Her source of strength was her trust in Christ. Earlier she had written in her journal that it was through the "blood of Christ" that she could conquer all her foes. "If I let go this prop I am undone forever." By 1846, however, both Dart and Eynon were in need of a rest. He had a painful leg as a result of riding and standing so much and Dart was in a "delicate state." Both exhausted, they spent some time in Kingston and in 1848 returned for a visit to England, where they spoke extensively on the Devon and Cornwall Circuits. They were accorded a magnificent welcome, and they gave addresses and led prayers that were "pervaded with a sacred glow of spirituality."[22]

There is little information about Dart's activities in the late 1840s and the early 1850s, although it appears that her ministry was severely curtailed. The obligatory missionary reports and letters, sent back to the home office in England and published in the denominational journal, were generally signed only by her husband after 1841. Earlier in their mission, both of their names had appeared at the bottom of the journal excerpts. Dart became known affectionately as "dear Mother Eynon," and from 1852 to 1855 her name appears in the Cobourg church elders' minutes occasionally in the role of mediator, but never as a preacher. One year Eynon, as pastor, had written letters to two of his parishioners about their deteriorating relationships with each other. Four months later, Sisters Higgins and Gilbard were still not speaking, and Dart was asked to bring about a reconciliation. On another occasion, as the membership was becoming lax in its observance of class and church attendance, she was asked to try to persuade two women and one man to return to the society as "full" members. There is no conclusive evidence that she was not preaching at this time, but this appears to have been the case. She was not in good health but neither was her husband, and both were advancing in age.[23]

Dart died in 1857 at the age of sixty-five years. The inscription on the marble column in the Bethesda cemetery near Bowmanville reads:

Elizabeth Dart
Born in Cornwall, England
April 1792
Entered the Bible Christian Itinerant
Ministry 1816
Married to the
Rev J.H. Eynon
Mar 18, 1833
And Proved a
Devoted Wife, Zealous Christian
And generally beloved
Died In
Little Brittain [*sic*]
Jan 13, 1857.[24]

The prodigious amount of work she had accomplished as an itinerant, however, was quickly forgotten by the denomination. The tombstone inscription, which suggests a difference in Eynon and Dart's work, is likely from a later era after the acceptance of the use of the term "Rev." Whereas she is referred to as "Elizabeth" in the "itinerant Christian ministry," John is "Rev. J.H." But even in 1857, when the *Bible Christian Magazine* noted her death, she was described only as the "wife" of John Hicks Eynon and a "devoted Christian." The annual Conference *Minutes* reported that "she took a lively interest in the cause"; and the denominational paper, the *Canadian Statesman*, mentioned that she was a "very devoted Christian," a "superior woman," and a "superior teacher," but made no reference to her itinerancy. As time went on, she generally received even less recognition. The history of the Bible Christians written by William Luke in 1878 notes five women briefly by name. Dart is not one of the women. The series of *Observer* articles in 1883 pointed out this gap in the official church records, placing Dart's contribution to the Bible Christian Church before its readers. But in a memorial to Eynon, who died in March 1888, the *Canadian Statesman* referred to her briefly and anonymously only as a "heroine in the missionary cause." The *West Durham News* devoted two long columns on its front page to Eynon's life and work in the "christian Ministry." Dart, however, is described as a "young lady" who "went from place, to place, warning sinners to flee from the wrath to come" and who became Eynon's "useful" wife. She was a "great worker, and untiring in her effort to do good" and a "fit companion" for her husband, the newspaper continued. The *Minutes* of the London Methodist Conference also paid tribute to Eynon, and noted that a "lady evangelist" who later became his wife was "his fellow-labourer" and gave him "advice, encouragement, and aid in proclaiming to the settlers in the wood the message of Divine mercy." Who she was, it does not say. According to the article, however, Eynon was in "the ministry." The distinction between evangelist and minister was evidently important. Other accounts suggest that evangelism was a step along the way to "the ministry" and therefore of a lower order. At that time, there were other unordained evangelists, but no unordained "ministers." In a later biographical sketch of Eynon, complete with photograph, in the *Christian Guardian* in 1904, there is no mention at all of Dart.[25]

Not all historical accounts, of course, omitted references to Dart's ministry or gave her such limited credit. The *Centennial of Canadian Methodism*, published by the

General Conference in 1891, noted that "Mrs. Eynon took work as regularly and as successfully as her husband," travelling from township to township, preaching and "sustaining the services." In his history of Canadian Methodism, J.E. Sanderson mentions that Dart preached, and F.W. Bourne provides a full account of her and other women in the Bible Christian ministry, especially in Great Britain.[26]

There is no concrete evidence that Dart was discriminated against in Canada because of her sex; however, only a few extracts from her Canadian letters and journals are extant. According to legend, when she was challenged as to whether she had been ordained to preach, she replied, "No, but I was fore-ordained." But Paul Robins, another Bible Christian itinerant, wrote from Peterborough in 1847 that the Society there would not tolerate a woman in the pulpit, even though they needed more preachers. "The Sunday I am in the country there is no person to address the people but Sister Heard and my wife," he explained, "and there appears to be a prejudice in the minds of the people against female preaching."[27]

Paul Robins' wife, Ann Vickery (1800-1853), ministered at the same time as Dart in England, first appearing on the Conference itinerants' roster in 1820. Like many of the women preachers she had been converted at age nineteen. Like Dart, she suffered from ill health, but she maintained an active ministry in London, the Norman Isles, and other towns and villages throughout the country. A highly motivated woman, Vickery felt obligated to do something for the Lord and for her "perishing fellow creatures." Her husband, Paul, experienced her as stubborn. He wrote that "Divine grace triumphed; and when she did submit, she submitted fully." Certainly she was an energetic woman. After her marriage in 1831, Vickery kept on preaching, many times carrying an infant to an appointment miles from her home, and handing it to a member of the congregation while she conducted the service. Afterwards, she picked up the child and walked back home. A nineteenth-century "superwoman," she did all her own housework except for a brief period after her second child was born. She prepared her Sunday meals in advance to avoid "bustle on the Sabbath," and she filled in for itinerants, making special arrangements for the care of her family. She preached, visited the sick, and led classes and prayer meetings. She had no sympathy for preachers who were "held back because of disagreeable weather."[28]

Robins, Vickery, and their sons emigrated to Canada in 1846, when Vickery was forty-six years old. John Eynon met them at Peterborough in May and noted that Robins and the children were well, but Vickery was not in good health. In the Canadian winter, she suffered even more. A thick cake of ice covered everything they put in their indoor cupboards; their breath froze on their bed clothes. Vickery carried water from her neighbour's well because they did not have one of their own. She cared for Robins when he became critically ill soon after he arrived, even though she herself was sick with rheumatism brought on by the frost and snow. Yet until the fall of 1847, she took her share of preaching on the circuits in Peterborough, Cobourg, and Darlington, at field meetings, in homes, and at protracted meetings. She had fewer preaching engagements than Dart, but Dart had no children to care for. The Bible Christian historian F.W. Bourne regarded Vickery and Robins as a ministerial team, for in describing their work in Canada, he uses the pronoun "they." A strong and outspoken woman, Vickery met with resistance, and from 1850 on she is mentioned only as a class leader, although leading both men and women. Indeed, even in this position, people reacted to her with strong feelings. In 1852, a class member,

Maria Carr, was rebuked for leaving the class she had been assigned in order to attend Vickery's. Another member, Brother Cosper, felt slighted when Vickery chose someone else to lead her class in her absence instead of choosing him. She died shortly afterwards, in 1853. The next year, Robins visited England, where he married Mary Ann Taylor, a "much esteemed" preacher. Taylor had been an intinerant for the Bible Christians in England for at least twenty years from 1832 to 1852, but there is no account of her working on any of the Canadian circuits after she came to Canada as Robin's wife.[29]

By the late 1840s, the Bible Christians in Upper Canada were well on their way to respectability. The population of Upper Canada doubled in the decade from 1841 to 1851, but the membership of the Bible Christian Church more than tripled from 1845 to 1855. After the union of the Methodist Episcopal Church with the British Wesleyans in 1833, the Bible Christian Church provided a welcome option for some of the more radical Canadians and Methodist immigrants who were disaffected by the conservative elements in the mainstream church. As the Bible Christian membership increased, however, more and better meeting places were built, and a more structured organization developed. This in turn led to more formal practices and less spontaneity. In 1841, Bible Christian preachers were granted licences to marry, and the denomination could secure chapels and burying grounds, giving it the recognition the members had been fighting hard to achieve. The type of meeting held in their church communities was also changing. Even in the 1850s, members were becoming irregular in their church attendance. In 1853, the Canadian mission became a self-governing Conference, and although it continued to attract members, it began to resemble more closely other more conservative Methodist denominations. Its growth slowed from 1855 to 1865, not quite doubling in numbers. By the early 1860s, structured Sabbath schools were emphasized, and there were far fewer protracted meetings, class meetings, and prayer meetings. Indeed, on April 12, 1860, the Cobourg elders' meeting passed a resolution that the "Females" in the church be asked to hold weekly prayer meetings. Ministry had become more formalized and professionalized, and that year, Conference developed a course of study for its ministers. By 1869, ministers were allowed to use the title "Rev.," although Paul Robins objected strongly to this custom, regarding it as a departure from the plainness and simplicity of the gospel. "If a man has real worth, he does not require this prefix," he declared. The Conference in 1872 recorded that several District meetings had noted "among our sisters, a deplorable conformity to the world in vain attire and a great neglect of class and prayer meetings." The denomination had blended into an increasingly conservative country. It was no longer a radical option. In 1884, when the Bible Christians entered the final Methodist union in Canada, they brought with them 6,918 members, only one and a half times the membership they had had two decades earlier.[30]

Elizabeth Dart Eynon and Ann Vickery Robins were only two of the many Bible Christian women preaching in Canada, some of them still active in the 1850s and at the beginning of the 1860s as local preachers. Few of their Canadian diaries and letters have been preserved, and their activity is visible mainly through brief comments by their husbands or other male itinerants. Most of them belonged to clergy couples, and the women had an active preaching ministry before their marriage.

Elizabeth Trueman Hoskin (1807-1882) preached for some time in Cornwall, England, before emigrating to the

Huntingdon area in Upper Canada, probably in the early 1830s. She began the Bible Christian Society there and preached for a number of years, "as long as her health held out." In fact, she was held in such high esteem that she was known to her community as the Rev. Mrs. Hoskin. Years later on her death in 1882, there was some embarrassment that she had been preaching, possibly because she was known as "Rev." The memorial tribute to her in the *Observer* reads very much like an apology, noting that she had preached because there was no one else to provide the early settlers with the "means of grace."[31]

Elizabeth Trick Henwood (1801-1872), one of the earliest Bible Christian preachers to arrive in Canada, emigrated in the spring of 1830, three years before Dart and Eynon. Her sea voyage from England on the brig *Friends* was described by her friend twenty-nine-year-old Elizabeth Peters. Elizabeth and William Peters and their three young sons, Thomas, William, and Nicholas, along with Elizabeth Trick Henwood and her husband Charles, and Maria and Thomas Hoskin(g) formed a close-knit group as they sailed together to Upper Canada. The Henwoods, Thomas Hoskin, and William Peters shared the worship services during the voyage. We do not know whether Maria Hoskin or Elizabeth Peters were also preachers. During the voyage, Elizabeth Peters was kept busy nursing her twenty-month-old son, cooking meals on the stove provided, sewing, knitting, writing in her diary, and caring for her other active children.[32]

After they arrived in Canada, Trick and Henwood preached for a number of years. Trick had been one of the first itinerants officially recognized by the Bible Christian Church in England in 1819. Newspapers reported that when she preached in Canada, she was as inspiring as the earlier saddle-bag preachers and created as much interest. In 1860 and 1861, both Trick and Henwood were listed on the Cobourg Circuit plan as preachers; he was third in seniority and she was fourth out of a list sometimes as long as twenty-nine. From January to July and October to December 1860, and from January to July 1861, months when preachers' plans are available on which they are both listed, Trick was assigned only sixteen preaching appointments, whereas Henwood was allotted forty-one. The discrepancy could have been due to the fact that she gave birth to twelve children, including one set of twins, and much of her time would have been spent managing the large household. However, in 1860, the youngest children were the twins, then fourteen years old and well able to care for themselves and help with domestic chores. Three of the other preachers who are listed with initials for their first names on those same plans may have been women. Generally at that time, it was customary to use only last names for the men and last names and initials for the women.[33]

There are other references to women conducting religious services on board ships on their voyages to Canada. This preaching activity suggests that these women had expectations of continuing their ministry when they reached their adopted country. John Williams' journals reveal that he was part of a group of Bible Christian preachers who arrived on the brig *Andus* in the spring of 1848. His wife, Elizabeth Riden, his sister-in-law Sister Parker, and another Sister Riden all preached during the voyage as much as Williams himself, to the delight of the captain and the crew.[34]

There are only traces of information about other preaching women. Mary Ann and John Kemeys joined the Eynons in "spreading the gospel" in 1834 in Upper Canada. Mr. and Mrs. John Adams emigrated to Prince Edward Island in the 1830s where they were both responsible for a great revival in the Bedeque area. They soon went to Upper Canada where Mrs. Adams preached around Exeter in 1834. A Sister Heard was preaching in the Peterborough area in the spring of 1848. Sarah Rippin (1824-1883) and her husband George, both preachers in Devon, emigrated to London and later Putnamville in Upper Canada in 1846, before proceeding to Ohio in the fall. Later in 1851 in St. Thomas, they were two of eight local preachers. Ruth Stovold Woodger (1818-1889) had been preaching in the 1840s in England for the Bible Christians where she earned the disapproval of members of the Church of England. A male minister wrote to her expressing his surprise that "one so modest" should be "guilty of the impropriety of preaching." Ruth emigrated with her husband to Woodstock where she preached for the Primitive Methodists and assisted at a number of revivals. In 1853 she joined the Bible Christians in Mitchell where she was well accepted in the pulpit, although how regularly she preached, we do not know. Susan Nan(ce)kivell, who had preached in the Cornwall area in Great Britain, was listed as a local preacher at Orono near Oshawa in 1857, and Mary Nicholls Green preached with her husband and sometimes supplied for him around Pickering in 1859. Green had been an itinerant in England at the beginning of the Bible Christian movement.[35]

In the later years, some of the women appeared only as guest preachers on special occasions. The widowed Mrs. Andrew Cory was invited to participate in the dedication services for a new church at Darlington. The small original chapel built in 1848 had been turned into a vestry for a much larger brick one in 1855. It was reported that as part of the celebrations, Mrs. Cory "made remarks," whereas Mr. Draper and Mr. Frayner "preached." Two Sundays later, however, there were three special "sermons," by Mr. John Hooper, Mr. Henry and Mrs. Cory.[36]

A number of Bible Christian women had an active ministry in Prince Edward Island, although the denomination never maintained much of a foothold there. The Abbotts held services in their house, and the Bryentons and the Adams were both considered talented preaching couples by the first missionary Francis Metherall. Martha Jago Sabine, who came from Cornwall, England to Canada in 1830, created "quite a stir" in Charlottetown by preaching in the market-house in the early 1840s, although she "did much good." Frances and William Calloway and Isabella Armstrong Harris and her husband William Harris arrived later in 1844. Armstrong preached for a few years but soon was widowed with a small child. The Calloways returned to England in ten years, but while they were in Canada, both preached extensively. According to William Calloway's journals, his wife took a number of engagements, drawing particularly large congregations. She appears to have been more adept at preaching than at some household chores, according to her husband's description of her efforts to put up a "Moschetto blind around the bed." She was "not so well skilled in putting them up as the Americans are," he wrote, "for numbers of them [mosquitos] found their way in, just as it was getting light." Another woman, Sister Buxton, led revivals as late as 1860.[37]

Ann Copp Gordon's story, recorded by her daughter, provides the fullest account of any of the Canadian Bible Christian women preachers. Copp (1837-1931) was the only Bible Christian woman preaching in Canada as late as the 1870s. Possibly because she was a public figure in the early twentieth century, her exploits did find their way into Canadian newspapers. Her experiences are interesting from the point of view of how expectations within the Bible Christian Church and in Canadian society coloured her own attitudes to speaking and preaching, and how men and women

75

reacted to women in the pulpit in the late nineteenth century.

Copp considered that she had been ordained in Devon in 1855 when she was designated a Bible Christian preacher. Her father disapproved of her career, but when he finally heard her preach on the eve of her departure to Canada in 1857, he was overawed. "Had I known my Annie had such ability, she would never have gone to Canada," he declared.[38]

Unlike many of the early Bible Christian women preachers, Copp was from a reasonably well-to-do family background and was brought up in a large stone house in Bideford in the north of Devon. Her father was a master builder, a "pillar" in the Established Church. Raven-haired, dark-eyed Copp was the "belle of the parish." She was drawn to the Bible Christian denomination, but because she feared her father's wrath, she entered their chapel only after her conversion at age sixteen. Like that of Elizabeth Dart, her spiritual struggle had been long. One night on her knees in her own home, she prayed in despair that she would not rise until she had been blessed by God. Almost instantly, she felt a presence at her side, "a vision of the Saviour, clear and unmistakable." The "weight" she had borne for months "lifted like the sun breaking through the cloud," and she was filled with a "light" which she claimed never left her through "persecution, loneliness and years of dire poverty."[39]

She joined the local class and followed the pattern of many other English women: because she converted to Methodism, she was forced by her father to leave home. Methodist literature has many stories of young women who were beaten or banished because they attended Methodist services against their parents' wishes, and these stories were held up to women as models to emulate. Soon after her conversion, Copp was entered on trial as a preacher in March

1854. Her speaking ability and deep spirituality were quickly recognized by the Bible Christians. A year later, she was "ordained a lay preacher" and walked seven miles to chapels to teach, preach, and lead services. The effort was exhausting, and two years later, when she was twenty, she set sail for Canada to regain her health and visit a brother in London, Ontario.[40]

On the London Circuit, Copp was welcomed as a preacher. She and Brother Heard led a six-week revival in Dereham that was so successful that the members planned to build a second chapel in the township although they had only recently opened their first one. She joined Paul Robins' church and in 1859 married Robin's assistant, Andrew Gordon. They shared services as a ministerial couple, and some said that she was much superior to her husband. Her speaking was quiet but "convincing" and always "with an evangelistic note." The well-known Canadian women's rights and temperance leader Nellie McClung described her preaching as a "mother speaking to erring children." Copp ministered in the countryside and in towns, in Tweed and Port Hope, and in 1868 preached the Conference sermon at Port Hope to the assembled ministers, wearing a black silk dress she had made for the occasion. Even though she was a successful preacher, a few male ministers suggested that "it was too much to ask of the little woman." Others said "let the little woman win her spurs," and "win her spurs" she did.[41]

In 1870 and 1871, Copp and Gordon caused a "bit of a flurry among other established Methodist bodies," preaching in the streets in Belleville. Around this time, she also preached the anniversary sermons on Sunday and gave an address the next Monday at Lindsay, Ontario. The sermons were easy for her, but the thought of making an "address" was terrifying. At that time, it was more acceptable for women to deliver a guest sermon than to make a public speech to a mixed audience: the sermon was similar to the work of an evangelist and within the purview of a talented spiritual woman, but an address conveyed a more authoritative tone. She was even more frightened when she discovered that she was sitting on the same platform with Chief Justice Benson of the Supreme Court of Canada. Quickly she slipped off the platform and ran to the parsonage where she gulped down the whites of two eggs, one whipped and the other plain. She had heard that the white of an egg loosened "muscular tension" but was not quite sure how the white should be eaten. Justice Benson introduced her as "the first woman he had ever heard speak on a public platform."[42]

Although Copp dreaded some situations, it appears that she was never too intimidated to stand up for what she believed. Nor was she afraid to be different. In Pickering, Ontario she burst into song at a Quaker service she attended in 1877, precipitating a heated debate among the Friends over singing hymns in their Meeting House. She studied phrenology, and according to her daughter, she had highly developed intuition and psychic abilities. She paid attention to her dreams. Like those of Elizabeth Dart, Copp's dreams were often precognitive. Once when it was thought that she was critically ill with consumption, she dreamed that she should not follow her doctor's prescription. After throwing the medicine bottle out the window, she called in a person considered to be a "quack" doctor and was healed with herbs. It turned out that the regular doctor had misdiagnosed her condition.[43]

An energetic woman like other women preachers, Copp managed her own housework and cared for a family in addition to her career. She brought up three children, clothing them in made-over garments which she sewed at night "so fast that her needle became heated and shone like a bar of fire." Economy was stressed as a virtue "particularly becoming and useful in the female," and a minister's wife needed to be economical. After her husband's death, she became active in the Temperance movement and often spoke in concert with Nellie McClung in the early twentieth century.[44]

Copp died in Winnipeg in 1931 when she was ninety-seven years old. By then she was well-known. The local newspapers had printed a story about her almost every year on her birthday when she was in her nineties. They referred to her preaching career, noting that she had often preached at three circuit points on Sundays. The stories indicate, however, that society has a short memory about women preaching. Unaware that women preached extensively in the early days of Methodism, the writer of one of the articles explained that as one of the first women to preach, Copp attracted wide attention. Indeed, according to another article, she was probably the first woman to preach in Canada. In fact, she was one of the last of the nineteenth-century Methodist women who preached in Great Britain and in Canada, beginning her career in each country in the late 1850s at a time when very few women in the Bible Christian or Primitive Methodist groups were still active in the pulpit. The newspaper stories also emphasized her role as a mother and homemaker, for this was where society believed women were meant to be. "Outside the Church the centre of her life was in the home, which she loved and cared for, and here was where she really reigned," wrote one biographer. Another indicated only that she took "the pulpit herself when the need arose – which she did for one whole year." The idea that a woman would preach other than to fill in in an emergency had long disappeared.[45]

How many Bible Christian women preached and exhorted, led classes and prayer groups cannot be determined. Few journals and letters survive to tell their story. But those that remain describe or suggest a vast amount of activity with results equal to those of their male counterparts. Most of them belonged to a clergy couple sharing the work load, successes, and failures, and it is clear that their husbands encouraged them and took pride in their accomplishments. In the late 1840s, some of the members of their church resisted their preaching. At the mid-point of the nineteenth century, few women were preaching regularly, and by the latter half of the century, the memory of their work had virtually disappeared.

In the Bible Christian *Observer* in 1884, a few months after the completion of the biographical series about Elizabeth Dart, Rev. S.J. Allin defended women, declaring that they had shared equally with men "the honour of preaching and sending the gospel" to others. "What women do," he wrote, is of "supreme importance," for "what woman is, we may truly say, is largely what the measure of civilization is." And in an address to the Bible Christian Conference in 1884, just prior to the last Methodist union in Canada, the Superintendent of the Bowmanville district, Rev. G. Webber, reminded the delegates of women's contribution, which by then had all but been forgotten. "Where God has endowed a woman to preach don't let us keep her out of the pulpit," he pleaded, assuring those present that a woman could both preach and be a mother. "I don't think a woman unfits herself for the noblest work on earth by standing in the Christian pulpit," he added. Yet at that time, women were not encouraged in the pulpit. Instead, the *Observer* printed articles encouraging Bible Christian women to remain in the home. "Thank God," the paper noted, "some of us have old-fashioned mothers." It was not until 1936 that the first woman was ordained in The United Church of Canada, the denominational heir of the Bible Christian denomination.[46]

Ann Copp Gordon (1837-1931), Bible Christian preacher, and her husband, Andrew. (Photo: The United Church of Canada/Victoria University Archives, Toronto.)

Tombstone in Bethesda Cemetery, Bowmanville, Ontario, commemorates Elizabeth Dart Eynon (1792-1857). (Photo courtesy of the author.)

BIBLE CHRISTIAN PREACHERS' PLAN; COBOURG CIRCUIT. 1861.

"BRETHREN, PRAY FOR US."—PAUL.

PLACES.	Time.	April. 14	21	28	May. 5	12	19	26	June. 2	9	16	23	30	July. 7
COBOURG,	2½	21	2T	14	19	12	2	22	1c	23B	3	13	1	18
"	6½	2	2L	1	1A	2s	8	1	1	2B	2	1	8	2
Friday,	7¼	2		1		2			1E		2		1	
PRECIOUS COR'R,	10½	21	23	20	A1s	21	27	22	18	13B	2	24	1	18
Monday,	7		2T	1		2			1		2		1	
GUIDEBOARD,	10½	12	1T	22	2A	14	1s	21	2	*	1c	22	2	8
"	6	9	27	21	18A	1	15	13	3	*	5	14	21	1
Thursday,	7	2		1		2			1E		2		1	2
ZION,	10½	1T	27	2A	18	1c	16	2s	4	1B	5	2	21	1
"	6	25	1L	12A	9	22	16	23	26	*B	15	22	2	9
Tuesday,	7	2		1		2			1E		2		1	2
PORT BRITAIN,	2½	1T	22	22	23A	24	9	2s	26	*B	9	17	25	1
Monday,	7	2		1		2			1E		2		1	2
CAMBOURNE,	2	2T	23	1	1A	2	27	1s	18	2B	2	1c	12	2
"	6½	5	13	20	19A	21	2L	19	13	5	20	24	15	7
Tuesday,	7	2		1	1E		2		1		2		1	
PORT HOPE,	10½	24	2	21	23A	3	18	1	1c	*B	12	14	19	4
"	6½	1T	22	2	2A	14	1s	2	2	1	1	2	1	8
Friday,	7½	2		1E		2		1E		2		1E		2
PLAINS,	10½	2T	14	14	27	2s	13	1c	15	21B	18	1	23	2
"	6	19	14	13A	27	19	20	21	12	21B	18	5	23	21
Wednesday,	7	2		1E		2			1		2		1	
AINLEY'S,	2½	23	1T	15	2A	22	1	24	2s	*B	1	23	2	25
Wednesday,	7	2		1		2			1		2		1	
TRELAWNEY,	2½	22	15	2T	3	1A	25	9	17	1	22	2s	26	1

Preachers' Names.

1 CHAPPLE.
2 STEVENS.
3 Henwood.
4 E. Henwood.
5 Cullis.
6 Hoar.
7 Cole.
8 Gilbard.
9 Brown.
10 Dodge.
11 Giddey.
12 M. Giles.
13 Ward.
14 Jex.
15 Giles.
16 Williams.
17 Doney.
18 Jewell.
19 Snelgrove.
20 Kay.
21 Roberts.
22 Wade.
23 Tom.
24 Grose.

PROBATIONERS.

25 Tamblyn.
26 Harness.
27 To be supplied.
* Conference Preachers.

REFERENCES.—s. Sacrament; L. Lovefeast; T. Renewing Tickets; A. Quarterly Collection; B. Chapel Collection; c. Sabbath School Addresses; E. Elders' Meeting.

☞ The next Preachers' and Quarterly Meeting will be held (D.V.) at Guideboard, on May 13th. Preachers will meet at 9½, the Society and Circuit Stewards at 10, A.M. At 3 P.M. R sermon will be preached. A large gathering of the friends from all parts of the Circuit will give great pleasure to the Pastor and others.

☞ The District Meeting will be held at Port Hope on 15th and 16th of May: due notice will be given of the religious services. The Conference will be held at Bowmanville, to commence first Thursday in June. Some of the Conference Preachers may be expected in this Circuit June 9th.

The 1861 Cobourg Bible Christian Preachers' Plan lists Elizabeth Trick Henwood (1801-1872). (Photo: The United Church of Canada/Victoria University Archives, Toronto.)

IV.
FROM ITINERANT TO GUEST PREACHER:
CANADIAN PRIMITIVE METHODIST WOMEN

*Shall Woman Preach? Of course let her preach.
She has the talent, the heroism and the perseverance for the work . . . Where shall she
preach? Anywhere throughout the world . . .
Has she the authority to preach? Yes, undoubtedly . . . Shall she be ordained? Now, we come
to a pause . . .*

Christian Journal, 23 January 1874, p.l. c.5

As in the Bible Christian Church in Canada, women played a prominent role in the early days of the Canadian Primitive Methodists. Some of them were itinerants as they had been in England, but most of them were guest preachers or preached only part-time. However, women like the Canadian-born Jane Woodill Wilson (1824-1893) and Mary Ann Lyle (1797-1862), an emigrant from England, were among the most gifted and popular preachers in nineteenth-century Upper Canada.

"My mother had little respect for girls who sat with their toes in the fire waiting for some man to take care of them,"

Jane Agar Hopper, the Canadian Primitive Methodist historian, pointed out in her memoirs. Girls and boys had to share equally in chores, Hopper continued, and all the members of her family were expected to take their turn leading worship at home. The situation was the same in early Primitive Methodist churches in Upper Canada. Men and women were both called upon to serve as itinerant and local preachers. The British historian William Townsend noted that women were used extensively not only as local and itinerant preachers in the Primitive Methodist tradition, but as missionaries as well. Nathaniel Watkins and his wife, the first official missionaries to Upper Canada, were also the first clergy couple to serve the denomination in that country. Nathaniel's wife, however, had a very limited preaching role in the new country.[1]

The Canadian Primitive Methodist Society began after William Lawson preached in the market square at York, Upper Canada in 1829. A gifted speaker, he attracted a large crowd, and a small Society was formed. Lawson had had a chequered religious career. He was brought up in the Church of England, yet as a teenager, he was attracted to the Wesleyan Methodists and began preaching for them at Brampton, England when he was twenty years old. He was soon expelled for attending a camp-meeting, and in 1822 he joined with the Primitive Methodist Society, which had begun eleven years earlier. On April 14, 1829, Lawson, his wife Ann Atkinson, a bonnet maker, and their children set sail from Maryport, Cumberland on board the brig *Dykes* for the Port of Quebec. Two months later, they arrived in York, and almost immediately, Lawson was leading a class of seventeen Primitive Methodist men and women in his house. Ann Atkinson, a gifted singer, assisted at all the services, although with seven children surviving infancy and four who died, there must have been little time for work outside the home.[2]

The new Canadian Society asked the parent body in England to send out a missionary preacher, and in August 1830, one year after the first contingent of Primitive Methodist missionaries had been sent to New York, Nathaniel Watkins and his wife arrived in York, Upper Canada. Watkins claims to have had successes in increasing the membership, doubling the size of the Society in a few months. Both he and his wife preached to congregations described by Watkins as "attentive." But he was not cut out for pioneer life. Quickly becoming discouraged by the climate and the impassable roads, in 1831 he joined his sister, Ruth Watkins, who was working as a missionary in Philadelphia and New York. Lawson and other Primitive Methodists in York probably encouraged his departure. While they admired Watkin's zeal and diligence, they considered him to be so illiterate that it was "painful to sit under him."[3]

Both the new Canadian and American Societies were plagued with lack of support from the English body. Rumours were rife, and charges flew back and forth across the sea. In 1835, Ruth Watkins referred to a report that was circulating in England from Canada and evidently made derogatory comments about some of the workers on the American mission. In Upper Canada, the itinerant William Summersides and other Primitive Methodists met on September 6, 1836 to discuss a letter they had recently received from England, accusing the Canadian Society of being "rebellious." They agreed that they still needed help from England simply to maintain their present position, but they wondered about joining with the Methodist Episcopals, who had remained separate when the rest of the Canadian Methodists joined with the British Wesleyans in 1833. They decided against it, and even with their problems, the Canadian

Society flourished. Like the Bible Christians, they, too, attracted dissatisfied Methodist Episcopal members to their ranks after the union in 1833 with the British Wesleyans.[4]

In 1833, another clergy couple emigrated from England, becoming of much greater assistance to the young Society than Nathaniel Watkins and his wife had been. William and Mary Ann Lyle arrived in York with their children after an extremely fatiguing journey. It had been hoped that the sea voyage would help William Lyle recuperate from an attack of cholera. They were both preachers. He had begun as a Bible Christian minister in England, afterwards teaching school before joining the Primitive Methodists. Mary Ann Lyle had attended both Wesleyan and Bible Christian services but was converted in the Bible Christian denomination when she was twenty through hearing a woman preacher. She preached for the Bible Christians and married William Lyle when she was twenty-six.[5]

Mary Ann Lyle continued to preach in Canada, although her appointments were sometimes infrequent. On the "Sunday Plan" of the Canadian Brampton Mission in 1836, her husband was assigned thirty-two preaching spots as the number one preacher. She was number seven, with only one service scheduled. On the preachers' plan of the Toronto Mission in 1839, however, she was listed as a preacher, although one of the most junior, eighteenth out of nineteen. William Lyle was set down as an exhorter and was scheduled to speak between two and four times every Sunday between April and June, a total of thirty-two appointments. Mary Ann Lyle was limited to seven preaching engagements. In 1843, on the Brampton Circuit, he was again number one on the list of preachers with a very full schedule, and she was number twelve with only a couple of assignments. Presumably the household demands on her time were greater than on his, although their lifestyle was indeed simple. At the beginning of their Canadian ministry, the couple and their three daughters and one son lived on the Etobicoke Circuit in a humble shanty covered with slabs. One room contained study, kitchen, dining room, parlour, and bedroom. In 1836, William Lyle received approximately $288.00 to cover his salary, house rent, expenses to maintain a horse, and an allowance for four children. By contrast, William Summersides, also with four children, was allotted $341.40 the same year. It is reported that the Lyles had a combined income of only $240.00 in 1837, although available records do not note how much of this was designated for Mary Ann Lyle.[6]

The first Canadian book of *Doctrines and Disciplines* published in 1833 for the young church advocated a frugal and simple lifestyle. There were general rules for the conduct and dress of all its members, and some rules specifically for local and itinerant preachers, both men and women. Like the other early Methodist societies, the Primitive Methodist Church demanded a plain, simple, hard-working, and sober existence, and serious conversation. No man or woman was allowed to remain in the society who attended "vain and worldly amusements," wasted their time at public houses, bought "unaccustomed [luxurious] goods," or was dishonest. Plain dress was "strongly recommended" for all members but required for preachers. Male travelling preachers were instructed to wear single-breasted coats, plain waistcoats, and their hair in a "natural" form. Female travelling preachers were admonished to display "patterns of plainness of dress." Local preachers had to be properly certified; itinerants were required to keep and submit regular journals. Preachers' salaries varied. A single man was to be paid from £4 4s. to £5 7s. a quarter or from $67.30 to $85.60 a year, while a woman's salary was set at significantly less, £2 10s. per quarter or $40.00 a year. It is probable that only single women were paid. In addition, both men and women on salary received room and board. A married man was to be paid twice the single man's salary, but any male itinerant whose wife carried on their business while he travelled received less. Presumably it was felt that his financial need was not as great. However, the assumption was that women were quite capable of looking after business concerns.[7]

There is nothing to indicate how long Mary Ann Lyle remained on the preaching schedule. Later on, it appears that she was invited to speak mainly on special occasions. She preached at the opening of the chapel at Bolton's Mills in 1845; in Nassigoway township on the Guelph Circuit in 1846; and again at the opening of a church in Claremont, where she took the theme, perhaps appropriately, of "Wood, hay and stubble." She was affectionately called "the venerable mother in Israel"; when she died in 1862 in her sixty-fifth year near Clareville on the Etobicoke Circuit, her funeral procession is said to have extended more than a mile. The *Christian Journal* paid tribute to her, reporting that four male ministers conducted the funeral services on "this impressive occasion," but no mention is made of her preaching. In a funeral tribute, one of her sons-in-law called her a "prophetess" and noted that she had "a position of some prominence" in her church. However, the memorial for William Lyle in the *Christian Journal* in 1874 virtually ignored her except for one reference to an illness in England and to her death which left him "homeless," the implication being that a home without a wife was simply not a home.[8]

Another Primitive Methodist preaching couple, Mary Ann and William Towler, had gone to the United States from England in 1846. William Towler was in that country as a general superintendent only a short time when he became ill.

In addition to taking care of seven children, Mary Ann Towler looked after her husband's extensive correspondence and preaching when he was sick. He soon died, and after his death she moved to Toronto where she opened a day school in 1848 and continued to preach on special occasions. In June of that year, she was the guest speaker at the anniversary of the Yorkville Sunday schools, and later she preached at least three times at the opening of a chapel on the Hamilton Mission, on Sunday, Monday, and Tuesday. Each successive appearance seems to have drawn a larger crowd than the one before, yet her audiences continued to be astonished at her "calmness and ability." In 1851, she was still sought after and preached the anniversary sermons for the Hope Chapel Sunday school. Other Methodist groups accepted her as a speaker, for on at least one occasion she appeared on the same platform with Wesleyans and members of the New Connexion.[9]

The most popular couple preaching for the Primitive Methodists in Upper Canada at that time may have been Jane Woodill and Isaac Wilson. Woodill's father was a zealous "Ranter" as the Primitive Methodists were called, and his religious enthusiasm and disciplined life-style were ridiculed by some of his neighbours. A silly rhyme was circulated:

> *Robert Woodill killed a pig*
> *To make the Ranters fat and big*
> *When they all sat down to eat*
> *Robert had to eat the feet;*
> *When the pig was eat and all*
> *Robert swore his share was small.*

When he and his son-in-law were building a new barn, they agreed not to serve the customary alcoholic beverages at the barn-raising. The neighbourhood turned out to "watch the fun," certain that the barn would never be built. William Proudfoot, a Presbyterian minister, had raised a barn on his farm in Middlesex County in 1833 and reported that although ninety men came to the three-day "bee," about two-thirds of these came for the sole purpose of drinking whisky and never once helped to lift a log. "Many of them got drunk," he complained, "and there was such a quantity of swearing and low buffoonery that the whole thing was very painful." Yet, at Robert Woodill's "bee," even though his daughter served only sandwiches and coffee, the barn went up before dark. As the workmen went away, they shouted, "Hurrah for the temperance barn!" Among the Primitive Methodists, Robert Woodill was highly respected. His name appears on the Etobicoke Circuit as a preacher in the 1840s, and he was the local postmaster.[10]

Robert Woodill and Mary Pickering had emigrated from Yorkshire, England to "muddy York" in 1819. Five years later, they moved north where they cleared one hundred acres of land and gradually put up farm buildings. Jane Woodill was born that year. When she was eighteen, her name first appeared on the Etobicoke Circuit Plan as a preacher. Seven years later, she married a first cousin, Isaac Wilson, who had also emigrated from Yorkshire, but later than the Woodills. His family settled in the Toronto area in 1831, and five years later they too moved north to what was by then known as Woodhill.[11]

Immediately after Wilson's conversion at age seventeen, he began exhorting and leading prayer meetings. Crowds gathered to hear him. When Jane Woodill was appointed to preach in her home church, it too was always packed. It was even said that she was intellectually "superior" to her husband and that he did "half as much preaching" as she did.

Like the other itinerants, Jane always dressed in gray, brown, or black and preached wearing a plain bonnet without any flowers on it.[12]

Woodill and Wilson led a busy life, supporting each other in their ministry. They had four daughters and one son, and often when Woodill was away preaching, her husband kept the youngest with him in his Sunday school class. In fact, he held the position of Sunday school superintendent for thirty-one years. The family were all active in church activities, playing the organ, singing in the choir, and the children carried the organ from their home to the church and back every Sunday. Both circuit preachers, Woodill and Wilson were often separated from each other. They travelled long distances north, and Woodill's Spanish spotted horse Toby achieved a certain notoriety. He was as gentle "as a kitten" when she rode him, but every time her husband tried to ride, the horse would run away. Woodill thought nothing of riding thirty miles and preaching two or three times on Sunday. Their home was a haven for other clergy, and Woodill became known as "Mother Wilson." She cared for the sick and the poor and had a reputation as a good and fearless nurse. When a local Wesleyan family fell ill with scarlet fever, she was the only person who would help. She changed her clothes in the woodshed after each visit to prevent the spread of germs. Not long afterwards, in 1876, because of its financial plight, the local Wesleyan church asked to join with the Primitives, and Woodill's care of that family is said to have been partly responsible for that unusual union.[13]

Although Woodill and Wilson travelled, much of their ministry was at the Salem Church, north of Tullamore. They began the first class in the kitchen of their home and such large religious revivals took place there that in 1848 a log church was built on their farm. By 1862, this had been replaced by a small but substantial brick building with all the materials and much of the labour donated by the members. The stone for the church had come from the Wilson's property.[14]

As with the Bible Christian movement around the Cobourg-Peterborough area, the 1840s and 1850s were the zenith of Primitive Methodist activity around Toronto. Good preachers were in demand. New chapels were being built and were rapidly paying off their debts. Both Woodill and Wilson had numerous engagements. In 1854, she preached the opening sermons at the Bolton church, and nineteen years later, she was asked to lay the cornerstone for a more modern church there. There were love-feasts, church openings, prayer meetings, field meetings, ticket meetings, and services indoors and outdoors. In the 1850s, camp-meetings were also still popular. Jane Agar Hopper described one held in the Township of Blenheim in June 1853 from Wednesday until the next Monday when the meeting broke up early because of wet weather. Families lived in tents in the bush "like a little worshipping village," she noted. At six in the morning, the first bell rang as a signal to prepare for breakfast. At eight it rang for family prayer in the tents. At ten, two, and seven, the people were called to public worship at a large square in the centre of the tent village. At ten at night, everyone retired, but some could be heard praying and singing throughout the night. Just before they broke up the camp, the participants marched around the campground singing, "Now here's my heart and here's my hand, To meet you in the heavenly land . . ."[15]

Unlike the Lyles, Woodill and Wilson appear to have been reasonably comfortable and financially secure. When the congregation at Salem wanted an organ, Wilson went to Toronto to buy it and kept it in their home. They added land to their farm in 1868. And when the neighbouring Wesleyan church was in disrepair, Wilson offered that congregation $500 of his own money to repair it. The donation had to be refused because no other funds could be raised. In later memoirs, their children mention that they always had a maid because Woodill was often away. The family was "well-connected." One of Woodill's relatives was "Squire" Woodill, and among the guests invited to his home for salmon fishing in the summer and hunting in the winter were the parliamentarian D'Arcy McGee and the journalist George Brown.[16]

Even though Woodill's preaching appointments were apparently limited in her later years, she was remembered as a preacher. A plaque in the brick church built on their farm reads:

> Sacred to the memory of a
> Beloved mother
> Jane Wilson
> Who was for 40 years teacher
> preacher and class leader
> in this church
> Born in little York now Toronto
> Feb 20 1824
> Fell asleep in Jesus July 17 1893
> She was truly a Mother in Israel
> Being full of the Holy Ghost
> And of faith.[17]

There were a number of women in the Primitive Methodist tradition who preached in Canada, but it is difficult to determine their names from the Preachers' Plans available because generally the initials of the preachers were listed instead of first names. Thomas Adams' journals in the *Primitive Methodist Magazine* in 1844 mention that his wife began a "female class" in the Niagara district where he was stationed, and Sister Murray was helping "push the work forward." Ruth Stovold Woodger (1818-1889) preached at Woodstock in 1851 where she was well accepted until she joined with the Bible Christians. Jane Agar Hopper gives a number of illustrations of women as money collectors, prayer leaders, and exhorters. Mrs. Markham exhorted in the 1840s; Mrs. C. Amy and her daughter Mrs. Harper led in prayer and at revivals; and Hannah Ward and Mrs. Jacob Camplin both led in prayer. Mrs. Stephenson, Hopper wrote cryptically, "had great help in her husband." Unfortunately, there is no indication of what she did except that she "brought much of the early Primitive Methodist fire across the ocean." She does tell us how her husband helped her: "he could arouse a prayer-meeting or class-meeting wonderfully." Even in 1881, Ann Swales and Jane Fletcher were listed on the Pickering Circuit as preachers, numbers five and sixteen respectively, out of fifty-one preachers. However, an examination of the plan available from April to July of that year shows that no preaching appointments had been scheduled for either woman.[18]

Women took an active role in the Primitive Methodist denomination for a few decades after it was transplanted to Upper Canada. Yet as in the Bible Christian groups, a shift occurred in the kind and quantity of women's activity that paralleled a change in the structures and customs in the denomination itself. As early as the late 1840s, women were restricted in their church activity. In a report of a meeting in an issue of the Primitive Methodist *Evangelist* in 1848, the writer noted the "superb style" in which the "ladies" managed a tea after the speeches. In the same newspaper in 1851, a "young, lovely and sensible mother" explained to the writer of a report on Missionary Societies that "I am a missionary in my nursery." The *Primitive Methodist Magazine* held up this same Victorian role model in an article entitled "Thoughts of a mother." The writer confessed: "Should I be asked, what has been the object of my thoughts in the morning, what has occupied my mind most during the day, to what have all my plans and employments referred . . . I should instantly answer, MY CHILDREN." Presumably, Primitive Methodist women heeded this advice and spent their time in house work and mother work, for on the winter 1856-57 Toronto City Circuit Plan, only one class out of twelve was led by a woman, Sister Kent.[19]

Jane Agar Hopper pointed out that in the 1850s the term "Rev." was very rarely used, but it became commonplace in the next decade. Camp-meetings were popular in the 1850s, but by the 1860s more energy was being put into a new newspaper and a Book Room, and in the *Minutes* of the Conference in 1863, for the first time the delegates were listed separately as lay and ministerial. The denomination still used local preachers, but they were accredited only after writing out their doctrinal position. A theological institute began, and the ritual of laying on of hands for ordination was being considered. Hopper wrote that by 1860 the earlier simplicity of the society was lost.[20]

In the "Ladies Department" of the Primitive Methodist *Christian Journal* in 1860, women were advised to "read newspapers" so they would "have something to talk about." An exegesis of a well-known biblical passage about women's relationship to men, 1 Corinthians 11:10, described the position of women as one of "curiously subordinated equality." What women could and could not do was being hotly debated, and in September of the same year the paper printed a defence of women entering the medical profession on the strength of a report that a Mrs. Winslow, a "nurse and physician" for thirty years, had compounded a soothing syrup for teething children. Behind this argument was the importance of the discovery. It was believed that many children died each year during the process of teething or at least became "debilitated" or "diseased." Newspapers commonly printed sermons for women, and the next year a front page "Sermon To Young Women" by a Primitive Methodist minister in Philadelphia set out the responsibility of women to society: "domestic economy" and the "economy of grace." The future of the nation, he wrote, depended on the spiritual piety of women. The Canadian Primitive Methodist newspapers echoed the conservative Canadian attitude towards women and their station in life. Women were expected to function in their proper sphere, that of housewife, mother, and spiritual guardian of the home. Gone was the early concept of equality in the home and in the church that Hopper described.[21]

Some of the male preachers would not accept women in a preaching role, believing that femininity and preaching were not compatible. As James Garfield, later president of the United States, responded in the 1850s to Antoinette Brown, the first woman ordained in the United States:

> *There is something about a woman's speaking in public that unsexes her in my mind, and how much soever I might admire the talent, yet I could never think of the female speaker as the gentle sister, the tender wife or the loving mother.*[22]

Even Mary Ann Lyle's sons-in-law had difficulty with women as preachers, although they were careful not to criticize her personally. At her funeral in 1862, one son-in-law, R.L. Tucker, also a Primitive Methodist preacher, expressed a concern that *"female preachers"* often lacked *"meekness, charity* and *domestic qualities."* This was not the case, he quickly pointed out, with his mother-in-law. Even though she "occasionally expounded the Word, and exhorted sinners to flee from the wrath to come," he noted, she was never "dictatorial and assuming" but always "modest and diffident." Tucker continued that it could be useful for a woman to be "public" occasionally as long as she could also "blend" this with a domestic life and a "meek and quiet spirit" and be a pattern of an exemplary wife and mother. His mother-in-law, he explained, was so correctly "diffident" that she was "unwilling to address the public while ministers were present" and "for many years she refused to preach in the presence of her own husband." If indeed this were true, it could explain why her preaching appointments in Canada were so limited. Another son-in-law and preacher, William Clarke, confirmed that Mary Ann Lyle was "modest and retiring," but disagreed on the extent of her activity. She *"frequently* addressed public assemblies," Clarke wrote. He agreed, however, that "she looked upon this as a sort of exception to God's usual way of working, and only felt justified in it when there was apparent need for her help." "Only a sense of duty," he added, "could have overcome her natural diffidence and nerved her for this work." Evidently, both men were imbued with the general belief of that time that all women were by nature shy and modest and unfit for the demanding and unwomanly occupation of preaching.[23]

A controversy over whether or not women should be allowed to preach appeared in the pages of the *Christian Journal* during the next decade. In 1873, the paper reprinted a talk given by the American Luther Lee under the heading "Woman's Right to Preach the Gospel." Lee, a Wesleyan

Methodist minister who had preached the sermon for the first woman to be ordained in the United States, argued in the affirmative, pointing out that the scriptures did not forbid women to preach. Indeed, he stated, the scriptures gave sufficient proof to allow it, and he noted that women possessed all of the qualifications necessary for the ministry. A few months later, a "lady contributor" raised the same issue, arguing that without question women should be allowed to preach anywhere throughout the world. They have the "talent, the heroism and the perseverance," the writer pointed out. It was not even necessary for women to be licensed, she went on, for they had been commissioned and given the authority to preach eighteen centuries earlier. In a strangely illogical manner, however, the author continued that women should never be ordained, for the Bible was "explicit and unequivocal" in its refusal to ordain women. Had Jesus intended to begin a "female ministry" the writer stated, one of the Marys mentioned in the New Testament would have been given a place among the twelve disciples.[24]

In his *History of the Primitive Methodist Connexion* published in 1880, J. Petty presented the history of the denomination without mentioning the contribution of any of the women preachers or itinerants, except for one brief reference to "Miss Smith who assisted Mr. Russell." In fact, Elizabeth Smith had been an extremely popular preacher, and according to her husband, Thomas Russell, she had her own demanding itineracy both before and after she married. Written eight years after J. Petty's work, H.B. Kendall's history was almost as exclusive, although he did refer to Sarah Kirkland, the best-known of the English itinerants, and "Miss Watkins." Even Hopper, whose study of Canadian Primitive Methodism recovered a number of the women, confused Ruth Watkins and her brother Nathaniel. Hopper wrote that the English Conference had replied to William Lawson's request for a missionary for Upper Canada by sending "Rev. R. Watkins, who was then in New York," and on the same page referred to this person as "Mr. Watkins." Ruth Watkins had been in New York as one of the first missionaries sent to America, but it was her brother Nathaniel and his wife who came to Canada from England the following year. Like the Bible Christians in Canada, the Primitive Methodist Society became permeated with Upper Canadian conservatism in the latter half of the nineteenth century, and the records of the Primitive Methodist women's extensive and successful labours were all but lost.[25]

Jane Woodill Wilson (1824-1893), Canadian Primitive Methodist preacher. (Photo courtesy of Betty Ward; The United Church of Canada/Victoria University Archives, Toronto.)

Beware of False Prophets—Matt. vii. 15.

PLACES OF PREACHING.	HOURS.	OCTOBER. 2	9	16	23	30	NOVEMBER. 6	13	20	27	DECEMBER. 4	11	18	25	PREACHERS.
Willington's	10½	—	. A	—	DC	—	A	—	G	.	A	.	J	—	A. W. Lyle
Smith's	2	—	AS	—	O	—	AT	—	F	—	A	.	D	—	B. D. Berry,
Churchville	6	—	A	—	—	—	A	—	A	.	A	.	—	—	C. M. Smith
Hemphill's	10½	A	. F	—	AS	—	BT	—	A	—	B	.	A	—	D. W. Lawson
Springfield	3	A	. 1	.	A	—	B	—	AC	—	B	.	A	—	E. W. Smith
Streetsville	6	A	. 1C	—	A	—	B	—	A	—	B	.	A	—	F. T. Turley
Whitsall's	10	—	D	—	1C	—	F	.	B	—	H	.	B	—	G. M.A. Lyle
Paisley's Churchville	2	—	D	—	1T	—	—	BC	—	—	.	B	—		H. M. Watson
Clarage's	2	F	. R	—	F	—	DC	—	J	—	. F	.	G		
Woodhill's	10	C	. 2	—	D	—	AC	—	C	—	. A	.	D		REFERENCES.
Rains,	2	C	. 2	—	D	—	AC	—	C	—	. A	.	D		
Albion,	6	—	. 2	—	—	—	A	—	—	—	. A	.	—		C. Collection.
Nichols's	10	B	. J	—	B	—	C	—	NC	—	. D	.	B		S. Sacrament.
Heglar's	2	B	—	—	B	—	—	—	NC	—	.	A	B		T. Tickets.
Tecumseth	10	—	—	2	—	B	—	AC	—	B	.	A	—		
Loyd Town	6	—	BS	—	2	—	BT	—	A	—	B	.	A	—	

A Day's Meeting will be held at Streetsville, Oct. 16th, No: 1 D F G. Quarterly meeting at Loyd Town Oct. 9th. At Hemphill's Oct. 30th. And the preparatory Quarter-day at Lawson's Nov. 24.

Mary Ann Lyle (1797-1862), Primitive Methodist preacher, is listed on the 1836 preachers' plan. (Photo: The United Church of Canada/Victoria University Archives, Toronto.)

Salem United Church, where Jane Woodill Wilson preached, began as a Primitive Methodist Church in 1861. (Photo courtesy Betty Ward; The United Church of Canada/Victoria University Archives, Toronto.)

V.
WOMEN SETTLE DOWN:
THE CANADIAN METHODIST
EPISCOPAL CHURCH

The good wife is one, who, ever mindful of the solemn contract which she hath entered into, is strictly and conscientiously virtuous, constant and faithful to her husband; chaste, pure, and unblemished in every thought, word and deed; she is humble and modest from reason and conviction, submissive from choice and obedient from inclination; ... she makes it her business to serve and her pleasure to oblige her husband ...

The good husband ... attributes [his wife's] follies to her weakness; her imprudence to her inadvertency; he passes them over therefore with good nature and pardons them with indulgence ...

Christian Guardian, 28 November 1829, p.13

I t is ironic that the Canadian Primitive Methodist and Bible Christian movements, which allowed women preachers at least for a few decades, were spawned in British conservative society, while the Canadian Methodist Episcopal Church, which appears to have offered little encouragement to women as leaders, came to Canada from the more liberal atmosphere of the United States.

There is, however, some evidence of women preaching in the Methodist Episcopal Church in Canada, especially in the early years. Other women, while not actively preaching, held leadership positions and indeed may have been more active than the available information describes. Records indicate that a few male pastors were sympathetic to women preaching. One intriguing conversation between an American Quaker minister and a Methodist in 1819 suggests that there were Methodist Episcopal men who were trying to persuade women to preach. After a visit to a Methodist meeting house close to Yonge Street in York, the Pennsylvania preacher, Edward Hicks, wrote in his memoirs:

> *I was led to speak of the rights of women – that they were one in Christ with men, and entitled to equal privileges, and that I had heard the Gospel preached by them in greater sweetness and power than I had ever heard from the lips of men. There was a precious silence covered the meeting, which seemed only interrupted by the suppressed weeping of some of the women. After the meeting ended, our kind Methodist friend took me by the hand and said in substance, "Dear brother, you ought to preach that sermon a dozen times over. Why we have been contending with our women about their right to preach."*[1]

In 1810, not long before this conversation took place, American-born Ellen Bangs Gatchell (d.1857) was exhorting in the Niagara region "like a streak of red-hot lightning." Her speaking gifts evidently surpassed those of her itinerant husband, Joseph Gatchell, and this is said to have pleased the members of their congregation. It is likely that he, too, found her abilities attractive; for Joseph Gatchell had been brought up as a Quaker, a denomination which had encouraged women leaders from its beginning in England in the seventeenth century. He was more radical than many of his co-workers, "impassioned" and "excitable," and later he was the only itinerant to vote in 1833 against the union of the Methodist Episcopal Church in Canada with the more conservative British Wesleyan stream. For this he suffered severe censure. The 1835 Conference *Minutes* reported that he had withdrawn "under very dishonorable circumstances" and was dropped from their records "without further notice." Ellen Bang's brother, Nathan, also supported women speaking in public. He had married Mary Bolton, who chafed at the restrictions put upon women in the New Testament Pauline writings. And he was a lifelong friend of the American evangelist and preacher Phoebe Worrall Palmer. Nathan Bangs and Palmer had attended the same catechetical class as children, and later he had acted as an unofficial president at the crowded weekly theological discussions in her house. "Why should any one oppose another, even though a female," he exclaimed in his journal. "I cannot but rejoice in whatever instrumentality God shall use for the salvation of souls," he wrote.[2]

Ann Dulmage Coate McLean's (b.ca.1777) story has some similarity. She, too, emigrated to Canada from the United States and her first marriage was to Samuel Coate, also a Methodist itinerant with a Quaker upbringing. Dulmage and

Coate were a stunning couple, the "handsomest pair" in Canada, and were reported to have superior intelligence and outstanding talents. The historian George Playter compared her to Abigail, an Old Testament woman described as being "of good understanding and of a beautiful countenance." Coate, who also was admired for his appearance, especially his long flowing hair, was likened to the biblical Absalom. An extremely popular preacher, Coate won converts by the hundreds in Canada until ill health forced him to leave the itineracy. He eventually became debtridden and died in England, leaving his wife and one daughter in Canada. Because of his debts and desertion of his family, Coate, like Joseph Gatchell, became an embarrassment to Canadian Methodists. Some historians later ignored the preaching successes he had had as a Methodist itinerant in Canada earlier in his life, while others referred to him as a "charlatan." We do not know precisely what role Ann Dulmage had in Canadian Methodism. It was not uncommon in the late eighteenth and early nineteenth centuries in the United States for Methodist women to travel on circuits with their itinerant husbands and help in the services, and when Ann Dulmage was first married, before she had children she accompanied Coate on horseback to his appointments. In 1804, she travelled with him to the Baltimore Conference. She also held meetings for women in her house.[3]

Margaret Bowes Taylor (1806-1859) is remembered better than either Ellen Bangs or Ann Dulmage, but the details of her work are just as elusive. Born in Ireland in 1806, she came to Canada in 1824 with her brother when she was eighteen, eventually marrying the Toronto merchant Samuel E. Taylor. Her brother, John George Bowes, served a number of terms as Toronto's mayor. She was repelled by the noise of camp-meetings, but at the same time was drawn to them, and at a camp-meeting in 1825 on the Yonge Street Circuit, she underwent an intense religious experience. This was the beginning of a deep commitment to Methodist activities, resulting in her involvement with the evangelist Phoebe Worrall Palmer and her husband, Walter Palmer, at camp-meetings in Ontario in the 1850s. Presumably, Bowes participated in the services with them, for she is described as "labouring" with the Palmers. At other times, she entered taverns and basement rooms, with at least one Methodist itinerant, to pray with the "denizens" of one of the "dirtiest" streets in Toronto, and she led as many as four Methodist classes at one time. She had a "remarkable gift of prayer," and when the Methodist Indian missionary Peter Jones was ill in 1856, it was noted that she prayed "most fervently" for his recovery. On her death in 1859, the *Christian Guardian* compared her spirituality to that of two renowned British Wesleyan women, Hester Ann Roe Rogers and Mary Bosanquet Fletcher. The men and women in her funeral cortège sang hymns all the way from her home to the church where the service was held. Margaret Bowes had requested that there be no mourning at her funeral.[4]

However, the best-documented woman preaching in Canada in the Methodist Episcopal tradition was Eliza Barnes (1796-1887), a dynamic and energetic Indian missionary teacher who came from the New England states in the 1820s and later married William Case, Superintendent of Indian Missions. The historian John Carroll wrote that she preached in a number of places after her arrival in Canada and was responsible for at least one revival. Carroll places her in the tradition not only of the fairly restrained English Wesleyan preacher Mary Bosanquet Fletcher, but also of the popular and rebellious Irish preacher Alice Cambridge and the equally iconoclastic English preacher Mary Barritt Taft. In fact, both

Alice Cambridge and Mary Barritt were still preaching when she began taking part in Canadian revivals.[5]

Barnes was born in Boston, Massachusetts on November 11, 1796. Most historians record her arrival at the Canadian Indian Missions in May 1828, when William Case returned from a fund-raising tour to the United States. But Barnes had been working at the missions at least a year earlier. In July 1827, the *Christian Advocate* reported that she was at Grape Island superintending the women in "knitting, sewing, and manufacturing straw hats." In October of that year she visited the mission, and she spoke in Albany, New York sometime before April 17, 1828 about her mission work. The newspaper noted that she had been "proclaiming the glad tidings of salvation" at Grape Island among the Indians the previous year. And the *Missionary Society Report* in 1827 notes that a salary of £14 had been paid to a "female teacher" who had been working for six months at the Credit Mission that year.[6]

In her first years as a missionary, Barnes travelled from mission to mission, supervising Indian women, organizing benevolent societies, and teaching children and adults. She made at least one trip annually to the United States to raise funds and make reports. The year 1829 is typical of her constant activity. In February, she travelled north with male missionaries on an exploratory trip to Holland Landing to discuss establishing a mission on Snake Island in Lake Simcoe. In March, she set out on a two-and-a-half-month tour of the New England states to raise funds and arrange for translation. By the middle of May, she was at the Rice Lake Mission, and two months later, she began a mission tour of Lake Simcoe and Lake Huron. In September she was working at the Grape Island Mission. In October she was at York collecting supplies for the Credit River Mission, and in December she organized a benevolent society for the Indian women at that mission.[7]

She was a successful fundraiser. In July 1830, she arrived back from the United States "richly laden." She had been to New York, Philadelphia, Baltimore, and Boston and had collected $1300 as well as donations of clothing and furniture. In March of the next year, she collected money for a mission house on the Grand River. She organized women's Dorcas Societies to raise money to spread religion among the native Indians. Dorcas Societies, named after the New Testament woman Dorcas who was "full of good works and acts of charity," were common in the United States. Barnes obtained the materials the Indian women in these societies needed to make moccasins, gloves, straw hats, and brooms, and when the products were finished, she took them to city bazaars. She was a much-admired, well-known, and tireless worker; in 1832 an anonymous donor gave $20 for a life membership in the Missionary Society for Miss Barnes, "the lady who is living among the Indians, teaching their little ones to read the good book." In fact, in James Youngs' 1830 *History of the Rise and Progress of Methodism in England and America,* "Miss Barns" [*sic*] is one of the few Canadian missionaries mentioned by name.[8]

Of all her skills and accomplishments, historians were most impressed by her preaching ability. At one time she created a "sensation" preaching in York. There were a number of revivals at the missions from their beginning in 1823 until 1827, and it is possible that she was a part of this activity. Upper New York State, familiar territory for her, was ablaze with religious revivals as part of the Second Great Awakening, and women were taking a leading role. Peter Jones' journals refer to a number of occasions when Barnes "addressed," "preached," or "exhorted" on the Indian Missions in Canada in 1828 and 1829 and on her American tours in 1829 and 1830. When she and her friend Hetty Hubbard (ca.1796-1831) arrived together at the Grape Island Mission in May 1828, both of them spoke, Barnes at a prayer meeting the first evening and Hubbard the next day. Barnes' speech was described as "much to the feelings of the assembly," and it was said that she spoke very "fluently." At a camp-meeting in Haldimand in June, she gave a theological "discourse" that covered a wide range of Christian thought – the "incarnation, death, resurrection and ascension of our Lord and Saviour." Again her hearers reported that she spoke fluently, with a strong voice, and "very figuratively." She was responsible for a great religious revival, such as was not seen again in the area for thirty years, and this sermon may have precipitated it. In 1829, she undertook a number of speaking engagements and caused a mild "Pentecost" at Yellowhead's Island in Lake Simcoe. The Indian missionary Peter Jones wrote of that occasion that it seemed as if "the very gates of heaven were opened to our souls, and the spirit of God descending upon our hearts." Jones saw a footpath appear "like a blaze of fire" and the whole camp, he wrote, "manifested the presence of God." One evening in February, she preached to a large gathering of Indians at Holland Landing "with her usual eloquence," and also exhorted. Later that month, she "addressed" the "whites" in the Mission House at a meeting on Grape Island, although it is recorded that at the same time Peter Jones "preached" to the Indians in the chapel. And in May, she spoke in the John Street Church in New York City to the Dorcas Missionary Society about her "trials and sufferings" on the Indian Missions. The next year she spoke twice in that same church with "simplicity and artlessness" and so "fervently" that many of the congregation were reduced to tears.[9]

John Carroll wrote that Eliza Barnes was "tolerated" as a preacher. But the Methodist educationist and temperance

111

worker Letitia Creighton Youmans reported that Barnes had been a successful preacher in the United States, and when she came to Canada she was greatly sought after for camp-meetings and services in private homes. Youmans recorded the reminiscences of one woman whose doorway became the "pulpit" for one of Barnes' sermons. The inside of the house was filled with women; the men stood in the large yard in front of the house. The text she took was from Ezekiel's "vision of the waters," the woman recalled.

> *"When the preacher [Barnes] spoke of the spread of the Gospel, and quoted in raptured accents,* the waters were still rising," *said the old lady, "I fancied I could still see the waters of life flowing in until the earth was filled with the* glory *of God."*[10]

Youmans pointed out that in spite of Barnes' popularity, a number of the male preachers objected to her speaking "in the Church," especially William Case, who at first refused to sit on the platform with her. There are no references to her preaching after 1829 in Canada, and only two speaking engagements are recorded for her later in the United States, both in 1830. Carroll wrote that she "settled down" soon after she came to Canada, probably because she married the widowed William Case in 1833 at the home of a friend in Belleville. In her diary she referred to her wedding very briefly and somewhat perfunctorily:

> *[August] 13th. Tuesday I went in company with Mr. Case to Belleville, where I stopped until the 28th. There we were married.*

Her entry a week earlier had noted that "her trials were neither few nor small," but what her trials were can only be speculated. A gifted preacher, she stopped preaching abruptly and "settled down." Unlike the Bible Christian Elizabeth Dart Eynon, whose preaching activity continued after marriage, Barnes was thrust into a "companion" stereotype of minister's wife in the more conservative Methodist stream. Her first and only child, Caroline Hetty, was born the next year and named after her friend Hetty Hubbard, William Case's first wife, but Caroline died almost eleven months later. Barnes continued teaching household and "domestic duties" at the missions where they lived. After her husband's death in 1855, she lived for five more years in their house in Belleville until she could no longer maintain the mortgage payments. She died April 16, 1887 at the age of ninety-one.[11]

Barnes was not the only female Indian missionary who spoke in public. Susannah Farley Waldron (1802-1890) and Hetty Ann Hubbard were both considered to be extremely gifted, with "rare gifts in speaking and prayer." Like Barnes, Waldron was from the New England states and had been teaching at Grape Island even before 1828 when official records note the beginning of female teachers. Perhaps she, too, had imbibed New England revivalism, and like many of the American women had been encouraged to preach in the United States. Hubbard was from Springfield, Massachusetts, about seventy miles from Barnes' birthplace, and she had been baptized at age twenty into the Congregational Church. She, too, was a competent speaker but a more retiring and less public figure than Barnes, and most of her work appears to have been confined to teaching home economics and singing at the Grape Island Mission School. In his diary, Peter Jones refers to her speaking only once, when she arrived at the Indian Missions in May 1828 with Case and Barnes. Likely

Case's aversion to women speaking in public had some influence on her, too. A year after she arrived at the Grape Island Mission, she married him in New York City. Barnes was part of the small bridal party, as her only bridesmaid. The next year, Hetty had a daughter, and she never regained her strength. She died only two and a half years after her marriage, at about thirty-five years of age.[12]

Eliza Barnes, Hetty Ann Hubbard, and Susannah Farley Waldron are only three of some twenty-five women mentioned in early record books, newspapers, and journal accounts who held leadership positions on at least six of the Methodist Episcopal Indian Missions in Upper Canada from 1827 to the early 1830s. How many of them preached we do not know, but they led worship, initiated and supervised women's groups and taught school at the River Credit, nineteen miles west of York; at Grape Island in the Bay of Quinte, six miles from Belleville; at Rice Lake, twelve miles north of Cobourg; at the Lake Simcoe Mission at the "Narrows" today known as Orillia; on the south side of Lake Huron at the Sahgeeng; and at the Muncey Mission on the River Thames. Many of them are recorded without first names; most have left few details of their activities: Sally Ash (Mrs. Sabine Frazer); Miss Bayles; Mrs. John B. Benham; Nancy Brink; Sophia Cook (1798-1849); Margaret Dulmage (1803-1873) (Mrs. Sylvester Hurlburt); Phoebe [Phebe] Edmonds [Edwards]; Miss Farley, a sister of Susannah Farley Waldron; Miss French; Miss Huntingdon; Miss Kunze; Sarah Lancaster; Mercy Miner Manwaring (1809-1891) (Mrs. Andrew Moffatt); Mrs. McMullen; Miss Pinny; Miss E[mma or Elizabeth] Rolph; Sarah Rolph (1797-1829) (Mrs. George Ryerson); Miss Sealy; Eliza Sellicks [Sillick, Scelec]; Miss Stockton; Miss Verplanck; and Miss S. Yeomans. Undoubtedly other women whose names are lost, perhaps forever, were actively involved.[13]

That Barnes was considered different from the other women is evident from the fact that her exploits were recorded in greater detail. The Missionary Society recorded her salary under the special heading "Miss Barnes" rather than the usual designation "female Teacher," even though she received a female school teacher's wage.

Barnes also appears to have been more aggressive than most of the other women, but no more daring. Women who chose a missionary career in that era needed courage and a spirit of adventure, for they had to endure great hardships and often risked their lives. Indeed, only those missionaries who were physically fit were able to tolerate for any length of time the conditions the mission field imposed.

Travel was hazardous, and the work demanded frequent trips by land and water between the missions. Margaret Dulmage Hurlburt worked for twenty-one years as a missionary. At times in the late fall she was so drenched by water on canoe trips that gloves would freeze to her hands. Barnes and Miss Verplanck were thrown from a wagon travelling between Rice Lake and the Credit Mission, and Barnes and Phoebe Edmonds had a terrifying moment when a sudden gale almost capsized their schooner on "Lake Koochecheeng" [sic] en route to visit mission sites.[14]

Housing was often primitive, supplies were scarce, and loneliness was a part of many of the women's daily existence. Waldron was often short of food. Once she was unable to offer a visiting clergyman anything at all to eat. She lived on Indian Missions for twelve years, and on one trip from Whitby to the Muncey Mission she travelled with two children by canoe and on horseback through mire and bush and over logs, harassed continually by mosquitoes, only to reach a vermin-infested mission house that she had to scrub with turpentine to make livable. Mrs. John B. Benham taught school in a bark "wigwaum" at the Sah-geeng Mission on Lake Huron in 1831; she lived sixty miles from the closest white settlement, and newspapers reported that she did not see another white woman for a year. A New Yorker, Miss Bayles, was isolated at her school half the year in 1833 because of ice. Sally Ash and Barnes taught in a seventeen-foot-square school house on Rice Lake in 1828. The six-foot-high sides and roof were made of ash and cedar bark fastened to upright posts. Indian women wove bark carpeting and the men built a clay oven. Ash and Barnes not only taught twenty-five girls "domestic economy" and how to read, sew, knit, and braid straw in this tiny building, but they lived in it as well. Shortly after it was built, the house caught fire, and the women had a narrow escape. That summer, Barnes lived in a wigwam on an island because of virulent fever on the mainland. In his early history, James Youngs reported a fire at the Mission on "Lake Simco" [sic] that forced the missionaries to flee to canoes in the water, and it may have been that Barnes was imperilled again. Mercy Manwaring shared one room with seven of her female students.[15]

Health care was inadequate. Infant mortality was high, and women often died in childbirth or suffered ill health as a result of the rigours of their existence. The Grape Island Mission near Belleville boasted a log hospital for women as early as 1828, and the River Credit settlement had a hospital building twenty by forty feet at least by 1829. Generally, however, physicians were distant. The closest doctor was forty miles from the mission on Yellowhead's Island. Missionary women who became ill or those who married and became pregnant might be bundled off to in-laws, friends, or relatives. Often, however, the missions took their toll. Credit missionary Sarah Rolph Ryerson, sister of the prominent Canadian physician and politician John Rolph, was the first woman to die exhausted from the work. Her husband,

George, was still devastated by the loss three years after her death. Sophia Cook taught for two years at the Credit Mission when ill health forced her to return to her home in Rochester, New York in 1834, although she did return to the Alderville Mission to spend the last years of her life there in the 1840s. Susannah Farley Waldron was left alone on a remote mission with a three-day-old baby in convulsions while her husband, Solomon, began a weeks tour of the missions. Missionary husbands had little time to devote to family crises, for the demanding work of the missionary cause came first. As Leonard Sweet noted in his study of eighteenth-century wives of ministers, "itinerants' indifference to their own well-being was matched only by their insensitivity to the welfare of their families."[16]

The classroom work itself was demanding. Classes were large and the work hours long. Sophia Cook taught reading, writing, arithmetic, geography, and grammar to almost fifty children at the Credit. Miss Pinny taught approximately fifty as well, and Miss Huntingdon had thirty students in her classes. There were thirty-eight girls in the school at the Lake Simcoe Mission in 1832, and Hetty Hubbard had thirty in her class on Grape Island four years earlier. Mercy Manwaring taught fifty Chippewa boys and girls in her school at the "Narrows" in 1833 and planned to leave unless she received an assistant. Andrew Moffatt was sent there to help, and they taught together, evidently with much compatibility, for they were married in December 1834. The women were not only in charge of weekday schools, but also instructed adults in the evening and organized a full programme for Sunday. Their days began at five o'clock in the morning in winter, at four in summer. On Sundays there could be as many as six sessions – prayer meetings, preaching services, and classes.[17]

Although newspaper accounts and missionary reports

described the North American Indian as wild, savage, barbarian, and dangerous, these stories were products of the prejudices of the era, and in fact the missionaries faced greater danger from travelling. There was some concern, however, at one time for the safety of the teacher at the Muncey Mission because of an initial resistance to the school by the Indians who were afraid that "white" schooling would prevent their children from learning how to hunt. Miss Farley was assaulted there by a drunken man who came to the school, "stove in the door," seized her, and tore her dress to shreds, and her brother-in-law, Solomon Waldron, faced a knife-wielding man in the church. But these appear to have been isolated instances.[18]

Not only were the women required to tolerate physical hardships, but there were strict moral and spiritual demands as well. Methodism was a "serious" business, and its missionaries were expected to be paradigms of piety and sobriety. Indian children were praised for their serious and prayerful deportment. "Those who play when they are young, will play when they are old" was a Methodist motto. But the women especially were called upon to be exemplary, and Methodist hagiography portrays the female teachers as living up to that ideal. Phoebe Edmonds was "a pious girl," and Sarah Rolph Ryerson an "accomplished, amiable lady, meek, kind and generous." Sophia Cook was said to be "a burning and shining light actively and zealously engaged in works of faith and labours of love." Eliza Barnes' diary displays an emotionally controlled formality. Three weeks after she married William Case, she was still referring to him in her diary as "Mr. Case." Not until a month after her wedding does she mention "my dear husband." And she referred to her sister teachers, with whom she had worked for several months, as "Miss Verplanck" and "Miss Cook."[19]

Bells, horns, and regular meal times were part of an extremely structured and rigid missionary lifestyle, since order, stability, and diligence were understood to be external marks of internal grace. Neatness, too, was supremely important. A high ranking visitor to the school at Grape Island in 1828 reported that the operations were in perfect order. "There was a place for everything, and everything was in its place," he wrote. Two years later, Peter Jones made a detailed inspection of all the houses there and found Margaret Dulmage Hurlburt's house "all neat like a white squaw's house" should be, "except that the tea kettle was out of place." The fact that she was sick in bed was no excuse! The Canada Conference of the Missionary Society noted the importance of setting an example of industrious labour for the Indians. Only in displaying "settled habits of industry" could this trait be encouraged in the Indians, and the accepted missionary theory was that settled tribes were more easily taught Christian precepts, educated, and civilized. "A roving life" exposed the Indians to temptations and reduced the chances of the "indolent savage" becoming an "industrious Christian." For all Methodists, however, settled habits were part of godliness. The denominational newspaper, the *Christian Guardian,* urged all men to stay at home as much as possible. "As a bird that wandereth from her nest, so is a man that wandereth from his place."[20]

High demands were placed on all the women, but minister's wives, as many of the missionary teachers became, were enjoined to be the "holiest" and "most spiritual" women in habits, conversation, and in their whole deportment. "Her prudence should equal her piety," explained the *Christian Guardian.* An early London Methodist Conference had spelled out the requirement that they be patterns of cleanliness and industry as well:

Let nothing slatternly be seen about her; no rags; no dirt; no litter. And she should be a pattern of industry: always at work, either for herself, her husband or the poor.[21]

Indeed, it seems as if missionary women were not allowed any human frailty, although occasionally there is a glimpse of something less than perfection. In his autobiography, Solomon Waldron mentioned that there had been disagreements between some of the missionaries and particularly between Eliza Barnes and Hester Ann Hubbard, both of whom were "passionately fond" of William Case, and both in turn his wife. Only when Hester Ann died, did the "painful struggles" between the women cease. And Solomon noted that his wife, Susannah Farley, gave up tea, tobacco, and alcohol in 1835. Evidently she had been using those stimulants for some time previously.[22]

Nor were the women permitted discontent. Public reports emphasized over and over again that they were "happy in their employment." For example, Mrs. Benham was "healthy and happy" in her "isolation" surrounded only by 150 "Indian souls." When Sally Ash and Eliza Barnes lived in wigwams on an island in Rice Lake in the summer of 1828, they were said to be "contented and happy in doing good." The women, however, can no longer speak for themselves, and we do not know if this was indeed the case. Of all the letters and diaries they must have written, only a brief extract survives from Barnes' journal in August 1833, the month she married Case. In terse, short sentences, she had written of unspecified problems. Three years earlier, when she had spoken at the John Street Church in New York City, it was reported that she talked about "her trials and sufferings" while "labouring" on the Indian Missions. Since most of the women stayed only a short time at one station, it could be that the women found the conditions intolerable. However, it was a Methodist practice to move ministers regularly from circuit to circuit, so this may have been a factor in the frequent moves of the women. In addition, ill health often forced them to leave a mission after a short stay.[23]

Even with the harsh working conditions, it should not be surprising that there were women in the forefront of this new missionary endeavour, "civilizing" and converting the Canadian Indians. First of all, the American and Canadian Methodist Societies had adopted Wesley's practice of separating sexes in worshipping congregations and in classes, although in sparsely populated pioneer communities this segregation could not always be enforced and gradually disappeared. But when the Canada Conference of the Methodist Episcopal Church set up Indian schools in 1825 to "tame the savages and Christianize the heathen," the authorities thought it proper that female missionaries be sought to teach the women and girls apart from the men and boys. Second, many of these missionary women were Americans, coming from a culture which accepted and encouraged an active role for women in many of its religious denominations, particularly during the early nineteenth-century religious revivals. Barnes, Farley, and Hubbard, apparently the first women to arrive at the missions, were from the United States, and many of those who followed had either lived in that country for a number of years or had been born there and emigrated as young children to Canada. Sophia Cook, Mercy Manwaring, and Mrs. John Benham were New Englanders by birth and had lived there for some time. We know that at least Barnes was preaching in that country before coming to Canada; possibly Hubbard and Farley were as well, as both were reported to be gifted speakers. Hubbard spoke briefly after she arrived in Canada and later in the United States when she and Barnes went there on fundraising tours for the Canadian Missions.

The polity of the Canadian Methodist Episcopal Church required the active participation of these women, but the acceptable norms of the church placed severe limitations on their activity. Never progressive in its attitude toward careers for women outside the home, the main body of the Canadian Methodist Church was becoming increasingly more conservative in that area. In spite of Barnes' obvious success and popularity among the people, by the end of the second decade preaching was clearly considered by church leaders to be out of bounds for women. Women promoted Christianity by the "eloquence which flows from subjection," noted the *Christian Guardian* in 1829. A woman preaching was considered to be an "eccentric effort," out of her "sphere." Even leading family devotions in the absence of one's husband was a "privilege" for women and not a right, the paper pointed out. Women had a different role. Ladies "preach the precious gospel" by sewing gloves and moccasins, knitting mittens, making baskets and brooms, "Rev. Mr. Ryerson from the [Canadian] Mohawk mission" explained to the Dorcas Society in New York at its anniversary service in 1831. "Kindly affections and benevolence" were "doubly attractive when exercised by females," he suggested. After 1830, there are no more references to any of the missionary women preaching or speaking in public, and it is reported that Barnes "settled down" not long after her arrival in Canada.[24]

Other boundaries were imposed on the women. Most of the female missionaries were restricted to a teaching role and within that profession to a clearly defined area: instructing women and children in elementary education and "domestic economy" or how to keep house. At Grape Island in 1830,

Miss French taught the girls to make their own clothing; the boys learned arithmetic, English grammar, writing, and geography under a male teacher. Mercy Manwaring had the care of the younger boys as well as the girls there in 1833 during the summer months while the male teacher took the older boys into the field to teach them agriculture. In 1834 she taught only girls, although she had been teaching both sexes while waiting for an assistant. At the Credit River in 1828, Sarah Lancaster, described as a "pious young lady from York," taught her pupils to read, sew, write, and knit. Much of the women's time was taken up with supervising the activities of the Dorcas Societies – groups of women who gathered together to make hand-crafted goods for sale. The money raised was used at the missions for school supplies and other expenses. Some other women in addition to Barnes did have broader responsibilities and were not as limited. Margaret Dulmage taught classes of men as well as women and travelled with her husband, Sylvester, on pastoral visits. In 1829, a woman, Miss Stockton, was hired to work at Grape Island introducing the Pestalozzian method of instruction, a system which was to be used by both male and female teachers.[25]

For the most part, however, as the nineteenth century progressed, Episcopal Methodists became more inclined to define for women a role of submissive virtuous housewife and benevolent charity bazaar lady. Woman's proper sphere is in the home, the *Christian Guardian* assured its readers in 1829. Housework is a woman's "peculiar and appropriate employment" and demands her full attention, the paper noted. Week after week, the denominational newspaper hammered home the role of woman in Christian society.

*The wife is not expected to go into the field, the
workshop or the counting house.*

*To the middling class of life there is no female
accomplishment more valuable than house-
wifery.*[26]

God had placed woman in the home to serve and submit,
the newspaper pointed out, in order to eliminate the perpetual
strife which would result from equality, but in any case, women
were not considered to be strong enough emotionally or
physically for the more rigorous outside jobs. Women are
"subjected to the trials of disobedience and weakness of a
feebler constitution" wrote the editor of the Methodist *Christian
Advocate*. The *Colonial Advocate* explained that:

*There is a delicacy of fibre in women, and a
susceptibility of mind which make them feel
more acutely than the other sex all external
influences. Hence their whole system is often
violently affected with hysterics and other va-
rieties of nervous weakness.*

And in the opinion of the *Christian Guardian*, a "Good
Wife" makes it her business to serve and her pleasure to
oblige her husband, whereas a "Good Husband" attributes
his wife's follies to her weakness.[27]

Not all women were willing to fit into this stereotype and
to accept the advice offered by the "Ladies Department" of
Canada's best-known religious journal. One woman in 1829,
who found the *Christian Guardian's* view of women offensive, summarized it in these words:

*Honour us; deal kindly with us. From many of
the opportunities, and means by which you
procure favourable notice, we are excluded.
Doomed to the shades, few of the high places of
the earth are open to us. Alternately we are
adored, and oppressed. From our slaves, you
become our tyrants. You feel our beauty, and
avail yourselves of our weakness. You com-
plain of our inferiority, but none of your behaviour bids us rise. Sensibility has given us a
thousand feelings, which nature has kindly
denied you. Always under restraints we have
little liberty of choice. Providence seems to have
been more attentive to enable us to confer
happiness than to enjoy it. Every condition has
for us fresh mortifications; every relation new
sorrows. We enter social bonds; it is a system of
perpetual sacrifice. We cannot give life to others without hazarding our own. We have
sufferings which you do not share, cannot
share. . .*[28]

In 1833, two women wrote that women in other countries
had much greater opportunities:

*Women in this country are not sufficiently
considered, they who in every other land have
attracted to themselves the consideration of
all, have here been neglected and left in oblivion.*

Much to the amusement of the *Advocate* editor, another
woman wrote what was described as "a spirited letter of

reproof" to that paper for publishing so many degrading lectures for wives and ladies and none for husbands and gentlemen.[29]

Given this climate, the Indian Missions offered exciting alternatives for women to step beyond the commonly accepted mould in spite of the restrictions imposed on them by the official policy of the Episcopal Methodist Church. Organizing Dorcas Societies enabled them to develop their leadership and organizational skills. And a salaried teaching career outside the home would be an appealing possibility, not only for women within the church, but in society as well. In her studies of Canadian schools in the nineteenth century, Alison Prentice points out that it was not until 1871 that an equal number of men and women were teaching in public or common schools in Upper Canada. In 1835, a small Upper Canadian government commission recommended that women should be trained as teachers because "that best fits" a woman "for that domestic relation she is primarily designed to fill." But even by 1851, only 20 per cent of all teachers were female. Although women were considered to be more suitable for nurturing infants and very young children, there was a question as to how effective they were in "governing" school-aged children. Indeed, before 1840 there were very few schools at all, and most education took place at home with voluntary instructors. Some women advertised in the *Christian Guardian*. The Misses McCord had a Day and Boarding School in 1831, and Mrs. Sarah Foster a similar establishment. But these situations, even in secular society, were few.[30]

The female missionaries were hired as teachers, and were clearly differentiated from male missionaries in the missionary society account books. The women were paid less than the male teachers on the missions, but it was customary in society to pay women smaller salaries. In fact as more women entered the teaching profession in the public schools, their salaries declined as a percentage of men's. In 1851 in Toronto, a woman was paid 69 per cent of a man's salary; by 1861, she was paid only 41 per cent of his salary. It has been suggested that in the latter part of the century, school trustees discovered that they could hire two female teachers for the price of one male, and they began hiring more women, and paying them less proportionately. Something similar may have happened at the Mission Schools, although fewer women were hired in the later years than in the early 1830s. In 1832, non-Indian male school teachers were paid between £37 10s. and £40 per year. Women were paid on the average £29 5s. or approximately 75 per cent of the salary received by men. Later, in 1850, a female teacher at the Grand River received only £15 per year, whereas the male teacher was paid £50. The woman received only 30 per cent of the man's salary. There is, however, the example of Sophia Cook who was paid £46 to teach at the Alderville Mission in 1844; this compares more favourably with the male teacher's salary of £50 per year. In any event, in 1832, the women at the missions were paid more than the Indian missionary teachers. Two native Indians, Peter Jones and John Sunday, who were internationally acclaimed missionaries, were paid only £25 a year to do the same work as their non-Indian brothers and sisters. Moreover, the female missionary teachers received a considerably higher wage than the female itinerants travelling in the same territory for the Primitive Methodist Church. These latter women received only £10 a year, although they were given free room and board in addition to their stipend. There is no record as to whether or not the Methodist Episcopal missionary men and women received free room and board, but one might assume this was indeed the case, considering the makeshift quarters in which they sometimes found themselves. (See Table 2)[31]

It is not possible to tell if all the female missionary teachers were paid, but it is probable that only the single women were. Many of the year-end statements list only "female teacher" beside the wage with no name. The first women to teach were single. Working on the missions provided an option, at least for a few years, to the norm of marriage. Generally, singleness was not well thought of. Celibacy, the *Christian Guardian* noted, is like a fly in the heart of the apple. It is confined and "dies in singularity." On the other hand, marriage is like a "useful bee." It feeds the world "with delicacies" and "promotes the virtue of mankind."[32]

Leonard Sweet notes that marrying a minister in the nineteenth century was a passport to "influence, deference and power," and that many women considered themselves fortunate to be a minister's wife, although an itinerant's wife was not such a favourable prospect. Most of the women, such as Hubbard and Barnes, did marry on the mission field, although some like Cook – a respected career woman all her life – remained single. Many of those women who did marry, married missionaries or ministers, and it is likely that they would be expected to continue their work without pay, as part of the duty of a missionary's wife. Women such as Barnes, who had been active before, found marriage in the Canadian Methodist Episcopal tradition not an opening to influence and power but a downgrading of their position and led to public silence.[33]

Table 2 – Comparison of Selected Male and Female Salaries in Upper Canada

	FEMALE	MALE
Secular school teacher, 1833		£37 10s.
Non-Indian school teacher, 1832 Methodist Episcopal Indian Missions	£29 5s.**	£37 10s.-£40**
Non-Indian missionary, 1832 Methodist Episcopal Indian Missions		£50**
Indian teacher/missionary, 1832 Methodist Episcopal Indian Missions		£25**
Itinerant preacher, 1832 Primitive Methodist Church	£10*	£16 16s.-£21 8s.*
Farm labourer, 1831		£26-£36*
Millwright/engineer/artisan, 1831-33		£72-£92
Domestic servant, 1831-1833	£9-£18*	£24*
Church of England clergyman, 1831		£100-£300
Roman Catholic Bishop, 1827-43		£400
Average salary, 1851 School teacher, Toronto	£73 2s.	£105
Average salary, 1851 School teacher, province	£33 10s.	£55 2s.

*The itinerants and servants received room and board. The farm labourers were given board. **Possibly includes room and board.[34]*

While it is true that teaching school on the missions permitted Methodist Episcopal women to have a career, it is also the case that in society at large in Upper Canada, teaching was not a prestigious position. Some considered teachers to be on the same level as household servants. As late as 1835, it was said that a student respected a "school master" "just as much as one bear does" its hunters.[35] Although the female missionary teachers earned considerably more than female servants, they were paid salaries approximately the same as those of good experienced male servants and farm labourers. On the missions and in Methodist circles, however, the missionary teachers, and especially those who were also preaching, were highly regarded and experienced adulation in the workplace. Indians flocked to greet them when they arrived at missions. Indian children and other missionaries' children bore their names, and Missionary Society members revered them. Their obituaries depict them as being without fault, and they became part of a Methodist missionary hagiography while still alive.

There were other rewards for the women who worked on the missions besides the more tangible benefits of a career, salary, and high praise. Devout Christians of that era had seized upon the idea of "rescuing" and transforming the "perishing" Indian as a romantic and glorious notion. Even more than that, converting the Indians assured the missionaries of rewards in heaven, for on the "great day of retribution" all those who had saved even one soul would be acknowledged. The women would be amply repaid for any sacrifices they had had to make.[36]

Missionary women often exhibited Indian children to awestruck assemblies who marvelled at the children's ability to learn and at their metamorphosis. Psychologically, the teachers must have received tremendous gratification for the part they played in this transformation. It was not uncommon for school children to be examined in public for as long as three days at a time, but an examination of Indian children would have been a novelty. In the fall of 1827, at the third anniversary gathering of the Canada Conference Missionary Society, fourteen children from the River Credit school displayed samples of their writing, read from both the New Testament and the English Reader, spelled words of four syllables, and sang hymns and repeated the Lord's Prayer and the Ten Commandments in English and in an Indian language. The next year, Hetty Hubbard "examined" twenty Grape Island school children in the Kingston chapel before a large, interested audience. A newspaper report of the event noted that the clean, well-behaved children were very recently part of a tribe of Indians who had been "grasping at the intoxicating bowl" and "wallowing in filth about our streets." In the early spring of 1829, Barnes and Hubbard took six of their pupils with them to New England. In New York City two thousand Sabbath School teachers and pupils listened to the Canadian eight-year-old Indian boys and teenaged Indian girls read from the New Testament, answer catechetical questions, and spell. One child spoke to the whole assembly.[37]

While the women were accorded high status in one context and were encouraged in their public appearances, they were often referred to only anonymously by Methodist officialdom. Mission reports tantalize with the paucity of detail about the women's work. There are passing references to faceless spinsters known only by their father's last name or missionary wives identified by their husband's name. Male teachers and missionaries by contrast generally rated an initial or first name. In 1832, when Sylvester Hurlburt wrote to William Case from Grape Island on the progress of the mission, he noted:

> *the female school was never doing better; the girls love and respect their teacher, and so they should, for she feels deeply interested for them, and takes much pains to instruct them and improve their manners.*[38]

Typically, the teacher's name is not mentioned by Hurlburt nor by Case, who published the letter. She might have been Miss Verplanck or even Hurlburt's wife, Margaret Dulmage. The *Christian Guardian* paid tribute in 1830 to an "anonymous pious lady" who laboured at several mission stations and travelled extensively to aid the society, in all probability referring to Eliza Barnes.[39] Perhaps the *Guardian*, which advocated a more secluded existence for women, was caught between wanting to give her the credit that was her due and at the same time was loath to hold up her lifestyle as a model for other women to follow. As a result of the sparse and scattered references to the women's work, few of their lives can be pieced together, and most are known only as Indian teachers, such as Miss French and Miss Huntingdon.

In 1833, the Methodist Episcopal Church united with the British Wesleyans, the conservative stream of Methodism that had passed legislation in 1803 prohibiting women from speaking in the pulpit in the London Conference. Some women continued to work on the missions after 1833, although their numbers were substantially reduced. The union disrupted the publication of the Missionary Society Reports, and when they appeared again, there were few references to salaries for women school teachers. Reports from the missions published in newspapers rarely mentioned women, and the extant journals indicate that most of the women who taught after 1833 were supportive wives of missionary husbands. Even Eliza Barnes restricted her activities after her marriage to the widower William Case in 1833. Described as a woman "possessed of a powerful mind" she, nevertheless, appears to have adjusted to the expected model of a Canadian Methodist Episcopal minister's wife, quietly teaching household and domestic science at the missions where they lived. As the *Christian Guardian* had pointed out, "Matrimony is a covenant . . . But to one party at least, [it] is a state of submission." With at least one missionary couple, however, it appears that the wife was the more prominent church worker. When the Chippewa Indians were relocated from the Narrows to the Rama reserve in 1839, both Mercy Manwaring Moffatt and her husband, Arthur, resigned. He went into business, and she continued to be involved in "church work." Later, she was credited with establishing the first Methodist church and Sunday school there.[40]

By 1834, it seems that the brief period of heady activity for women in the Canadian Methodist Episcopal Church was over. Preaching women were no longer acceptable, and American teachers had for many years been especially suspect of "inculcating habits of subordination" imbibed in the United States. Canadian Methodist Episcopal women settled into a more conventional Victorian existence in the Wesleyan Methodist Church in Canada, the name adopted by the union of the Methodist Episcopal Church and the British Wesleyan Methodists in 1833.[41]

The Methodist Episcopal Church, however, continued in Canada. Although Ellen Bangs' husband, Joseph Gatchell, had been the only itinerant to vote against the 1833 union, other Methodists had already severed their relationship and formed a continuing Methodist Episcopal stream. There is no doubt that this continuing denomination was perceived as being more liberal and radical, for the Canadian Primitive Methodists considered joining with them in 1836. Why they decided against it, we do not know. According to an American newspaper, the *Northwestern Christian Advocate*, Emma Richardson was licensed as a local preacher by the Canadian Methodist Episcopal Church in 1864, five years before Maggie Newton Van Cott in the United States. Evidently, Richardson soon preached only in the United States, for she appears to be known only in that country. She was still active in 1873 when her license was renewed by the American La Crosse District Conference.[42]

By the late nineteenth century in Canada, few Methodists in the newly united Methodist Church would have argued with the Haligonian minister John Weir in favour of itinerant women preachers, even though a small number of women evangelists accepted invitations as revival speakers at that time. Weir suggested that both male and female lay preachers should be dispersed throughout the Methodist Church to combat the defections taking place to the Salvation Army, and that these preachers could come from their present ranks of male and female local preachers, exhorters, and class-leaders. It is not clear, however, where those female local preachers and exhorters were, for at the time of union in 1884, even in the more radical groups such as the Bible Christians and the Primitive Methodists, few, if any, women preachers remained. The Bible Christian preachers had already been forgotten, and it appears that the few women listed on Primitive Methodist plans had no appointments.[43]

In the Methodist Church of Canada, a union of all the other Methodist denominations including the Wesleyan Methodists, most references to the preaching contribution of the women who had preached in the years before 1833 had disappeared. Susannah Farley Waldron's memorial in 1890 notes that she and her husband "toiled together" for forty years and that she "rendered valuable aid to her husband in the work of God" but makes no mention of any speaking. Earlier, in 1862, the historian George Playter noted only that Eliza Barnes Case was an adventurous missionary woman, although a few years later John Carroll did include scattered references to her work and recorded that she made addresses. Her obituary in the *Christian Guardian*, however, pointed out only that she "labored for 8 or 10 years among the Indians at Grape Island as a pioneer missionary." And when Annie Stephenson wrote her history of Methodist Missions in 1925, she mentioned only that Miss Barnes was a teacher at Grape Island and Miss Hubbard at Rice Lake.[44]

In 1860, an anonymous writer who described Methodism in Canada from 1820 to 1860, noted that Methodist women "never presumed to preach." The "good" they accomplished, he wrote, was in visiting in houses, gathering together in classes, and praying at prayer meetings. A Methodist woman, he reported, might have read other women a sermon or added an exhortation of her own, but never had she stepped over the bounds of acceptable behaviour by preaching. Evidently, the anonymous writer was not familiar with the long history of women actively preaching in the late eighteenth and early nineteenth centuries in Great Britain.[45]

Methodist Episcopal preacher Eliza Barnes Case (1796-1887) and her husband, William. (Photo: The United Church of Canada/Victoria University Archives, Toronto.)

Mercy Miner Manwaring Moffatt (1809-1891), teacher at the Methodist Episcopal Indian Missions, and her youngest son, Charles Henry. (Photo: St. Paul's United Church, Orillia, Ontario.)

Eliza Barnes Case and the other missionaries narrowly escaped a fire at the Canadian Indian Missions. James Youngs, *History of the Rise and Progress of Methodism in England and America,* p.417. (Photo: The United Church of Canada/Victoria University Archives, Toronto.)

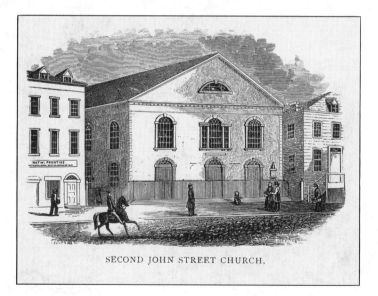

SECOND JOHN STREET CHURCH.

John Street Church, New York City, where Eliza Barnes Case preached during her American fundraising tours. J.B. Wakeley, *Lost Chapters Recovered From the Early History of American Methodism,* p.580. (Photo: The United Church of Canada/Victoria University Archives, Toronto.)

VI.

INCHING TOWARDS ORDINATION:
IN THE UNITED STATES OF AMERICA

"I'll go over to Canada for a wife when I marry," said a young south shore farmer to his friend. "When I come home at night she'll have a nice blazing fire on, and a clean kitchen, and a comfortable supper for me; but if I marry a New Yorker, it'll be when I come home 'John, go down to the well for some water, to make the tea'; or 'John, go and bring some logs to put on the fire to boil the kettle.' No, no, a Canadian woman's the wife for me."

Canadian Statesman, 12 February 1857, p.1

I n the first half of the nineteenth century, Methodist women preachers from Great Britain emigrated not only to Upper Canada but also to the United States, where many of them continued preaching to mixed reactions. Generally, in spite of resistance, they made greater progress in the United States than in Canada, inching their way towards ordination before the turn of the century. Whereas the government of Upper Canada was bent on preventing

139

rebellion and preserving the status quo, the United States had been born of revolution and peopled by radicals seeking freedom from restraint and authority. As a result, women were able to function more freely in the latter country than they could in the former, especially in public spheres generally considered by Victorian society to be the preserve of men.

American women had a reputation of being outspoken and assertive. Travelling throughout Canada and the United States in the late 1830s, Anna Brownell Jameson had recommended to a man looking for an educated but energetic wife in Canada that he look instead for a "spirited" woman from the New England states. Unfortunately, she wrote, British Canadian women displayed "a want of cheerful self-dependence, a cherished physical delicacy," and "a weakness of temperament" considered by that society to be "essential to feminine grace and refinement." This kind of Canadian woman, she explained, was totally unsuited to Upper Canada and pioneer living.[1]

But while the lively American woman was more appealing to Jameson, who was independent and adventurous, that type of woman was an aggravation to others. In 1834, the editor of the *Christian Advocate* reported that a "female correspondent" had written a "spirited letter of reproof" accusing the paper of treating women differently than men in its columns. In fact, the editor remarked facetiously, the writer seems to think that the paper degrades women because she has read many lectures directed towards "wives and ladies" but not one "respecting husbands and gentlemen." Another reader supported the paper, suggesting sarcastically that the "female correspondent" must be suffering "from an injudicious bias of early education," and that her mind "may have imbibed prejudices and jealousies on the hackneyed and still debated subject, 'the rights of women,' which are not easily obliterated."[2]

While assertive women could be annoying to many Americans, women preaching were especially irritating. In his mid-century *Compendium of Methodism*, James Porter explained that there was nothing wrong with women speaking in public, as long as they were careful not to "usurp any authority" over men. In his opinion, the problem of women preaching was not the speaking itself, but the manner in which women spoke. It was "indecorous" for a woman to "be contending with a man in public," Porter exclaimed. A woman could teach, edify, or comfort, he explained, "as long as she does not find fault with men." A woman could "prophesy," he continued, as long as it was not done in an "immodest or masculine" manner. Women, he concluded, "must not be kept from speaking," but they must not speak "too loud or too long."[3]

Women, however, had been preaching in the church in the New England states since the seventeenth century. By the late nineteenth century, the American Methodist temperance worker Frances Willard estimated that at least five hundred women "evangelists" had occupied pulpits in the United States, *excluding* an estimated three hundred and fifty Quaker women. Many of the women who preached had come from Great Britain, seemingly undeterred by the hazards of ocean travel, including six weeks in confined quarters, contagious diseases, and the lack of fresh food.[4]

Dorothy Ripley (ca.1767-1831), described by the *Christian Advocate* as the most extraordinary woman in the world, crossed the Atlantic nineteen times between England and the United States, eleven of these trips between 1825 and her death in Virginia in 1831. Brought up as a Wesleyan Methodist in Whitby, England, Ripley left that denomination because of opposition to women preachers. A free spirit, she travelled and preached as she felt called. She maintained a loose affiliation with both Quakers and Methodists, although she never would submit even to the direction of the Quaker Society. Ripley, however, is one of the few women whose biographies appear in Harmon's Methodist *Encyclopedia.*[5]

Of a rebellious nature, she befriended other preachers who refused to fit into the accepted mould. The tall, pock-marked, asthmatic Methodist preacher Lorenzo Dow was one of the recipients of her kindness. He, in turn, vigorously defended her against all opposition. Those who tried to block her were nothing but "religious bigots," he declared, "of narrow, contracted minds; for little minds are only capable of little things." Ripley championed many causes in the United States. She visited the prisons and described the horrors in the jails. "The rattling chains never can be obliterated from my mind," she wrote in her journal. She abhorred slavery. On one occasion, she went on board a slave ship and berated the owner. A black woman "praised God" that she had lived long enough to see a woman in the pulpit preaching "Jesus Christ." Ripley preached to the Oneida Indians where the crowds were so great that in order to be seen and heard she had to stand up in a cart in the blazing sun. One of the women there told her not to be discouraged even though many Americans believed a woman should not preach.[6]

Presbyterians, Methodists, and Quakers in the United States invited Ripley to speak to their congregations. In one six-week period alone, in New York in 1805, she slept in thirty different homes and filled forty-six appointments. In 1806, the Speaker of the Legislature of the state of Maryland offered her his chair to speak, and later that same year Thomas Jefferson invited her to address the United States Congress. Her contemporaries referred to her preaching appointments, but in her memoirs, she wrote that she objected to using the word "preach." She equated following a prepared text with preaching, whereas she claimed that she spoke only extemporaneously as and when inspired by the Holy Spirit:

> *I did not approve of the word "preach," because I never prepared anything for the purpose . . . for I pray, and give my heart and tongue for God to inspire and speak by.*[7]

Many of the early women preachers were from denominations other than the Methodist Church. The New Hampshire Freewill Baptists provided Sally Parsons (b.ca.1780) with a horse, saddle, and bridle so that she could travel "so much further" to exhort, pray, and preach. Later, when she married another Baptist minister, Benjamin Walton Randall, she was presented with the horse as a wedding gift. Clarissa Danforth Richmond (b.1792), another Freewill Baptist, was the "preaching sensation of the decade" from 1810-1820. She attracted vast crowds throughout the New England states and in the Canadian Eastern Townships, leading a religious revival in 1819 which lasted sixteen months. Chapels from other denominations were opened to allow her to preach, as was often the custom for popular preachers. In the early 1830s, the Baptist Martha Spaulding also preached in the New England states and in the Eastern Townships. At least four other women were known to be preaching in that denomination during this period. Dorothy Ripley had written in her diary in 1806 that the baptist [*sic*] ministers were "free from those prejudices that prevail over many, against women officiating in the Gospel with them." The Christian Church is also reported to have had at least six female travelling evangelists before 1833, including Ann Rexford, who was given a new chapel of her own in New Jersey. And some women were preaching in the pulpits of the Congregationalists, Universalists, and Presbyterians.[8]

The Methodist Episcopal Church

Methodist histories suggest that the Methodist Episcopal Church was not as receptive to women preachers. However, women appear to have been more active than official church records allow. The historian Nathan Bangs refers to a woman who began exhorting in the middle of one of his sermons in 1796. He stopped preaching "and let God send by whom he will send." There is other evidence that women were exhorting in 1810 and had taken an equal part in Methodist meetings by 1812. Several Methodist woman were preaching regularly in New York before 1825. Contagious religious revivals, a "Second Great Awakening," had been erupting in the United States since 1790, spreading westward from New England until at least 1837. Women formed the backbone of these revivals, and many women were encouraged to exhort and preach. In fact, historians have estimated that as many as two-thirds of all the participants were women. The Methodist itinerant John Hudson reported that he had mostly women in his meetings in the first decade of the nineteenth century. When he went to Sela's Creek, he found that all the men had gone to the races except one who was blind. Consequently he met in the school house with the women, mostly "young ladies of respectable appearance." With women in the majority, it is not surprising that they took on leadership functions as they had in the Methodist Church in the eighteenth century in England.[9]

Eleanor Dorsey, wife of a prominent New York judge,

accompanied a circuit rider in house-to-house visitation. She is credited with bringing in forty new converts to Methodism in one day. Fanny Butterfield Newell raised two children, but this did not prevent her from travelling with her itinerant husband through Vermont and Maine. Married in 1810, she began exhorting on her wedding day, and afterwards when she travelled and shared the ministry with her husband, Ebenezer, she attracted crowds of people who came to hear her call penitents to the front of the church. Amey Scott accompanied her husband and exhorted sometime after 1826. Both Elizabeth Cantrell and Mrs. William Baker also travelled with their husbands, exhorting at the close of their husbands' services, Cantrell in the 1830s in New Jersey and Mrs. Baker in Arkansas. But one of the most famous ministerial teams was Deborah Millett and her husband. Millett began exhorting in 1819 after her marriage to Edward Taylor, and by 1859 she was preaching sermons. She was so well received in Boston that she was known as the Reverend Mrs. Edward T. Taylor. Judith Mathers, Susan Hermes, Mrs. Thompson, and Jane Perry were also among a long list of early nineteenth-century women preachers.[10]

In the face of this activity, however, American mid-nineteenth-century Methodist biographers and historians played down women's role in the church. Though George Coles believed that the "most heroic followers of Christ" were "Females" [sic], yet in his accounts of English women who preached and worked closely with John Wesley, he either avoided referring to their preaching or devalued their work. He wrote that Sarah Willis Stevens "instructed the ignorant," that Sarah Crosby "held public meetings," that Ann Cutler was a "non-commissioned itinerant," that Mary Woodhouse Holder "worked with her husband," that Elizabeth Ritchie Mortimer was "useful," and that Sarah Mallett Boyce "preached for an hour when in fits." "Wesley," wrote Coles, did not want any women to "assume the character and title of a preacher." In fact, after initial resistance, Wesley recognized and supported women in preaching roles. Gabriel Disosway, writing in 1861, four years after Coles, is even more selective in his study of Methodist women. Of the British Wesleyan preachers, the only one included is Mary Bosanquet Fletcher, who led "public meetings." Disosway downplays women's role in early Methodism even more than Coles. Therefore it is possible that they also understate the work of some of the American women they describe in leadership positions – such as the "useful" Kentucky feminist Sarah Low Norton (1790-1856), who "was able to argue intelligently"; Elizabeth McColloch Zane (b.ca.1748), who "read sermons," exhorted, and took over in the absence of a preacher; Sarah Pigman Griffith (1783-1845), who accompanied her itinerant husband from 1811 onward; and Virginia resident Sarah Roszel (ca.1751-1830), who led public meetings, exhorted, and read sermons. The "useful" designation was often applied to women who preached in the Methodist church. Wesley had described itinerant preacher Sarah Crosby as "useful" and suggested to Eliza Bennis that she become "useful" by organizing and leading some classes. An English preacher and friend of Wesley, Bennis died in the United States in 1802, evidently "having called people to repentance."[11]

At the time that Coles and Disosway were writing, many members in the Methodist Episcopal tradition assumed that women would not preach, and it was natural for these historians to interpret their sources from a mid-nineteenth-century mind-set. Coles pointed out that he was not aware of any women who even led Methodist classes in the United States. "The practice . . . does not obtain in this country," he explained, and as far as he knew, very few women were even praying out loud in prayer meetings.[12]

In his vignettes of American Methodism, James B. Finley recounted a story of two "pious" women who found themselves isolated in the country without access to church or pastor. Meeting in the woods to pray and talk about their spiritual life, they were overheard one day by a hunter. Reminded of the "instructions and prayers" of his "pious mother," the hunter implored the women to lead a prayer meeting in his cabin for his neighbours. "What Christian," asked Finley, would have believed that "any good would have resulted from such a meeting" led by women? But the women spoke and a revival began. Forty men and women were converted in a two-week session which continued without intermission. The news spread. A male itinerant arrived and according to Finley, the women "cheerfully" entrusted the work to him. One wonders, of course, if the women were that relieved to hand over the work after such success. "How improper" it had all been, suggested Finley, how "abhorrent to every Christian" that the "Holy Spirit" had sanctioned a work brought about by such "improper agencies." "How shocking to delicacy," he exclaimed, that women had spoken "in public, especially in such a mixed assembly."[13]

The Victorian model of the modest, pious, and domestic woman who ministered in the home, shielded from the rigours and unsavoury aspects of the public milieu, had evolved as a result of the industrial revolution, which effectively separated the home and the workplace. The public sector became the arena for men. In Victorian society, men and women believed that motherhood was the role assigned to women since the beginning of creation, and although religion was more natural for women than for men, women's main religious function was to train their young at home in Christian morals and precepts. As Disosway pointed out,

147

"woman and piety" were "sacred names," and "the bliss of home, of a sainted mother's love" was for him the most potent force in society. Women had been charged with their sons' spiritual growth and conversion and in this way, it was argued, women were ultimately responsible for the shape of world events. It was a duty which could not be dismissed lightly. The prayers that God listened to most of all, noted Coles, were "those of the devoted mother pleading for her wandering child." Mothering, however, did not have to be confined to the home but could be extended to the community. As Coles explained, women were not useful or powerful "in the same way as preachers of the Gospel" but in other nurturing ways such as "Mothers [sic], class leaders for their own sex, visitors of the sick and poor, Sunday school teachers, tract distributors, collectors" and as wives of missionaries and ministers.[14]

The expectations of the church and society for women and what women did in reality, however, did not always mesh. Many women did not limit their ministry to mothering roles. For example, Miss Miller, "a lady preacher from the Northern States" was admired by the itinerant George Brown, a young Methodist Episcopal minister. In 1826 and 1827 she undertook an extensive tour around Pennsylvania and was sought after as a preacher at quarterly Conference Sunday morning services. Although she was "highly recommended" by a number of Methodist preachers, Bishop Soule called her a "strolling girl" with no authority to preach. But she spoke from the "altar" and drew larger crowds than the bishop. Eventually she married a Methodist Episcopal minister, William A. Smith. George Brown was more liberal than many of his co-workers. In 1829, he spearheaded the formation of the Methodist Protestant Church in the Ohio valley, a splinter group which advocated more involvement of the laity in church government and limited authority for the bishop. In 1866, after three years of discussion, the Northern Indiana Conference of the Methodist Protestants ordained Helanor M. Davidson, although a later motion to ordain women was defeated by the General Conference in 1871.[15]

In his research, Leonard Sweet found that on many occasions women preachers were asked to conduct funeral services; that many Methodist churches invited women preachers for "prime-time" Sunday morning worship; and that Methodist presiding elders sponsored women, and quarterly Conferences invited them to preach. Nancy Towle, an unordained Christian Band preacher from New Hampshire, preached to Methodist congregations around Pennsylvania in the 1830s; she also preached to Lutherans and Dutch-Reformed Baptists. After ten years as an itinerant, she claimed that only in Frederick, Maryland had she ever been prohibited from preaching in a church. Although Towle was often invited by the Methodist people to preach in their congregations, preachers sometimes attempted to stop her. Her travelling companion was Thomasine O'Bryan, one of the daughters of William O'Bryan, the founder of the Bible Christian Church.[16]

Phoebe Worrall Palmer (1807-1874) firmly believed that she had been sanctioned to preach. "That God has called me to stand before the people, and proclaim His truth, has long been beyond question," she declared. Converted to Methodism, Worrall began speaking in 1829, and for years she held "Tuesday meetings" in her New York home, promoting the doctrine of holiness or perfection. This was not unlike Wesley's idea of sanctification, the state of perfect love, or willful action without sin. The historian Nathan Bangs, her childhood friend, acted as an unofficial president of these gatherings and "pronounced her teachings substantially orthodox and Wesleyan." He believed that opposition to her stemmed from a lack of understanding of her opinions. "Why should anyone oppose another, even though a female," Nathan Bangs conceded in his diary, if that person had been instrumental in "the conversion of sinners and in the sanctification of believers." Worrall became widely renowned as a preacher and camp-meeting speaker travelling from the 1850s to the 1870s throughout Canada, the United States, and Great Britain with her physician husband.[17]

A number of women, spurred on by revivalist fervour, served as American missionaries in the early part of the nineteenth century, both with the Indian tribes and beyond the continent. The surviving sources do not reveal whether or not these women preached as did some of the American women who went to the Canadian Missions in the 1820s. Jane Allen Trimble (1755-1839) worked with the Wyandottes in the Ohio Conference, as did Harriet Stubbs a little later on. The presiding elder, James Finley, described Stubbs in language similar to that used to describe the Indian teacher and preacher Eliza Barnes Case, who won the admiration of the Canadian Wesleyan Indian converts in the late 1820s. Stubbs was known as the "pretty red-bird" and regarded as an "angel-messenger sent from the spirit-land." According to Finley, she had "more courage and fortitude than any one of her age and sex." He wrote that she was "intrepid" and the "idol of the whole nation." Although she is recorded as a teacher of Indian girls, these titles suggest a fairly assertive personality and unusual activity. In 1829, Lucy Richards (b.1792) was teaching the New York Oneida Indian children the alphabet, reading, and the New Testament. Natio Curtis Barnum (1812-1853) was also "useful," teaching the Indian women domestic economy around the 1830s. On New Year's Day, 1834, Sophronia Farrington, a teacher employed by the

Boston Auxiliary to the General Methodist Missionary Society, arrived in Monrovia, Liberia with two other couples to become the first single missionary woman sent overseas by the American Methodists. After twenty attacks of fever, she reluctantly returned to the United States the following year, and in 1836 was replaced by Ann Wilkins (1806-1857), a thirty-year-old widow from New York State. Marcella Russell was sent to Rio de Janeiro in 1837, and a Mrs. Jenkins to Buenos Aires three years later. A "strong" woman, Jenkins' services were soon terminated because of her refusal to follow her superintendent's orders. In 1851, Sarah Hale compiled a monumental work which noted all of the distinguished women from creation to her time, eventually revising her final section to include women up to 1868. She listed all the women who had worked for missions, both at home and abroad, for the American Board of Foreign Missions, the Baptist Mission Union, the Protestant Episcopal Society, and the Presbyterian Churches, but she was unable to obtain the names of the Methodist Episcopal women even though she made repeated requests to that denomination's Missionary Board. As Hale pointed out, the Methodist Board published the names of all of the financial donors to world mission but neglected to "honour" those women who gave "of their living."[18]

Enthusiastic and committed as the Methodist Episcopal women preachers were, they often held back in the face of opposition and abuse. Miss Miller begged to be excused from a preaching obligation when she heard that the bishop who opposed her would be in town, but the presiding elder insisted that she keep her appointment. When Methodist preachers all suddenly developed "colds" at a protracted meeting where Nancy Towle was scheduled to speak, she gracefully withdrew and the preachers quickly recovered from their illness. A number of Methodist male preachers had no use for women who "screamed loud" and "frothed at the mouth," terms James A. Garfield used to describe women preachers.[19]

However, despite some resistance in the denomination in the nineteenth century to women preaching, the Methodist Episcopal Church in the United States was one of the earliest to officially sanction women preachers. In 1869, Margaret Newton Van Cott (1830-1914) was given an exhorter's licence by the New York Conference, and a preacher's licence the following year, even though she had sought neither. She had started preaching in 1866 after the death of her husband. Initially, she had been afraid to attend a Methodist class meeting because she would have to speak, but she soon overcame her reticence. During her first year as a preacher, she delivered 335 sermons, added five hundred new church members, and travelled three thousand miles. At least fourteen other women were licensed and engaged in an active preaching ministry in the 1870s, including Anna Oliver, Jennie Fowler Willing, and Amanda Smith. In 1880 their licences were withdrawn, but full-fledged ordination was permanently recognized in 1889.[20]

The Primitive Methodists

Whereas the early Methodist Episcopal Church gave limited official recognition to women preaching, the Primitive Methodists occasionally published accounts of their women preachers' activities after missionaries were first sent to the North American continent. One of the most intrepid and controversial of these women was Ruth Watkins (b.1802). In spite of her courage, she wept as her vessel set sail from Prince's Dock in Liverpool just before noon on June 19, 1829, the only single woman in the first group of missionaries sent to minister to the Primitives already in America. Forty-two days later, she stepped onto land in New York City, having suffered on the voyage from fear and nausea. The captain told her that in his fifteen ocean crossings in that ship, never had he experienced such rough seas during the summer. The small band of seven adults and two children comforted each other briefly and then got on with their work. Watkins carried out an exacting ministry around New York and Philadelphia, until sick, virtually destitute, disillusioned, and feeling totally abandoned by the English Missionary Society, she retired in December 1832.[21]

The published journals and letters from Watkins and her co-workers omit the dark side of their stories. The Hull and Tunstall Circuits in England had contracted to support the missionaries, but they were often negligent in paying their salaries. Made up mainly of poor women and men, the Primitive Methodist Society had enthusiastically begun the mission but was financially unprepared. It sent its missionaries to America with inadequate funds. While enough money had been scraped together to buy hymn books to send over, the missionaries had to borrow money to pay the duty: 26 per cent for stitched books and 30 per cent for bound books. With their remaining funds, they could afford to rent only a cellar in the "back part of the city." The 1829 *Primitive Methodist Magazine* contained a plea to all their British members to make extra contributions to pay for their mission expenses. Yet in 1835, William Samson wrote to the "Brethren at Hull" on behalf of the other itinerants asking for more money. He explained that the cost of living in America was extremely high, that Americans expected them to dress better, and that the dirt from the dusty roads and the perspiration that resulted from the summer heat shortened the life of their garments. Other Societies were offering more attractive wages. Preachers needed at least $260.00 a year to live in the United States, William Samson pointed out. But in January 1836, he reported that he had received only $71.00 the past year as salary, $59.68 to cover travelling expenses, and $16.00 for house rent, a total of $145.68. Hardly enough, when the most recent doctor's bill for his wife, Eliza, had been $11.00. However, at least by 1852, male married preachers were to be paid an annual stipend of $260.00 along with a small allowance for children, although a station could reduce this if necessary. Single male preachers were to be paid only $100.00 a year, and female preachers only $60.00 a year. In 1835, Ruth Watkins wrote that she had received only $16.00 from England since she had been in America, and this in 1830 or 1831. She had been given an additional $13.00 from the American stations. One hundred dollars "would have saved those Missions at the North [of New York State]," Ruth declared, "but we could receive no communication from home."[22]

The lack of home support led to certain abuses. Society members quarrelled in Philadelphia over whether the station there should be considered a circuit or a mission. Money which had been collected to buy land for a church building was being held by a few members who would not give it up. At Newark, William Samson had initiated a lawsuit to try to regain possession of the Society's property there, valued at $6,000. The itinerant George Parsons was accused of misappropriation of funds, and letters hinted at "mysterious affairs" of which "every preacher" was suspected. The members at Albany had been able to raise only $900 of the required $1900 to pay for their church when another society offered to bail them out if they turned over the buildings and joined with it. Only Ruth Watkins stood firm and would not be compromised. The trustees and the other preacher, her brother Nathaniel, changed their allegiance.[23]

It was a hard life. Six hours had to be spent in study and eleven in pastoral duties, leaving a maximum of seven hours sleep a night. The preachers were required to visit twenty different families each week, in addition to services, classes, and other work. A preacher was fined fifty cents a day plus loss of salary for negligence. In the summer months, the heat was oppressive. "I felt as though my blood almost boiled in my veins," Watkins wrote the second week in New York City. After walking ten miles outside Philadelphia to an appointment, Ann Wearing noted, "I find I could better walk in England ten miles, than five in this country. The roads and climate are different."[24]

But in spite of the lack of funds, the disagreements, and the working conditions, Watkins undertook an active ministry. She preached from the church pulpit or out of doors, often three times a day; she led classes and week-long prayer meetings, held "love-feasts," and opened new stations. The itinerant William Summersides wrote in 1830 that she was "very useful" and "well received." By December of that year, the Primitive Methodist missionaries had opened a church in Philadelphia, and the Church Board there wrote to New York to see if Watkins could extend her stay with them longer than had been scheduled.[25]

Watkins alternated with Wearing on the Philadelphia and New York Circuits for periods of four to six months, although there were brief times when they worked together. A man, seeing them together in the pulpit one Sunday, said they reminded him of "the women who looked into the sepulchre." Wearing had been a Wesleyan preacher in Devon. She had a more pastoral approach to ministry than Watkins, concentrating on families and seeking out the unchurched.

"More good is done by family visiting than by the public ministry," she wrote in her journal. The people are able to speak more freely, she explained, "and the preacher gets into confidence with the people." She preached in small alley-ways, although some "delicate people were offended," in jails and poor houses, and visited in hospitals. Church-goers often lacked an intense loyalty to any one denomination, and Methodist Episcopals, Quakers, Baptists, and Presbyterians welcomed her, and along with Roman Catholics, attended her services. She had a thirst to find out about different aspects of life and a love for all people. She attended a black people's meeting where she listened to them preach, exhort, pray, and sing. She found them "sincere and happy." She was invited to a Methodist Episcopalian camp-meeting and went out of curiosity "as well as a desire to get good to my soul." To reach the campsite she travelled ten and a half hours by sloop on a river and walked three miles. There were three thousand men and women and 180 tents at the four-and-a-half-day meeting. At times Wearing found that her work was a "heavy cross," yet she was consoled by her "happiness" and "inward satisfaction."[26]

The reports of Wearing's ministry end abruptly. The historian John Acornley wrote that the itinerant Edward Wearing returned to England in 1831. Edward Wearing could have been a relative of hers or John Acornley may have confused the name.

Acornley also mentions that Watkins married a Methodist Episcopal minister at that same time, but her later corre-spondence makes no mention of this. In 1831, she was asked to open new missions and did so around Albany and Troy. But the cold weather, lack of money, and long walks in the snow were too much for her, and by the end of 1832 her health was spent. Friends cared for her and nursed her back to health, but the lack of support and communication from the parent Society alienated her. In 1835, she sadly wrote to John Flesher and William Clowes, the denomination's leaders in England:

> *I have loved as dear as my life the P. M. cause,*
> *but I never can in future join it nor incourage*
> *[sic] anyone else to join it in this country.*

Watkins disappeared from historical accounts. Years later, in paying tribute to the first courageous missionaries to North America, the Canadian writer Jane Agar Hopper referred to her as Mr. R. Watkins.[27]

Even with its internal problems, the Society continued, and women participated actively both in the industrialized Eastern cities and on the frontier. T. Newton and his wife, who had been on the preachers' plan in Derbyshire, England continued to preach in Philadelphia after they emigrated to the United States in 1830. Mrs. Suddard preached there, too, until her husband, a Primitive Methodist itinerant, joined the Methodist Episcopal Church as a minister. Ann (ca.1807-1889) and George Parker were both itinerants for the American church. Sister Sutton was speaking in Albany in 1831, and in 1842 Eliza Fletcher was one of six people received into the professional ministry. Somewhat later, Mary Holt Livsey (ca.1837-1896), who had been an active preacher throughout Lancashire in England, continued after she emigrated to the United States, although marriage "interfered somewhat" with her ministry.[28]

H.M. Knowles was sought after as a preacher, often holding her services in the open air to accommodate all the people who wanted to hear her. In spite of her popularity, however, the available records of her work, mainly in her husband's journals and letters, refer to her only by her initials. She and her husband, William, arrived in New York with the first group of missionaries. Even though she was expecting her first child, she took her share of preaching engagements. The parent body in England, however, accorded her less status than her husband. The broadsheet prepared by the Primitive Methodist president, James Bourne, to announce the first group of missionaries to New York referred only to "our respected Brother and faithful Minister, the Rev. William Knowles" and "our respected Sister, Ruth Watkins," ignoring H.M. Knowles. Even though Watkins was accredited as an official missionary, she was not described as a "Minister" or given the title of "Rev."[29]

In his first year as a missionary, William Knowles wrote back home that New Yorkers were opposed to open-air preaching and that it was never done except for annual camp-meetings. He was told that he "would lose his character" if he preached outdoors, but, he confessed, "if this be the case, it is already gone." In 1830, the English Missionary Society asked William and H.M. Knowles to open a station at Cincinnati, Ohio. In response, they set off on a seven-hundred-mile trek with a new infant. They took turns preaching to crowds of "Old Methodists," "Associate Methodists," and people of other denominations, estimated by William Knowles to have been from two thousand to three thousand women and men. Their young child accompanied them to services. Methodist Episcopals welcomed them into their homes. After H.M. Knowles preached, the people kept asking, "when will she preach again?" Many young people were attracted to their message but, recorded William Knowles, "influenced by their parents they joined other denominations." The first fall, H.M. Knowles caught a severe cold from preaching in a log barn where the space between the logs was wide enough for her husband to put his arm through. They were both ill for some time during the second year in their new station.[30]

In 1840, the young Society became independent from the English Church. Yet six years later, William Towler, his wife Mary Ann Proctor, and seven children arrived on the sailing ship *Montezuma*. On salary from the parent church, Towler was to assume the duties of general superintendent of the United States Missions. He was paid very little and had to practise the most rigid economy. The family slept on the floor, and lacking enough chairs, most of them stood up to eat their meals. The kitchen work table doubled as Towler's desk. He travelled extensively throughout the United States and Canada, but the demands of the job and inadequate funding from England resulted in illness and his death less than a year after he had arrived. When he was sick, his wife, "a lady of culture and refinement," took his services and looked after much of his correspondence. Later she preached in Canada.[31]

It was not unusual for wives to fill in when their husbands were ill. In Pennsylvania, William Wood's wife preached when he was sick, but unfortunately she took sick, as well, and her husband was unable to provide what he felt was the necessary care. On a salary of $69.60 a year, he often had to resort to "begging." Money, evidently, was so scarce in the Bloomsburg congregation, that Wood quarried the stone himself to build their church. It is estimated that he was required to take up to ten regular services each week in addition to funerals and other pastoral duties, walking approximately sixty miles.[32]

Even with these opportunities for preaching, there is no question that the American Primitive Methodist women in the United States soon lost the equality that the early Primitive

Methodist women had in England. Almost from the time that the first missionaries arrived in New York City, an air of respectability appeared in the new Societies. In April 1832, Ruth Watkins had noted at a convention that year in New York City that some of the members wanted to discard the Primitive Methodist rules, but she insisted on retaining the "old Rules." At the end of 1835, William Samson had written that the itinerants needed more money to dress better, even though they were instructed to wear plain dress. Indeed, some of the preachers were enticed to join other denominations that paid better salaries. The New York Conference in 1849 decided that women could not vote or speak at official meetings even though the Conference in 1852 set a salary for women preachers. In the 1870s, women were invited to preach on anniversaries and at other celebrations and were engaged as supplies when the regular pastors became ill. By the early 1880s, however, they were hired by Conference staff as travelling evangelists, and one of them, Caroline Watson from Toronto, is credited with converting 1,132 men and women in a period of two years and three months. However, experiencing some resistance to her preaching in 1884, she and one of the churches in Michigan later left the denomination and joined with the Methodist Episcopals, finding them more liberal in their acceptance of women preaching.[33]

Obviously, not all Primitive Methodists opposed women preachers at that time. As in the Methodist Episcopal Church, in spite of opposition, the women gained ground. In 1886, John Acornley from the Eastern Conference remarked that not only did they permit women to preach about "the realities of eternity," but they were "ahead of the universe" in the "principle of women's rights" by allowing a woman to speak and vote at their annual meeting. Two years later, the Rev. E. Humphries, another minister from the same Conference, again pointed with pride to the position of women in their denomination. Whereas the Methodist Episcopal Church had rejected women delegates at their meetings, the Primitive Methodist denomination already had two Conferences where women delegates had equal rights with men. "And why should they not?" he asked in an address to the Western Conference, pointing out that since women made up most of the membership and were the best workers, it was only justice to allow them equal representation in church courts. And by the following year, the Primitive Methodists had ordained their first woman minister.[34]

Methodist Protestants and Other Denominations

A variety of other Methodist groups in the United States accepted the gifts women had to bring to the pastorate, although not without some opposition from other denominations and within their own ranks. Hannah Pearce Reeves (1800-1868), one of the early Bible Christian preachers in England, itinerated in Ohio for the Methodist Protestant Church from her arrival in 1831 to the year of her death. Born in Devonshire, she was the third child in a large and apparently talented family. Her mother was an excellent cook and a business woman who owned her own store. Her father had two farms and a malting business, managing extremely well until he became an alcoholic. Initially Pearce entered the "gloving business," but after her conversion to Bible Christian Methodism, she became a parlour maid for the son of Canada's first lieutenant-governor, John Graves Simcoe. There, she learned "cultural niceties" until she became an itinerant preacher at the age of twenty-five. As an itinerant, her life took on a different complexion. She picked blackberries in order to eat. On one mission she walked thirty miles each day. Exhausted after two years of demanding work, she rested for a year in order to recover her physical strength. In Kent, she met the American William Reeves, who had been taken by a Wesleyan to hear her preach. Claiming that he was impressed by the fact that she preached without any notes, Reeves asked her to marry him. That same year she sailed to the United States from Bideford, somewhat apprehensive about her future. In the United States, however, Reeves and Pearce both preached for the Methodist Protestant Church, and he defended her against any opposition. They travelled on horseback, sometimes together, sometimes to separate appointments. She was called a "modern marvel" and Conference offered her her own circuit, but she declined, preferring to share the work with her husband. Like other women preachers, she took her second son, Samuel, to church when she preached. He waited patiently until after the sermon when he went up to the pulpit to join her. Someone else then closed the service.[35]

The confusion in women's roles in the Methodist Protestant Church illustrates well the mixed reactions to women preaching in the United States. By 1866, the Northern Indiana Conference had ordained Helanor M. Davidson, although the General Conference defeated a motion to ordain women in 1871. In 1880, Anna Howard Shaw (1847-1919) was ordained in the New York Conference, where she ministered in a church in Massachusetts. Four years later, the General Conference ruled her ordination out of order. Nevertheless, in 1889, Eugenia St. John, who had been a pulpit supply for her ailing husband, was ordained by the Kansas Conference.[36]

There were a number of prominent women preaching in the African Methodist Episcopal Church. Jarena Lee, backed by Bishop Richard Allen, was preaching in the 1820s. Male ministers exhorted for her, and elders took her on their circuits. Zilpha Elaw itinerated throughout the New England states, supported by both black and white male ministers. Born into slavery and later freed, a woman known only as "Elizabeth" (b.1766) began preaching in 1808 and continued for fifty years.[37]

When the Wesleyan Methodists ordained women is not clear. One historian notes that women were fully ordained in the denomination as early as the 1860s. Another source, however, notes only that when a woman was ordained an elder in 1864, the General Conference refused to forbid it. Earlier, in 1853, the Wesleyan Methodist preacher, Luther Lee, had preached the ordination sermon for the first woman minister in the Congregational Church, Antoinette Louisa Brown. In his address, Lee declared that they had not gathered together to confer a right on Brown to preach the gospel. "If she has not that right already," Lee said, "we have not the power to communicate it to her." The only role the participants had, he continued, was "to subscribe our testimony to the fact, that in our belief, our sister in Christ, Antoinette L. Brown, is . . . authorized, qualified, and called of God to preach."[38]

The founder of the Free Methodists, B.T. Roberts, argued in favour of ordination of women as early as 1860 when that denomination began. That church licensed women as local preachers in 1873, but granted them full ordination only in 1974.[39]

Nevertheless, before the turn of the century, American Methodist women had been accepted for ordination in a number of denominations, although the road had been rough. The Victorian model of a passive and submissive woman had permeated American society as it had Great Britain and Canada, but the more liberal environment of the United States had enabled a number of women to step outside the mould and shake off some of society's constraints.

REV. WILL^M KNOWLES. RUTH WATKINS.

THE
Primitive Methodist Connexion
TO THE INHABITANTS OF
NEW YORK,
AND OF THE
UNITED STATES OF AMERICA
IN GENERAL SEND GREETING.

Friends and Brethren,

THE LORD having in his Providence raised up the Primitive Methodist Connexion, in Old England, and made it an instrument, in his hands, of turning thousands and ten thousands unto righteousness, and many of its members having emigrated to the United States, it was judged providential to appoint a regular Mission. We have accordingly sent over our respected Brother and faithful Minister, the Rev. WILLIAM KNOWLES; as also our respected Sister, RUTH WATKINS, who has laboured much in the Lord. And we trust they will be made useful in the Gospel of our common LORD, and will meet with that kindness and respect among you, that you, under similar circumstances, would expect from us.

Signed in behalf of the Conference of the said Connexion.

James Bourne, President.

Hugh Bourne, Secretary.

N. B. The History of the Primitive Methodists may be had of either of the persons above mentioned, with any other necessary information. Bemersley, near Tunstall, in Old England; Printed at the office of the Primitive Methodist Connexion, by JAMES BOURNE, June 8th, 1829.

Ruth Watkins (b. 1802) emigrates to the United States of America. (Photo: John Rylands University Library of Manchester.)

VII.
THE LEGEND OF BARBARA HECK

A stout opposer of the Methodists, hearing that his wife was in a prayer-meeting, rushed violently into the room, seized his wife, and dragged her to the door, when attempting to open it, he was himself seized with trembling, his knees failed him, and he fell helpless upon the floor, and was fain to beg an interest in the prayers of those very people whom he had so much despised and persecuted. He rose not until the Lord released him from his sins and made him a partaker of his pardoning mercy. This very man afterward became an itinerant minister.

Nathan Bangs, *History of Methodism in Canada*, p.53

Although Elizabeth Dart Eynon, Ann Vickery Robins, and other Canadian and American women did extensive pioneering work, the legendary "Mother" of North American Methodism was a woman who never preached but rather urged a man to fulfill his preaching obligation. She was the Methodist Episcopalian Barbara Heck, a woman who has been remembered and revered while the more outspoken North American Methodist women preachers were relegated to oblivion.

Barbara Ruckle Heck (1734-1804), twenty-six years old and recently married, arrived in New York City on board the ship *Pery*, in August 1760. Emigrating with her were at least twenty-four friends and relatives from Ireland, including her cousin Philip Embury, a lay preacher. The commonly accepted story explains that six years later, calling on Methodist neighbours, Heck discovered them playing cards. Sweeping the cards into the fire, she quickly searched out her cousin Embury. Sharing the "decadence" she had uncovered, she pleaded with him to preach "the word" at once that they might all be saved. After some hesitation, Embury did as she asked. They gathered a few people together to form the first American Methodist class. The Methodist Church had begun in the New World. Two years later, the first Methodist chapel in the United States was opened. Around 1778, Heck and her family fled the Revolutionary War, entering Canada at Montreal, and by 1785, with some of their friends, they had settled in the township of Augusta in Grenville County in Upper Canada. The first Upper Canadian Methodist class, led by Heck's son, Samuel, was formed in 1788. Two years later, William Losee, the first American Methodist itinerant to travel throughout Upper Canada, preached in the Heck's barn. Heck died in 1804, but it was not until 1866 that her descendants erected a cenotaph in her honour, selling photographs of the graveyard and her grave in order to pay for it. Later still, in 1909, a much more substantial monument was erected in Prescott, Ontario. The inscription credits her with bringing into existence both American and Canadian Methodism and notes that she "laid foundations others have built upon."[1]

Tracing the alterations in Heck's story throughout the decades and in successive Methodist histories illustrates the development of a myth appropriate to the contemporary view of women.

The oldest accounts of Methodism in North America either omit all reference to her or describe an elderly woman. One of the earliest known reports of the beginning of Methodism in the 1760s in New York City is a letter from Thomas Taylor quoted in a much later British *Methodist Magazine* in 1823. An early American Methodist trustee, Taylor described in 1768 how "it pleased God to rouse up Mr. Embury to employ his talent (which for several years had been hid as it were in a napkin)." There is no explanation of how God roused up Embury, and Heck is not mentioned as God's agent. Taylor's letter explains that Embury formed two classes, one of men and one of women. Later, when the class members realized the need for a church building, they all fasted and prayed "and called upon God for His direction." Evidently, at that time, Heck was not credited with a special role in the establishment of the first church in the United States. The editor of the *Magazine* in 1823, however, contributed other details that must have developed in Methodist circles sometime after Taylor's letter in 1768. According to the editor, an unnamed mother of an immigrant family, "a woman of a bold and independent spirit . . . much devoted to God" was made "instrumental" in "reviving their languishing spirits." This anonymous woman grabbed the playing cards out of the hands of the Methodist immigrants, threw the cards into the fire, and prostrated herself before Embury, entreating him to preach in his own house. According to this version, Embury had been one of the Methodists found playing cards. This same "elderly lady" received direction from God as to how to build the first worship house in the United States.[2]

Another early reference to the Heck family can be found in Francis Asbury's *Journal.* One of two Superintendents of American Methodism, Bishop Asbury travelled extensively throughout the United States and into Canada. In 1811, he wrote that he had called upon "Father Dulmage, and Brother Heck's [*sic*] – a branch of an old Irish stock of Methodists in New York." But there is no mention of Heck. In 1825, in reporting the death of Paul Heck, the *Methodist Magazine* noted only that "his pious mother was one of a small number who formed the first Methodist Society in America." Barbara Heck's husband, Paul, however, had died in 1795, and there is no record of a son called Paul. In 1846, in a memorial to Samuel Heck, John Carroll referred to the "religiously heroic woman who was instrumental in calling back the distinguished Philip Embury from a state of backsliding and prompting him to resume the exercise of a long buried talent." The woman's name was omitted, but Samuel Heck was said to have been her grandson.[3]

The historian Nathan Bangs knew the Hecks well. He often visited their Prescott home, and in 1818, speaking at the dedication ceremony for the second John Street Church in New York, he referred to Barbara Heck. Yet in his 1856 *History of the Methodist Episcopal Church*, Bangs alluded to two different women, one anonymously. He described how Embury and other Irish Methodist immigrants to New York had became lukewarm about their religion; how an unnamed "pious 'mother in Israel'" arrived the next year and found the Methodists playing cards; how this woman threw the cards into the fire, and turning to Embury demanded that he preach. According to Bangs' story, classes were formed and the new members determined to build a church. It was while they were deciding how to accomplish this, that "an elderly lady" who "fervently engaged in prayer" was directed by God to solicit subscriptions from wealthy citizens. This "elderly lady," Bangs continued, was a "pious" woman called "Hick [*sic*], the mother of the late Paul Hick." He also explained in a footnote that he personally had heard these facts from Mr. Hick and other members of the family living in New York, including children and grandchildren. J.B. Wakeley later remarked that Nathan Bangs had been writing the same account since 1824. The same information appeared in James Dixon's history in 1849. Quoting from Bangs, he repeated the incident and added that it was a pity that the name of the first woman had "not been preserved," but the "elderly" lady's name had been "rescued from oblivion," and she was "Paul Hick's mother." In 1857, in Smith's *History of Wesleyan Methodism* published in London, there was a brief reference to the story, but Barbara Heck's name was never mentioned. References were made instead to "a Christian woman," "an aged Christian matron," "the old lady," and "this mother in Israel," although Heck would have been only thirty-two years old at the time of the card-playing incident.[4]

As the 1860s approached and plans were made for centenary celebrations, American Methodists researched the beginning of their church in North America. In 1858 J.B. Wakeley collected little-known anecdotal stories for his *Lost Chapters Recovered From the Early History of American Methodism*. He included a chapter on Barbara Heck, virtually repeating the version of the card players and the founding of Methodism that Nathan Bangs had used. But this time, the story created a controversy which lasted from 1859 until 1866 in the columns of the *Christian Guardian*. There were four main points in dispute: the correct spelling of Barbara Heck's name – Hick or Heck; the existence of a son Paul; her arrival in Canada; and whether or not Embury had been one of the card players. The main antagonists were two historians, J.B.

Wakeley and John Carroll. After arguing the facts in print over a number of months, however, they came to an amicable settlement. In August 1859, they both signed a letter stating that there had been two Pauls – one a Paul Hick who died in New York, and the other a Paul Heck who had emigrated to Canada. Presumably, then, there were two Barbaras as well. Who threw the cards into the fire was a question they could not settle but left open to speculation. Wakeley agreed to publish a revised version of the story.[5]

Two other early Methodist historians remained aloof from the controversy. Abel Stevens noted that the debate was of interest chiefly to friends of the Hick and Heck families. "Our church history," Stevens explained, "has little concern with the particular matter in question." What he almost certainly meant was not that he was uninterested in Barbara Heck's role in the first Methodist Society, but that he was not prepared to argue over details. In a publication in 1869, *The Women of Methodism*, Stevens devoted thirty-seven pages to her. The other historian, the Canadian Methodist itinerant Egerton Ryerson was satisfied that the Barbara Heck who was buried in the churchyard a few miles from Prescott in Upper Canada had indeed begun Methodism in America. Recounting some of his travels in a letter to the *Christian Guardian* in 1839, Ryerson noted that he had visited the graveyard near Prescott to look at the graves of some of the "honourable dead." Among those buried, he wrote, was "Mrs. Hick [*sic*], the devoted matron who urged Philip Embury, (the first Methodist preacher in America), to lift up his voice in the City of New York in 1766." He visited her two surviving children and eulogized, "O my heart burned within me when I heard them converse about their sainted mother … I almost envied them the privilege of being thus related to the Founder of American Methodism." Later on in his report, he noted that "a majority of the members in this neighbour-hood are family connexions of the venerable Mrs. Hick, the mother of the American Methodist Israel." Even though Ryerson revered her and had visited with her descendants, he persisted in spelling her name "Hick." According to Carroll, who was writing in the 1860s, the itinerant Anson Green had suggested raising a Canadian memorial to her in 1839, but nothing had come of his request. A "Brother Green" had been travelling with Ryerson in 1839, and it is likely that he was Anson.[6]

Although Heck's involvement in the card-playing inci-dent and in the plan to build the church may have been part fact and part legend, by the 1860s they were common details of a story in circulation. The American Methodist Ladies' Centenary Association asked ministers' wives to canvas all the ladies for a donation of any amount from $1 to $1000 to build a residence at the Evanston Biblical Institute as a memorial to Heck. She was really the "Foundress of Ameri-can Methodism" the Association explained in 1865. "She called out the first preacher, convened the first meeting, and planned the first church edifice on this side of the Atlantic." Noticeable in stories published in 1866, one hundred years after Embury preached his first sermon, was the fact that he had not been among the card players but lived on "another street."[7]

Future writers embellished the account to suit their needs. In 1869, Abel Stevens pointed out that 1,972,000 men and women in the United States and Canada were members of the Methodist Church as a direct result of the work of Heck, a "devoted, obscure, unpretentious woman." He included, in his account, a centenary address by C.H. Fowler, who credited her with calling out the first minister, convening the first congregation, meeting the first class, planning the first Methodist church building, and "securing its completion." By 1880, W.H. Withrow was describing her as a prophetess who came to the United States "under divine impulse" and who might "even take precedence" over Embury in founding Methodism in the United States and Canada. An article in 1893 in the New York *Christian Herald* depicted Heck as a new Deborah rescuing the nation; a modern Abraham obediently setting out under God's command to an unknown land; a Christ figure sitting calmly in a boat while her "children nestled in terror at her feet" en route to Lower Canada; and the leader of a loyal British Protestant remnant escaping the tyranny of the American Revolution. On her arrival in Montreal, Heck was reported to have said to Colonel Burton, the military governor of the district, that "there are yet seven thousand who have not bowed the knee to Baal." By 1934, there was even a story that she was of "Royal Birth" of the House of Guelph, a descendant of Elector Frederick III.[8]

Heck had evolved from an anonymous eighteenth-century Irish emigrant to the United States to become the "Foundress" of Methodism in North America. Finally, with the emerging spirit of Canadian nationalism, she appeared as the late nineteenth- and early twentieth-century symbol of the United Empire Loyalist woman. Over the decades, the details of her story were altered to fit the changing paradigm of woman acceptable to and promulgated by mainstream society. If she did indeed throw the cards into the fire and take an active role in establishing the first class and the first church, her behaviour evoked no notice in the late eighteenth century. Her assertiveness must have been within the boundaries of appropriate feminine behaviour. The story of her contribution to the establishment of the Methodist Church was popularized only as the norm for women shifted to a less assertive role. At the same time that women were involved in intense preaching activity, in the 1820s and

172

1830s, she was evolving into the official Methodist model of the "True Woman," one who assisted the male preacher in many active ways but stood behind him and supported him in his preaching role. Instead of preaching, the official stereotype was that of a guardian of morality and a "custodian of conversion."[9]

As the legend unfolded and was embellished, the factor which remained constant in all the stories was the passive role Heck adopted in preaching the gospel. When she realized how "secularized" her friends and relatives had become, she did not speak to them herself but turned to a male lay preacher, although he had not been exercising his "gifts" for a number of years. This submissive demeanour was the kind of action put forward as the paradigm for women's behaviour during much of the nineteenth century and especially after the 1840s. Even though many women refused to be bound by this model, it was held up by mainstream Methodists as an example of how women should conduct themselves.

As the nineteenth century progressed, the mythology of the pious mother who remained at home nurturing her children took hold tenaciously on society. Women lost voting rights, were barred from the medical profession, and became mainly "decorative" and "spiritual" members of society. In her study of American nineteenth-century attitudes to women, Ann Douglas wrote that between 1820 and 1875, "American culture seemed bent on establishing a perpetual Mother's Day." It was at this time that Heck came into her own. Barbara Heck, the "Mother of Methodism," became the mother *par excellence*. Shunning the spotlight and the public role of preaching in contrast to more vocal American women, she stood behind Embury, encouraging him to preach instead. The "sublime work" of mothers, explained the editor of the Canadian *Methodist Magazine,* "is to nurse heroic souls and send them forth":

> *The great need of the world to-day is women who can worthily wear, as the queenliest dignity of her life, the hallowed name of mother; lifting it high above the defilement of earth; making it a potent spell . . . at whose . . . utterance temptation and sin shall lose its power. Mothers may write upon the loving palimpsest, a child's heart, lessons of undying wisdom that not all the vile chirography of sin can ever cover or efface . . . They may lay their hands upon the hidden springs of action which, more powerful than the Archimedian lever, may move the world.*[10]

The Methodist itinerant William Case, who opposed Eliza Barnes' preaching, also believed that the "Mother" was the most important influence in a son's life. It was a mother's tears, prayers, and religious devotion that often led men to the ministry, he wrote. "Who has not heard of the piety of the venerated Mrs. Wesley; of the faith of 'Mother Kent' of New England; of 'Mother Covel' of the Catskill Mountains; of 'Mother Ryerson' of Canada; and of many other 'mothers in Israel' and of their sons in the ministry," he exclaimed in a Jubilee Sermon. Egerton Ryerson, perhaps the most influential Canadian Methodist from the early 1830s on, became maudlin about his mother after her death. Describing two pairs of socks which she had knit for him, he wrote:

> *I scarcely ever put them on without a gush of feeling which is not easily suppressed. They*

every day reminded me of the hand which sustained my infancy and guided my child-hood, and the heart which has crowned my life with its tenderest solicitudes, and most fervent and, I believe effectual prayers. Praise be to God above all earthly things, for such a Mother![11]

Nineteenth-century Methodist historians commonly depict pious wives and mothers as the instruments of conversion for men and, therefore, the salvation of society. Writing about the beginning of a Methodist Society in Long Island in 1794 in his history of *The Methodist Episcopal Church* in the United States, Nathan Bangs gives a classic example. Bangs described how Mrs. Moore and two other "pious" women who gathered together for prayer every Monday evening, pleaded with God to send a minister to begin a Methodist Society in their community. Unable to come together one week, they prayed in concert but in their own homes, asking again for a preacher. This time Moore was confident that their prayers had been answered. Just then, the story continues, Wilson Lee, a Methodist preacher prevented from continuing his journey to New York, felt an unusual urging to go to Long Island. He made his way to Moore's home, and she immediately recognized him as the preacher God had promised to send. The two of them gathered some friends and neighbours together and a society was soon formed.[12]

The story is not unlike one in James Finley's *Sketches of Western Methodism* in which the prayers of two "pious and devoted" women were instrumental in beginning a society in Georgia just after the Revolutionary War. A woodsman, who had overheard the women praying and talking about their spiritual experiences, begged them to come and speak to his neighbours. As a result, a revival began. A Methodist itinerant soon appeared and organized a new society.[13]

In these two accounts the prayers of pious women resulted in the formation of a Methodist Society in a geographical area devoid of "the means for spiritual nourishment." The women, however, were only agents: they paved the way for a male preacher. The same theme runs through the story of the Irish immigrant Barbara Heck. She recognized the desperate need for religious support for the Methodist community in New York, and at her insistence Philip Embury preached in New York in 1766, beginning the first Methodist Society there. Variations of the story surfaced throughout the history of early North American Methodism. In Chicago, it was Lucy Walker Wentworth, the wife of a tavern keeper, who by herself gathered up groups of people to hear the itinerant William See. Even the indomitable American preacher, Hannah Pearce Reeves, covenanted with two other women to pray two hours every day for men to lead singing and take care of administrative matters for them. Their prayers were answered. A great religious revival took place, providing them with male assistance.[14]

The emphasis on Barbara Heck's passive role can be compared to the adulation bestowed on Hester Ann Roe Rogers (1756-1795) and contrasted with the lack of recognition accorded the preaching activity of other more assertive Methodist women such as Dorothy Ripley in the United States and Eliza Barnes Case and Hetty Ann Hubbard in Canada.

The Experiences and Letters of Hester Ann Rogers was one of a very few books available in 1812 from the American Methodist Episcopal Book Room. It sold for seventy-five cents. Hester Ann Roe was born in England, the daughter of a Church of England clergyman. Converted to Methodism when she was twenty-one years old, she married a Methodist lay preacher, James Rogers, ten years later. She bore seven children in eight years, dying in childbirth at the age of thirty-nine. The official record of her life circulated by the Book Room included the sermon preached at her funeral by Thomas Coke, the Methodist bishop who later presided at the Irish Conference when the restrictive legislation regarding women preachers was passed. Coke referred to Roe as a "mother in Israel," emphasizing her "usefulness" especially after her marriage, noting that she never "assumed the authority of teaching in the church." Instead, he emphasized, she visited orphans and widows and prayed for them. Her husband included his own memorial to her, agreeing that "her good sense, joined with that Christian modesty ever becoming her sex" led her to visit the sick, to teach only her own sex in private, and to pray whenever called upon. In his account in 1861, Gabriel Disosway described her as an "excellent mother," commenting on her "purity, patience, prudence, charity, generosity, and perfect resignation." Her church work, he noted, included meeting classes, instructing "penitents," and leading "believers to Christ." Roe rarely preached. In his story of women preachers in the early nineteenth century, Zechariah Taft omits any reference to her. This suggests that she was in fact a more retiring and much less aggressive woman than the other Wesleyan preachers, for Taft's admiration of assertive women is quite evident. It appears that she was a suitable model for Victorian women. By contrast, the story of Dorothy Ripley, who spent so many years preaching and travelling throughout the United States and actively promoted prison reform and the abolition of slavery in the early nineteenth century, has been omitted from all official histories. Indeed, one is hard pressed to find any references at all to most of the other women preaching in the early nineteenth century in the United States and Canada.[15]

Canadian Methodist Episcopal women had stopped

preaching around the time admiration for Barbara Heck began in that country. Egerton Ryerson and Anson Green were the first to hold her up as a role model for Canadian women in 1839. Were it not for the respect and approval of the Indian convert Peter Jones and his first-hand accounts of their preaching, Hetty Hubbard Case, Eliza Barnes Case, and Susannah Farley Waldron would probably be remembered only as pious women and Indian teachers. Barnes' obituary in the *Christian Guardian* in 1887 mentions her as a pioneer missionary at Grape Island, and the histories of Canadian Missions refer to each of them briefly as teachers. In 1925, in her official history of the Missionary Society of the Methodist Church, Mrs. Stephenson wrote that "Miss Barnes, in addition to the ordinary school work, taught sewing, knitting, straw-hat making and cooking . . . Miss Hubbard did the same." Yet by this time, halls had been dedicated to Heck, stories written, and monuments raised. Methodist officialdom ignored the examples of women preaching, instead praising other activities considered more normative for women. A description in 1860 of an involved Methodist woman published under the heading "An Elect Lady" noted that although she was intellectually endowed, "yet she never presumed to *preach*." Instead, she spent her time "in visiting awakened persons from house to house," in classes, in prayer meetings, in "collecting the poor and neglected of her own sex" and reading them a sermon or even "superadding exhortation and prayer." It was more acceptable for women at that time to pattern their lives after Heck than to emulate the early Methodist women preachers.[16]

BARBARA HECK.

Barbara Ruckle Heck (1734-1804), called the Mother of Methodism in North America. (Photo: The United Church of Canada/Victoria University Archives, Toronto.)

VIII.
THE DEVOLUTION

*Few can inflict a more deadly wound upon
society than the unprincipled woman; and
few can be more beneficial than a pious one.*

Christian Guardian, 11 June 1831, p.124, c.3

The stories of Methodist women preachers in Canada
and in the United States leave us with no doubt that
the women faced both enthusiastic support and hostility throughout the nineteenth century. But it is also apparent that after a heady period of activity in the first half of the
century, there was in general a marked increase in resistance
towards them and a noticeable decrease in the numbers of
female itinerants and full-time preachers.

When we compare how the women preachers were
received in the different Methodist streams and their level of
preaching activity, we see striking differences. First of all,
there is a large body of evidence that women were travelling,
exhorting, and preaching extensively in the Methodist Episcopal tradition in the 1820s and 1830s in the United States,
whereas only isolated instances can be found in Upper
Canada. Second, in Upper Canada, there was a sudden

cessation of what little preaching by women there was in the Methodist Episcopal tradition around 1830. In the United States, some women were ordained before the turn of the century. The third dissimilarity is the gradual disappearance of women preachers in both the Primitive Methodist and Bible Christian Churches in Canada, while in the United States in the Primitive Methodist and Methodist Protestant Churches, again women were ordained by the end of the century. (The Bible Christian Church was not transplanted to the United States as a church, although women preachers who had been Bible Christians in England emigrated to the United States and preached in other denominations.)

Historians who have analyzed the status of women have their favourite theories to explain why women lost power or position at certain periods in history. Increasing industrialization, urbanization, institutionalization, and professionalization, as well as the natural evolution of a religious denomination from a sect to a church, are all interrelated and have validity as phenomena that lessened women's acceptance as preachers by the middle of the nineteenth century in North America. Nor can we underestimate the power of the press and pulpit as a way of enforcing the "Cult of True Womanhood" which kept women more closely confined to the home. There are psychological theories as well, such as the fear of women's power – which in this case would mean the fear of women preaching. Indeed, all these factors are part of a complex set of circumstances which contributed to the diminishing of women's position in the nineteenth-century church, and they need to be briefly examined.

Industrialization and Urbanization

As industrialization and urbanization changed the face of

North America around the 1840s, women were thrust into new roles. Even in the less developed province of Upper Canada, a flood of settlers from the British Isles in the 1830s and 1840s accelerated the move from a pioneer community to a more urbanized society. Urban centres grew yet more rapidly after 1851. With this shift in demographics, women were not as frequently required to work alongside their husbands clearing land and establishing homesteads. Instead, as towns developed and families became prosperous, the middle class woman was encouraged to fit into the stereotype of the leisure class Victorian lady whose "proper sphere" was the hearth and whose influence was in the home as wife and mother. If she did become involved in the wider community, it was generally in a limited nurturing role such as that of Sunday school teacher or in newly formed benevolent organizations. Historians have noted that many opportunities previously available for women disappeared at that time. In both countries, women who had been able to vote lost that right. This happened around 1830 in the United States and in Canada between 1832 and 1849. Harsh abortion laws were enacted in Upper Canada in 1837, limiting the options of family size and confining women to child-rearing for a lengthy period of time. In the United States, women were discouraged from entering occupations and businesses that had formerly been open to them. At one time in the early history of that country, women had been butchers, silversmiths, gunsmiths, upholsterers, gate keepers, jail keepers, sextons, journalists, printers, "doctoresses," apothecaries, and shopkeepers of almost every kind.[1]

Institutionalization and Professionalization

The institutionalization and increasing professionalization in nineteenth-century society also resulted in a more limited role for women. Where once an apprenticeship had been adequate, new scientific knowledge made specialized training and knowledge a requirement for professions. Schools, newly established for this purpose, were closed to women. In the United States, women still practised medicine in the mid-fifties, but their acceptance was limited. Not only did graduation from a medical school become the criterion for obtaining a licence to practise medicine, but it allowed access to hospitals as well. And medical training schools were off-limits to women.[2]

Religious institutions, too, were transformed. In Upper Canada, new towns and cities required more sophisticated church buildings than the taverns and rude log houses where the earliest worship services had been held. As the population multiplied, so did the churches and the church structures. A variety of religious publications and newspapers appeared; religious head offices sprang up; Sunday schools proliferated. Even in the smaller "sectarian" movements, preachers were ordained and the gap between lay and clergy widened. Orderly camp-meetings held emotions in check. Mainstream Methodist clergy were allowed to settle on one circuit for up to five years although they had been shifted every six months in the late eighteenth century and moved every two years in 1828. Church meetings required the participation of "ladies" to "prepare tea" and supervise "well-filled tables."[3]

Church members, who had become more "respectable," prosperous, cultured, and educated than they had been in the early pioneer settlements, demanded a more educated clergy. This was particularly noticeable in the Methodist denominations in Upper Canada where members of the British governing class believed that Methodists were on the whole of a much lower class and that most Methodist ministers were illiterate. Methodist churches responded by establishing theological schools and requiring graduation from these schools as a prerequisite for ordination. Victoria College introduced a theological course in 1851. Since women were not accepted in a theological college, this served as another barrier to women's active participation in religious leadership roles.[4]

Salaries for Methodist ministers' wives decreased, indicating a devaluing of their work. In 1792, the General Conference of the Methodist Episcopal Church meeting in Baltimore had resolved that "the wife of a preacher" should receive $64, the same salary as a preacher. In 1816, Canadian salaries not only decreased for minister's wives, but they were no longer listed as such and were considered instead as salaries paid to the male ministers themselves, if they were married. By this time, married male ministers did not receive a double wage but were paid only $100 per annum compared with a salary of between $60 and $80 for single male ministers, although there were allowances for each child up to a maximum amount. "Economy," the *Christian Guardian* pointed out, was "a virtue proper for both sexes," but "particularly becoming and useful to the female." Evidently Methodist ministers' wives were expected to be even more frugal in the nineteenth century than in the eighteenth.[5]

From Sect to Church

The institutionalization of the church and the professionalization of the ministry are part of the natural evolution which generally occurs as a sect evolves into a mainstream church. Certainly this can be seen in the changing face of Methodism in North America in the nineteenth century, first in the Methodist Episcopal Church and later in other denominations such as the Bible Christian and Primitive Methodist movements. Early Methodist churches had displayed all the traditional characteristics of sects. Theirs was a radical ethic set over against the world. Methodist doctrines and disciplines emphasized a conversion experience, the claim of a direct personal relationship with God, a direct personal fellowship with each other, and an ascetic lifestyle. Striving for inward perfection, members displayed an unbounded religious enthusiasm not typical of other denominations such as the Church of England or the Presbyterians in Upper Canada. They adhered more rigidly to the idealism of the early church, valuing lay leadership including that of women. Sects, however, have a limited life expectancy. As membership increases, new generations are born into the religious faith often without the earlier prerequisite experiential conversion. Losing their other-worldly colouring, sects become noticeably less detached from the world and more accommodating to secular values.[6]

The Power of the Press and Pulpit

Women's position in the church was also affected by strong opposition from the pulpit and in the early nineteenth-century press to women's preaching. As more women became involved in preaching, more articles appeared prohibiting preaching and emphasizing that women should stay in the home. Elisabeth Fiorenza points out that an analysis of sermons and written ethical instructions on women's place and behaviour in the United States has shown that prescriptions against women's participation outside the home increased in direct relation to women's actual activity. The appearance of women preachers in the Methodist tradition in the eighteenth and nineteenth centuries proved no exception, and the question of whether or not women should be allowed to preach was hotly debated both in Great Britain and in North America at that time. Injunctions against women preaching were issued from the pulpit and in women's columns in journals and periodicals. Not only were these statements opposed to women in the pulpit, but they also insisted that women were not preaching and, moreover, had "never presumed to preach."[7]

Women in the nineteenth century received opposing messages. In Upper Canada in the 1830s, Methodist women were being assured that they were preaching the "precious gospel" by knitting socks and remaining in their nursery. Yet at the same time, the political writings of the radical British feminist Harriet Martineau were being circulated to the public and referred to in the press. In the 1850s, Canadian women presented petitions to the government asking for the right to own property; and the American Lucy Stone, head of the American Woman Suffrage Association and editor of the *Woman's Journal*, lectured on women's rights in Upper Canada. Yet at the same time, the Methodist Conference in 1852 reinforced the myth that attending Leaders' meetings was not proper for women and that Methodist women had never assumed such a public role:

> *Resolved, that although female Leaders have had charge of Female Classes, and have rendered great service as helpers in the Church also giving such [much] information from time to time to the Superintendents respecting their classes; yet female Leaders have never been regarded as Members of the Quarterly or Leaders' Meetings; Nor is it according to our usage, any more than according to the sense of Propriety entertained by our devoted female Lead-*

*ers, that they should take a part in the official
proceedings of such Meetings.*

As women in the Toronto District had evidently attempted to take a more active role in the decision-making
processes of the church, the Methodist Church felt it necessary to state that women had always acted according to the
Victorian sense of "Propriety," a dominant value at that time.[8]

In the nineteenth century, the arguments against women
speaking and taking leadership positions in the church were
louder and more frequent than those in favour. Partly as a
result of this hostility, most of the women, particularly in
Upper Canada, either stopped preaching completely or responded only to guest invitations to speak at special celebrations such as anniversaries or church openings.

Other women, of course, like the eastern Canadian Mary
McCoy Morris Bradley never did summon up enough courage to speak in the face of official church opposition. She
was convinced that God had called her to be a preacher, and
she was aware of biblical examples of "prophetesses." Still
she felt bound to yield to the restrictions her church placed
upon women. Her diary explains how she struggled to come
to terms with these conflicting demands all her adult life:

> *I thought if I had been a man, nothing could
> hinder me from going abroad to proclaim sal-
> vation to a dying world. O, how I longed to
> declare what God had done for my soul, and
> to invite Sinners to flee from the wrath to come,
> and lay hold on eternal life . . .*

But she was afraid to act against the church's expectations for women. "I was many times afraid lest the fear of

offending man, kept me from obeying the operation of the Spirit of God, which I felt in my heart," she confessed in her memoirs. Finally, believing it to be her only recourse, she decided to write her autobiography as a testimony to God's call.[9]

Fear of Women Preaching

In the history of the Christian church, one of the controversial issues has been whether or not women should be allowed to preach. Pauline passages from the New Testament have been dissected, defended, attacked, and critiqued either to uphold a woman's right to speak in church or to support the position that woman's place has been divinely decreed not to be behind a pulpit but in the home.

It has not been solely the difference in scriptural interpretation, however, that has fanned the flames of this religious debate. Over the centuries, there has been something particularly offensive or threatening about a woman preaching. As James Porter pointed out in his analysis of the question in 1851 in the United States, it is not that women must be kept from speaking, but that they must not speak "too loud or too long." The injunction against women speaking in church, he noted, only applied to women who were "contending with a man in public," who were finding "fault with men," or who were usurping "authority over them." As long as women were not "dictating" to men or were not perceived as being "disloyal to the men in public," he wrote, women could speak. But in Porter's opinion, women preaching fit the proscribed categories.[10]

Two elements in Porter's understanding of preaching are worth noting, particularly as it relates to women. First of all, preaching clearly conveys an authority far beyond that of ordinary speaking which is less "loud" and less "long." Since nineteenth-century women were admonished to be submissive to men and not authoritative over them, preaching was ruled out as a proper activity for women. "Nothing will increase your influence and secure your usefulness, more than 'being in SUBJECTION to your own husbands,'" the *Christian Guardian* informed its female readership in 1829 in its Ladies' Department. Indeed, in a later edition, the same paper pointed out that the subjection should be a "cheerful" act, remembering that since "woman was 'first in transgression,'" this "ruin was chiefly under her hand" and this subjection was "her just punishment." Although the line between preaching and evangelism was not clearly defined, evangelism was considered to be less authoritative than preaching. Women described as evangelists were tolerated at a time when women preachers were forbidden. As one late nineteenth-century historian wrote of Mary Barritt Taft in England, "her services as an evangelist led to her employment as a preacher." Second, while the *Oxford English Dictionary* defines the verb "to preach" primarily as "to pronounce a public discourse upon sacred subjects," there is a less desirable meaning, "to give moral advice in an obtrusive or tiresome way" as in the following conversation from 1834:

> *"Pray Mr. Lamb, did you ever hear me preach?"*
> *"Damme," said Lamb, "I never heard you do anything else."*

As one male churchgoer in the United States commented after hearing a woman preach, "Oh the sermon was all right, but you see I hear a woman preach six days a week, and on Sunday I like to get a rest." It is this pejorative understanding of preaching that is emphasized in Porter's description and which has been traditionally ascribed to women – from Geoffrey Chaucer's fourteenth-century depiction of the "Wife of Bath," described as a "prechour" to her numerous husbands, to a twentieth-century evangelist's equation of *Bobbed Hair, Bossy Wives and Women Preachers*.[11]

In the nineteenth century, the inappropriateness of women preaching was sharply contrasted with the appropriateness of domesticity or the "Cult of True Womanhood." Methodist women in both Canada and the United States fell heir to this stereotype. Many of the Methodist women preachers faced the challenges not only of overwork, hard living conditions, and economic deprivation as did their male counterparts but also the added burden of resistance because they refused to conform to the Victorian paradigm. By the middle of the century in both countries, Barbara Heck was more of a household word than were either Eliza Barnes or Dorothy Ripley.

Social Disorder

One other thesis needs to be explored for its possible relevance to the Canadian context. In her excellent analysis of women and religion during the period of the Second Great Awakening in the United States, Smith-Rosenberg suggests that religious disorder mirrors social disorder. Sects, revivalism, and other anti-ritualistic religious expressions, she maintains, are a response to social, economic, and political chaos or instability. Once individuals or groups have been accepted and successfully incorporated into the bourgeoisie or mainstream, they no longer have a need to destroy or challenge old institutional and hierarchical arrangements. In this way, Smith-Rosenberg explains how women who became marginalized in the process of industrialization and urbanization were especially attracted to revivalism in the first half of the nineteenth century. Adolescent women were particularly vulnerable because they were doubly marginalized. She claims that after women married and their families became successful and safely ensconced in the new middle class which emerged around the 1840s, and after society became more firmly urbanized and less in a state of flux, most women returned to more traditional religious expressions.[12]

Methodism and Politics

All of these reasons have something to say about the Canadian situation. Yet none by itself adequately explains why there were few women preaching in the Methodist Episcopal tradition and why these women suddenly stopped preaching around 1830. Nor can these reasons answer why, in spite of opposition, Methodist women were ordained in the United States beginning in 1866, and several others were officially licensed to preach. Yet in Canada, women were eased out of the pulpit in the different denominations in the second half of the century and were ordained only in 1936 in The United Church of Canada.

Both countries experienced the same trends towards urbanization and industrialization. In fact, the United States was substantially more advanced than Upper Canada, particularly in the East. If industrialization and institutionalization were major factors in the devolution of women's preaching activity, then women should have ceased preaching in the United States in the early nineteenth century. Yet many women were very active in the church in the New England states as well as on the western frontier. The professionalization of the ministry and the institutionalization of the church were phenomena that existed in both countries, with the United States again ahead chronologically. And women in both countries were bombarded with articles, columnists' advice, and sermons declaring not only that women's place had been divinely decreed to be in the home but that women in fact had always remained there. Passive, submissive role models were held up in both countries for women to emulate.

Smith-Rosenberg's theory is persuasive and helps explain why the Bible Christian and Primitive Methodist movements were successful in Canada between the 1830s and 1850s. Cholera in 1832, the influx of immigration, the shift from a pioneer country to a more urbanized country, the unions and separations in the Methodist Episcopal church, and the rebellions of the late 1830s all contributed to unsettled conditions that could explain the popularity of the more anti-ritualistic and sect-type Methodist denominations and women's prominent leadership roles in them. Yet this thesis cannot be applied easily to women's situation in the Methodist Episcopal Church. In spite of constant political and social upheaval, there is little evidence of women preaching in this stream in Upper Canada in the first half of the century, and an abrupt cessation of what activity there was occurred in 1830. In fact, while intense revivalism swept across the United States for several decades, very little took place in Upper Canada at all. There were camp-meetings and pro-tracted meetings and a brief period of revivalism at the beginning of the Indian Missions when Eliza Barnes was first preaching in Canada in the Methodist Episcopal Church. The same kind of activity also took place in the early years of the Bible Christians and the Primitive Methodists. Compared with the United States, however, revivalism affected a very small proportion of the Canadian population.

I suggest that the major difference that allowed women

greater progress in the United States was the political climate that permeated all of society, including its religious institutions. The United States had been born out of rebellion and encouraged democracy. "By no people are women treated with more respect and consideration than by native born Americans," a Cobourg newspaper noted. "An instance of one of them beating his wife rarely occurs." This was hardly an example of equality of men and women, but it did symbolize a dramatic difference in the American and Canadian mind-set. Although women in the United States had to work hard to swim against the current of the "Victorian leisured lady" paradigm, they did make some headway. On the other hand, the Upper Canadian governing *élite* was continually trying to prevent revolution, discourage democracy, and keep a lid on any kind of emotional religious expression. Because of the more conservative attitudes in that country, women slipped more comfortably into the Victorian mould. For example, the British immigrant Anne Langton gave up canoeing in 1839 not long after she came to Canada because her husband John considered a canoe to be "an unfit conveyance for so helpless a being as a woman." Having enjoyed her previous canoe rides, she confessed to being glad that John's "idea did not spring up earlier," but she did not travel in a canoe again.[13]

Women preaching in the Methodist Episcopal tradition in Upper Canada were caught in a double bind. Not only were they socialized into a less liberal atmosphere than in the United States, but they found themselves part of a Methodist stream that intentionally adopted a more conservative and rigid stance than its American counterpart in order to achieve more privileges and gain greater respectability. British Wesleyans in England had undergone a similar metamorphosis after Wesley's death in order to be more acceptable. But in order to understand why the Canadian Methodist Episcopals deliberately chose conservative policies, we need to review how they were received in Upper Canada in the late eighteenth and early nineteenth centuries.

When the first American Methodist men and women arrived in Upper Canada at the end of the eighteenth century, they were warmly welcomed. Many of them were British loyalists fleeing from the United States, a traitorous and rebellious country in Great Britain's eyes. The Methodist itinerants, who first came to Canada from the United States in the 1780s, were also enthusiastically received by isolated settlers and by people in pioneer communities who were devoid of almost any formal religious opportunities. The itinerants not only brought spiritual nourishment, but their style of delivery met the needs of a backwoods people. Whereas the few Church of England and Presbyterian clergy already in Upper Canada expected the people to come to worship services in established church buildings, Methodist itinerants took the services to the people. In a country where roads were either non-existent or treacherous, settlers lived miles apart, and the weather was either unbearably cold or too hot, the Methodist approach met with resounding success. Their emotionally charged services were far better suited to a spiritually starved, isolated and rough people than was a staid, reserved British liturgy. Later, in the early 1800s, when Methodist camp-meetings were introduced into Upper Canada from the American frontier, they provided social opportunities welcomed by families who had little access to social intercourse. Indeed for many adults and children, the outdoor camp-meeting and the later indoor protracted meeting provided breaks in an otherwise tedious and hard life and were eagerly anticipated as the social highlight of the season.[14]

Although the Methodist itinerants achieved an enormous

popular following in Upper Canada, many of the British governing *élite* had little use for Americans and especially for the Methodist clergy. After all, the eighteenth-century Methodist movement had been a damning critique of the sterile condition of the Church in England, and it was that church to which most of the government officials adhered. At the beginning of the nineteenth century, when democratic initiatives had only recently resulted in the overthrow of governments in France and the United States, the ruling classes in England understandably feared a movement that consisted mainly of the middle and working classes, and that appeared to provide these classes with a voice and a measure of equality. In 1794, Jacob Mountain, the Anglican Bishop of Quebec, had reported to the Secretary of State about the Canadian condition noting that:

> *The greatest bulk of the people have and can have no instruction but such as they receive occasionally from itinerant and mendicant Methodists, a set of ignorant enthusiasts, whose preaching is calculated only to perplex the understanding, & corrupt the morals & relax the nerves of industry, & disolve [sic] the bonds of society.*

The first lieutenant-governor of Upper Canada, John Graves Simcoe, assured the Secretary of State, the Duke of Portland, that it was his intention to render Upper Canada "as nearly as may be 'a perfect Image and Transcript of the British Government and Constitution'" and that "a regular Episcopal establishment, subordinate to the primacy of Great Britain" was in his opinion "absolutely necessary."[15]

After the war of 1812 between the United States and

Great Britain and the ravages of parts of Upper Canada by the Americans, to be an American and a Methodist in Upper Canada was seen to be a double threat to national security. In 1814, General Gordon Drummond, the administrator of the government of Upper Canada, reported that the Methodists were "itinerant fanatics, enthusiastic in political as well as religious matters," who came from the United States to Upper Canada deliberately to disseminate "their noxious principles." For a number of years after the war ended, Americans were officially discouraged from emigrating to Upper Canada, and at one point Lord Bathurst, the British Secretary of State for War and the Colonies, considered taking away the land of all those Americans who had entered the country since the war. Later on, in the opinion of the British, the abortive rebellions of the late 1830s appeared to justify these anxieties. The aptly named newspaper, the *Patriot*, noted in 1839:

> *Yankee missionaries have preached in the pulpit, at Camp Meetings, in the wigwams of our simple-hearted Indians, and at the family hearths of our unsophisticated yeomanry. Yankee schoolmasters have preached in our common schools; Yankee Doctors have preached at the bedsides of their patients; Yankee tavern-keepers have preached in their bar-rooms; Yankee stage-drivers have preached on the highways, and eke [sic] multitudes of Yankee squatters have preached in our backwoods. All these preachings have been for thirty years; and thus has the poison been unsparingly preached, promulgated, punched, poked and pummelled into the people from the whining schoolboy to the old gray beard.[16]*

Book after book by authors of British background who lived in Upper Canada or visited the country in the early nineteenth century described American Methodists as boorish, uncultured, unmannered, and above all, democratic, even as the writers begrudgingly admired American urban centres, technical advances, and their "greater number of comforts and conveniences." John Howison travelled throughout Upper Canada for two and a half years with brief visits to the United States. In 1821, he wrote that the Methodists in St. Catharine's "carry their religious mania to an immoderate height," holding meetings there three or four times a week. Their "fanaticism and extravagance," he felt, were "degrading to human nature." He criticized the Methodists for condemning card-playing and dancing, "while their own lives were, in many instances, one continued outrage against decency, decorum and virtue." Although more charitable toward the Methodists, William Cattermole, who also spent time in Upper Canada, wrote ten years later that it would be better to have Methodist preachers from England rather than from the United States. Republicanism, he noted, "is as natural" to Americans "as piety is to the English Methodist preachers." Catherine Parr Traill found the "Yankee manners" annoying and Howison wrote that Americans went to bed with their boots on. Even the iconoclastic Anna Brownell Jameson found "the frantic disorders" of Methodist love-feasts and camp-meetings much worse than she had imagined, although she realized that without the Methodist "religious teachers," the people would have been "utterly abandoned."[17]

The Presbyterians, too, had little love for their Methodist sisters and brothers. On coming to Canada in 1832, the Scottish Secessionist minister William Proudfoot was appalled at the "ascendancy" which Methodists had "acquired" throughout the country. "Their doctrines," he wrote, "are frightfully in opposition to the grand, the glorious doctrines of the Gospel." In fact he went as far as to declaim that:

> *Something must be done to dislodge these pre-*
> *tenders, these so distant [Methodist] preachers.*
> *The country will never become Christian till*
> *these fellows be dislodged.*[18]

Even working class British Methodists were outspoken in their criticisms of Canadian Methodist Episcopal preachers. Describing their experiences in attending a Methodist Episcopal chapel in York, a group of British families noted that

> *they submitted patiently for some time to laxity*
> *of discipline, and various indignities, together*
> *with the rudeness of vulgar and ignorant men*
> *who occupied the pulpit. They had never been*
> *accustomed in England to see ragged and*
> *dirty preachers with beards "that shewed like a*
> *stubble at harvest home," nor had they ever*
> *been outraged and disgusted, by seeing their*
> *minister put his finger on his nose, and lean*
> *over the pulpit first on one side, and then on*
> *the other, and blow like a snorting horse, and*
> *then wipe with the cuff or the lap of his coat,*
> *and after vociferating nonsense for an hour,*
> *sit down in the pulpit and cram his hands into*
> *his waistcoat pockets, and bring out of one a*
> *plug of tobacco, and a short pipe, and out of*
> *the other a Jack knife, and deliberately cut his*
> *plug, and fill his pipe, then light it at the pulpit*
> *candle and come down puffing away to salute*
> *his brethren.*[19]

By and large, however, at the beginning of the century, the ordinary Upper Canadian resident, whether of British or American origin, was more interested in eking out sustenance in the wilderness and in providing for a family than in considering the geographical origin of his or her neighbours. The Methodists, particularly, tended to be apolitical, and the early itinerants had no time or interest in politics. Indeed they had barely enough hours in any one day to fulfil all their denominational requirements of reading, visiting, preaching, praying, and theological reflection.

Methodist political involvement became acute, however, in the 1820s when Egerton Ryerson, a twenty-three-year-old Methodist itinerant only recently received "on trial," and the Venerable John Strachan, Archdeacon of York, who had been raised in the Presbyterian tradition and ordained in the Church of England, became embroiled in a public controversy that sent shock waves across the Atlantic Ocean and had ramifications that lasted until the final settlement of the Clergy Reserves in 1854. In fact, it resulted in the union of the Canadian Methodist Episcopal Church and the British Wesleyans in Canada, permanently changing the face of the Canadian Methodist Church.

While delivering the oration at a funeral service for Bishop Mountain in the summer of 1825, Strachan made outrageous statements about the current status of the Protestant religion in Canada and especially the Methodists. He inflated the strength of his own church, dismissing as inconsequential all other denominations except the Kirk and independent Presbyterians. Calling the Methodists "ignorant" and lazy, he noted that they had "no settled clergymen." He suggested that they probably had around thirty itinerants in all of Canada, but they were all "subject to the orders" of the American body and therefore "hostile to our [Canadian] institutions, both civil and religious." Archdeacon Strachan quite genuinely believed that the Methodists were filling the people's minds with "low cunning" and with "republican ideas of independence and individual freedom." In his opinion, this was anathema.[20]

He had waved the red flag. This was the third formal attack that Church of England clergy had made on the Canadian Methodists. The itinerants decided that they had suffered enough abuse, for they were also denied privileges such as the right to solemnize marriages and to hold land as a church body for chapels and cemeteries. They called on Egerton Ryerson to make a response. Much to the delight of his co-workers, he prepared a brilliant rebuttal that was published in the Upper Canadian left-wing newspaper, the *Colonial Advocate*. Proud of his own British background, Ryerson pointed out that the Methodist itinerants were loyal British subjects and that all but eight of them had been born or educated in "British domain." Of those, only two were not naturalized British subjects. He elaborated on the high quality of their training, hard work, and supervision, although the Methodists themselves recognized that their itinerants needed to become better educated. In 1825, the Second Canada Conference of the Methodist Episcopal Church resolved that itinerants needed to improve their minds "to meet the wants of society," and in May 1826, the *Colonial Advocate* found it necessary to print a course of study that was recommended as indispensable for Canadian preachers.[21]

Strachan made another stinging statement in the spring of 1828. He reiterated his stand on the need for confirming the Church of England as the established church in Upper Canada. In his opinion, it followed that this church was legally entitled to all the financial proceeds from the Clergy Reserves. Although the Canada Act of 1791, which had stipulated that one-seventh of all lands should be set aside as Reserves for the "support and maintenance of a Protestant clergy," made no specific connection between "Protestant clergy" and the Church of England, Strachan had succeeded in setting up a Clergy Reserves Corporation under Church of England administration. As editor of the newly established Methodist newspaper, the *Christian Guardian,* Ryerson continued the debate, arguing for a complete separation of church and state and the secularization of the Reserves. As a member of a voluntarist denomination, he believed that the Reserves should be sold and the proceeds used to support education.[22]

The Church of England, Ryerson wrote, "maintained ceaseless warfare against Methodism" in the early nineteenth century. Historians agree that intense pressures were brought to bear by that denomination in the ensuing controversy. In 1828, Sir Peregrine Maitland, the lieutenant-governor of Upper Canada, told the Mississauga Indians at the Credit River that if they persisted in attending Methodist camp-meetings, they would not receive a school or other government assistance. It is reported that Strachan also threatened the Indians, insisting that they give their allegiance to the Church of England. He helped fund the "Ryanites" who broke away from the Canadian Methodist Episcopal Church because the itinerant Henry Ryan believed the Canadian Methodists were too slow in dissociating themselves from the American parent body. Strachan, it was reported, wanted to stir up trouble among the Methodists. And because of his intense dislike for American Methodists, while he was in England he negotiated with the British Wesleyans to send more of their missionaries to Upper Canada even though this was completely out of his jurisdiction. Although he was a committed Church of England clergyman, Strachan admired the British Wesleyans, believing that they displayed "respectability" and a consistency of "organization."[23]

The Methodist Episcopals were involved in lobbying and political action of their own. In 1828, they separated from the American Methodists to form an independent Canadian Methodist Episcopal Church. This was not a unanimous decision. Out of 170 delegates, 105 voted in favour, 43 against, and 22 abstained. Nathan Bangs, whose sister had been preaching in the Niagara region, was one of those opposed. But those itinerants who favoured the separation from the United States believed that it would be politically advantageous for them. Like British Wesleyans who had taken earlier actions in England to be more accepted in that country, the Canadian Methodist Episcopals felt that this would give them more credibility and allow them greater privileges in Upper Canada. The Primitive Methodists noted that the Methodist Episcopal preachers exerted a "Wonderful Political influence in the Country." "Their Preachers," wrote William Lawson, "attend popular Elections and make violent Speeches and run all over the Country influencing the Electors." Indeed, the Methodist Episcopals obviously achieved some of the respectability they sought and influenced the governing body, for one year later they were given permission to conduct marriage ceremonies. Presumably with this separation from the United States, the Canadian Methodist Episcopal Church was perceived as having acquired more the "sober and regulated modes of thinking" that the Upper Canadian legislation had specified as the criteria for granting that privilege to other religious denominations in 1798. In 1828 as well, the Canadian Methodists forwarded a petition to the British government with eight thousand signatures, protesting against the claims of the Church of England. George Ryerson, who was in England on personal business, was asked to have it put before the British House of Commons.[24]

George Ryerson was the most liberal of five Ryerson

brothers who became Methodist itinerants in Upper Canada. While he was visiting England, he had opportunities to visit with the Wesleyans and was appalled at how reactive they had become. They were "too *churchified*," George wrote to Egerton, and too legalistic. "Every act is a legislative act, even on so trifling a subject as, whether a certain chapel shall have an organ, etc." In fact, he pointed out, "altogether I fear that the Wesleyan Conference [in England] is an obstacle to the extension of civil and religious liberty." Because of his observations, George Ryerson opposed any close affiliation with the British Wesleyans, recommending to his brother that they suffer "the temporary censure of enemies in Canada" rather than consider "the permanent evil & annoyance of having a Church & State Tory Superintendent" from England.[25]

Egerton Ryerson, however, declined to heed his brother's advice. More closely attuned to another brother, John, Egerton listened instead to his opinion. John Ryerson had been inspired to unite with the British one day while he was walking along Bay Street in downtown Toronto. He believed a union would be the only action that could achieve complete acceptance and harmony with the Upper Canadian establishment. As a result, Egerton Ryerson steered a course for the Canadian Methodists that united them in 1833 to the British Wesleyans. It is one historian's assessment that John Ryerson wielded more influence in the Canadian Conference than any other itinerant for almost thirty years, and it is said that Egerton Ryerson always sought his advice. Egerton himself wrote that he found his brother John to be "the most cool and accurate judge of the state of the public mind" of any man he had known in Canada. Whereas George believed the British Wesleyans were too conservative, John felt that the Canadian Methodists were too radical. George

Ryerson had been refused entrance into the Anglican priesthood and this may have helped shape his attitude. Moreover, George's wife, Sarah Rolph, the first Indian missionary teacher to die while at work on the Canadian Indian Missions, was a sister of the noted Reformer John Rolph. John Ryerson, on the other hand, had no use for the Upper Canadian Reform party, and in the 1836 election he worked hard to ensure that, as he put it, "not a ninny" of the Reformers would be elected in the riding where he preached.[26]

Only one itinerant voted against the 1833 union – Joseph Gatchell, husband of Ellen Bangs, who had preached in the Niagara district. Gatchell, more radical in his attitudes than the other Methodist male preachers, was dishonourably removed from the roll. But there were other after-effects. A group of itinerants who had already left in opposition to the union formed a continuing Methodist Episcopal Church that attracted more liberal Methodists and a number of American settlers. Mary Lewis Ryerson, John's wife, wrote that it was a good move for they took "the rubbish from our church." It was this body the Primitive Methodists considered joining in 1836 because of the treatment they had received from their own British parent body. And in this continuing Methodist Episcopal Church, a preaching licence was issued to Emma Richardson in 1864. George Ryerson became an elder and later an "Angel" (ordained bishop) in the Irvingite Church in Toronto, a denomination he had come upon in England that accepted women in leadership roles.[27]

The newly united Wesleyan Methodist Church in Canada adopted the same attitudes as those of the British Wesleyans in Great Britain. Camp-meetings were frowned upon. Local preachers could no longer be ordained as they had been when an emergency need for more preachers arose. Women who had been preaching on the Indian Missions became silent, and in fact few women remained even as teachers. Legislation against women preaching had been passed in England in 1803. Some women such as Mary Barritt Taft and Elizabeth Tomlinson Evans were still preaching in the 1840s in England; in Ireland, Alice Cambridge had retired only in 1830 and Ann Lutton preached throughout the 1830s. Yet Canadian women were discouraged from following their example as were Wesleyan women in Great Britain. Instead they were informed that women preached by knitting socks, and they were encouraged to be missionaries in the nursery. The church became more "autocratic" and lay members were not highly regarded. Many of the Methodists believed that they had been "sold" by the Ryersons.[28]

A number of men and women joined other more liberal denominations, although the Primitive Methodist itinerant William Summersides noted that there was "tumult and confusion" in all the denominations except his own. On the Yonge Street Circuit alone, membership in the newly united church declined from 951 to 578 between 1833 and 1836. Between 1833 and 1839, the church as a whole lost 5 per cent of its members while the population of Upper Canada increased. But the Methodists who entered the union did achieve a certain measure of the "respectability" they sought. They abandoned their voluntarist stance by accepting financial aid for the Indian Missions. The radical Reformer William Lyon MacKenzie included in his "seventh Report on Grievances," which he presented to the Upper Canadian Assembly in 1835, a statement that "payments of gifts, salaries, pensions and retired allowances" were being made by the government to Methodist clergy as well as to other denominations. In 1837, the Methodist Conference passed a resolution allowing the use of funding from the Clergy Reserves for other than for educational purposes. At the beginning of the following year, the President of Conference and the Superintendent of the Toronto District signed a statement that they saw no objection to the Church of England being recognized as "*the Established Church* of all the British colonies," which included Canada.[29]

However, the marriage of the Canadian and British Methodists was definitely not a happy one; in 1840, they separated. Even John Ryerson felt appalled at the changes he witnessed. "Never did high-churchism take such rapid strides towards undisputed domination in this country as it is now taking," he wrote to Egerton Ryerson. "Never were the prospects of the friends of civil and religious liberty so gloomy and desperate as they are now." The Indian Missions remained under the British Wesleyan jurisdiction, and among those preachers who remained with the Wesleyans was William Case. He had opposed women preaching: although both his wives – first Hetty Ann Hubbard and second Eliza Barnes – had at one time been preachers, both "settled down" shortly after they arrived on the Canadian missions. Although the Methodists had lost members with the union, by June 1841, they had a net gain of 663. A second and this time permanent union took place between the British Wesleyan Methodists and the Canadian Methodists in 1847, partly in an attempt to receive a share of the payments from the Clergy Reserves. By this time, British conservatism had firmly taken hold of Canadian society.[30]

There is no question that the union in 1833 with the British Wesleyans orchestrated by Egerton and John Ryerson helped seal the fate of women preachers in the Canadian Methodist Episcopal stream. The climate that was already not conducive to women preaching or even working outside the home became increasingly more restrictive. Certainly Egerton Ryerson gave them no encouragement. Like biblical literalists of his day, he subscribed to the concept that wives were to submit to their husbands, and he included this injunction in a later Canadian school textbook on Christian morals. Both he and John Ryerson educated their daughters to be genteel ladies by sending them to a French convent, and Egerton took his daughter Sophie on the traditional European tour to become more cultured. He favoured modesty in a woman and on the education of farmers' daughters, he wrote:

> *But let it not be imagined that I would wish to see farmers' wives and daughters lay aside country plainness and simplicity of manners, and attempt the silly foppery of city fashions and vanities. I have found, in more than one instance, that a city, or village, belle is as superficial and ignorant as she is fine and vain, while a well-educated farmer's daughter is as intelligent and well-informed as she is plain and modest.*

In 1842, when Egerton Ryerson became president of Victoria College, women were no longer permitted to attend classes there, ostensibly because of lack of space. He made allowances, however, for young men who had trouble learning the classics to attend. Although he realized that they would be able to stay at the college for only "one or two years' instruction," he insisted that room be made for them. He sincerely believed what he wrote in his own history of Methodism that the religion that declared that all were "equal in the sight of God" would "not refuse to acknowledge that all citizens are equal in the eye of the law." Yet because of his socio-cultural context, this did not fully apply to women. Formerly Upper Canada Academy, the school had been founded by the Methodists in 1836, the first Protestant institution of higher learning in Canada open to women. When the Academy was changed to a degree-granting institution, not only were women expelled because there was not enough room for them, but the two leading liberals on the Academy committee were replaced by more conservative members, and money was requested from the Upper Canada legislature. The union with the Wesleyans had dried up earlier sources of funding, mainly reform-minded Methodists.[31]

Egerton Ryerson had little love for Americans. He found their manners unrefined and disliked their democratic system of government. He formed a poor impression of the French in Europe because he felt they were unable to apply themselves, and he wrote in his diary that they were the "Yankees of Europe." His family had been driven from their New Jersey home during the American Revolution, and his widowed aunt's farm had been burned by American marines in 1814. And even though he had turned down an invitation to become a Church of England minister in favour of the Methodist tradition, his sympathies lay with the British. As he wrote to Jabez Bunting in 1844, "You will probably recollect that I . . . stated [in 1840], that my principles were strictly British, & such alone as could perpetuate British authority in Canada."[32]

Egerton Ryerson was authoritarian, and although he was applauded for the contribution he made, particularly to Methodism and to education in Canada, he also suffered extreme criticisms. He considered himself a moderate and on different occasions leaned in opposite directions. He displayed an anti-institutional bias when he criticized Jabez Bunting for introducing "laying on of hands" during the ordination ceremony, yet he resigned very briefly when the Canadian Church refused to relax the regulation of compulsory attendance at class meetings in 1852. As a result, he was subject to attack from all sides. The radical Canadian paper, the *Globe*, termed him a despot, and the Reformers at one point put a price on his head. The Provincial Auditor, John Langton, a British sympathizer, called him the "Pope of Methodism" suggesting that he mistook his profession since "nature intended him for a Jesuit." The British Methodist leader Jabez Bunting accused him of displaying "an utter want of integrity." Yet because of the influence he wielded, his pro-British attitude contributed to the increasing conservatism of the Methodist Church in Canada.[33]

Although women no longer preached in the conservative united Methodist Church, other women in Upper Canada were accepted as preachers in the more radical Methodist denominations, the Bible Christian and Primitive Methodist movements. When the "old" Methodists turned their back on their earlier voluntarist principles, "the torch of voluntarism" passed to the other sectarian groups attracting the more liberal-minded Methodists. But British conservatism was permeating all of Canadian society, and it was not long before most of the women preaching in these groups also left the pulpit and settled into more acceptable patterns of life. Women were scarcely heard of preaching in the Bible Christian Church beyond the early 1860s, although Ann Copp Gordon appears to have been an exception. And it was not long before the Primitive Methodists, as well, became too traditional to accept women in the pulpit. The natural institutionalization process occurred in these denominations as they evolved from sects to churches, yet it was mainly the conservatism of Canadian Methodism and of society that rendered them far less amenable to women in the pulpit than their sister churches in the United States.

APPENDIX A

Selected Nineteenth-Century Methodist Women in the United States and Canada

Name	Birth/Marriage/Death	Workplace	Work
Abbott, (Mrs. Abbott)	b. [England]	P.E.I., Canada	B.C. preacher
Adams, Elizabeth (Mrs. Henry Adams)	b. [England]	England/ P.E.I., Canada/ Upper Canada	B.C. preacher
Adams, (Mrs. John Adams)	b. [England]	P.E.I., Canada	B.C. preacher
Allen, Jane (Mrs. Trimble)	b. 1755 d. 1839	United States	M.E. Indian Missions teacher
Armstrong, Isabella (Mrs. Wm. Harris)	m. 1858	P.E.I., Canada	B.C. preacher
Ash, Sally (Mrs. Sabine Frazer)	m. ca. 1828	Upper Canada	M.E. Indian Missions teacher
Baker, (Mrs. William Baker)		New England	M.E. exhorter
Bangs, Ellen [Eleanor] (Mrs. Joseph Gatchel(l))	m. 1812 d. 21 Oct. 1857	Upper Canada	M.E. exhorter
Barnes, Eliza (Mrs. William Case)	b. 11 Nov. 1796, Boston m. 28 Aug. 1833 d. 16 Apr. 1887	United States/ Upper Canada	M.E. preacher/ Indian Missions teacher
Bayles, Miss	b. [New York]	Upper Canada	M.E. Indian Missions teacher
Benham, (Mrs. John Benham)	b. [New England states]	Upper Canada	M.E. Indian Missions teacher
Bennis, Eliza[beth] (Mrs. Bennis)	b. 1725 [England] d. 1802	England/ [United States]	W.M./[M.E.] "called people to repentance"

210

Bowes, Margaret (Mrs. Samuel E. Taylor)	b. 1806, Ireland m. 1828 d. 18 Mar. 1859	Upper Canada	M.C. - worker at camp-meetings/ class leader
Brink, Nancy		Upper Canada	M.E. Indian Missions teacher
Butterfield, Fanny (Mrs. Ebenezer Newell)	m. 1810	Northeastern United States	M.E. accompanied husband/exhorter
Calloway, Frances	b. [England]	P.E.I., Canada	B.C. preacher
Cantrell, Elizabeth (Mrs. William Calloway)		United States	M.E. accompanied husband/exhorted
Cook, (Mrs. Cook)		United States	A.M.E. preacher
Cook, Sophia	b. 1798, Pompey, New York d. 8 Sept. 1849	Upper Canada	M.E./W.M. Indian Missions teacher
Copp, Ann (Mrs. Andrew Gordon)	b. 19 Dec.1837, Beaford, Eng. m. 23 June 1859 d. 9 Aug. 1931	England/ Ontario/ Manitoba	B.C. preacher
Cory, (Mrs. Andrew Cory)		Upper Canada	B.C. preacher
Cox, Rebecca (Mrs. Jackson)		United States	A.M.E. preacher
Curtis, Natio (Mrs. Nelson Barnum)	b. 1812 m. 1834 d. 1853	United States	M.E. Indian Missions teacher
Dart, Elizabeth (Mrs. John Hicks Eynon)	b. 13 Jan. 1792, Cornwall m. 18 Mar. 1833 d. 13 Jan. 1857	England/ Upper Canada	B.C. preacher
Davidson, Helanor M.		United States	M.P. ordained preacher
De Merritt, Ella	b. 16 Aug. 1866, Ohio, U.S. d. 22 Apr. 1898	New England states	P.M. preacher
Dorsey, Eleanor (Mrs. Dorsey)		New York State	M.E. accompanied itinerant

211

Dulmage, Ann 1.(Mrs. Samuel Coate) 2.(Mrs. Archibald McLean)	b. ca. 1777, [New York State]	Upper Canada	M.E. class-leader/ accompanied husband
Dulmage, Margaret (Mrs. Sylvester Hurlburt)	b. 30 Aug.1803, [U. Canada] m. 1826 d. 13 June 1873	Upper Canada	M.E. Indian Missions teacher
Edmonds, Phoebe		Upper Canada	M.E. Indian Missions teacher
Edwards, P.		Upper Canada	M.E. Indian Missions teacher
"Elizabeth"	b. 1766	United States	A.M.E. preacher
Elaw, Zilpha (Mrs. Elaw)		United States	A.M.E. preacher
Evans, Rachel (Mrs. Evans)		New Jersey, U.S.	A.M.E. preacher
Farley, Susannah (Mrs. Solomon Waldron)	b. 19 Sept. 1802, Connecticut m. [11 Sept. 1826] d. Dec. 1890	Upper Canada	M.E. Indian Missions teacher
Farrington, Sophronia		from U.S. to Liberia	M.E. missionary
Fitzgerald, Osie	b. ca. 1813 [United States]	New England states	M.E./Holiness preacher
Fletcher, Eliza		New England states	P.M. preacher
Fletcher, Jane		Ontario	P.M. preacher
Ford, Elizabeth Atkinson (Mrs. Charles G. Finney)	b. ca. 1799 m. 5 Nov. 1848 d. 27 Nov. 1863	England/ United States	Holiness preacher
Giles, M. (Mrs. Giles)		Upper Canada	B.C. preacher
Gordon, (Mrs. James A. Gordon)		Ontario	M.C. supply preacher
Haviland, Laura	b. 1808 d. 1898	United States	Q./W.M. preacher

Heard, Sister (Mrs. Heard)	b. [England]	England/ Upper Canada	B.C. preacher
Hermes, Susan		United States	M.E. preacher
Hill, (Mrs. W.C. Hill)		United States	M.E. Indian Missions teacher
Holt, Mary (Mrs. Livsey)	b. ca. 1837 d. Oct.7, 1896	New England states	P.M. preacher
Hubbard, Hester Ann (Mrs. William Case)	b. ca. 1796, Granville, Mass. m. 4 May 1829 d. 24 Sept. 1831	Upper Canada	M.E. preacher/ Indian Missions teacher
Huntingdon, Miss	b. [United States]	Upper Canada	M.E. Indian Missions teacher
Inskip, Martha Foster (Mrs. John S. Inskip)		United States	Holiness preacher
Jago, Martha (Mrs. Sabine)	b. Cornwall, England	England/P.E.I.	B.C. preacher
Jenkins, (Mrs. Jenkins)		from U.S. to Buenos Aires	missionary
Kemys, Mary Ann (Mrs. John Kemys)	b. [England]	Upper Canada	B.C. preacher
Kent, Sister		Upper Canada	P.M. preacher
Knowles, H.M. (Mrs. W.M. Knowles)	b. [England]	[England] United States	P.M. preacher
Kunze, Miss		Upper Canada	M.E. Indian Missions teacher
Lacount, Miss		New England states	P.M. preacher
Lancaster, Sarah	b. [Upper Canada]	Upper Canada	M.E. Indian Missions teacher
Lee, Jarena	b. 1783, New Jersey, U.S. m. 1811	United States	A.M.E. preacher
Low, Sarah (Mrs. John Norton)	b. 1790 m. 1807 d. 1856	mid-west United States	M.E. -"useful" "argued intelligently"

Lyle, Mary Ann (Mrs. Wm. Lyle)	b. 29 Jan.1797, Cornwall m. 1823 d. 7 May 1862	England/ Upper Canada	B.C./P.M preacher
Manwaring, Mercy Miner (Mrs. Andrew Moffatt)	b. 1809, Connecticut, U.S. m. 28 Dec. 1834 d. 12 Oct. 1891	Upper Canada	M.E. Indian Missions teacher
Markham, (Mrs. Markham)		Upper Canada	P.M. exhorter
Mathers, Judith		United States	M.E. preacher
McColloch, Elizabeth (Mrs. Ebeneezer Zane)	b. 1748	United States	M.E. exhorter
McMullen, Sister		Upper Canada	M.E. Indian Missions teacher
Miller, Miss (Mrs. Wm. A. Smith)		midwest United States	M.E./M.P. preacher
Millett, Deborah (Mrs. Edward Taylor)	m. 1819	New England, U.S.	M.E. preacher
Murray, Sister		Upper Canada	P.M. preacher
Nan(ce)kivell, Susan	b. [England]	England/ Upper Canada	B.C. preacher
Newton, Margaret (Mrs. Van Cott)	b. 1830, New York City d. 1914	United States	M.E. licensed preacher
Newton, (Mrs. T. Newton)		England/ New England	P.M. preacher
Nicholls, Mary (Mrs. Thomas Green)	b. [England]	England/ Upper Canada	B.C. preacher
Opheral, Charity		United States	U.B. preacher
Parker, Ann (Mrs. George Parker)	b. ca. 1807, England d. 11 Nov. 1889	England/New England states	P.M. preacher
Parker, Sister	b. [England]	England/en route to Canada	B.C. preacher
Pearce, Hannah (Mrs. William Reeves)	b. 30 Jan. 1800, Devon, Eng. m. 5 July 1831 d. 13 Nov. 1868	England/ midwest United States	B.C./M.P. preacher
Perry, Jane		United States	M.E. preacher

Pigman, Sarah (Mrs. Walter G. Griffith)	b. 1783 m. 1803 d. 1845	United States	M.E. accompanied itinerant husband
Pinny, Miss		Upper Canada	M.E. Indian Missions teacher
Richards, Lucy	b. 1792	United States	M.E. Indian Missions teacher
Richardson, Emma (Mrs. Richardson)		Upper Canada/ United States	M.E. licensed preacher
Riden, Elizabeth (Mrs. John Williams)	b. [England] m. 1844	England/en route to Canada	B.C. preacher
Riden, Sister	b. [England]	England/en route to Canada	B.C. preacher
Ripley, Dorothy	b. ca. 1767, Whitby, England d. 23 Dec.1831	England/ United States	W.M./Q. preacher
Rippin, Sarah (Mrs. George Rippin)	b. 1824, Devon, England m. 1844 d. 11 Mar.1883	England/ Upper Canada/ United States	B.C. preacher
Rolph, E[lizabeth][1] or Rolph E[mma] (Mrs. Wm. Salmon)	b. 24 June 1796 [England] d. 18 Mar. 1835 b. 8 July 1797 [England] d. 1838	Upper Canada Upper Canada	M.E. Indian Missions teacher M.E. Indian Missions teacher
Rolph, Sarah (Mrs. George Ryerson)	b. 7 May 1799 [England] m. 1821 d. 10 July 1829	Upper Canada	M.E. Indian Missions teacher
Roszel, Sarah		Virginia, U.S.	exhorter
Ruckle, Barbara (Mrs. Paul Heck)	b. 1734, Ireland m. 1760 d. 17 Aug. 1804	United States/ Upper Canada	M.E.-encouraged preaching and classes
Russell, Marcella		from U.S. to Rio de Janiero	M.E. missionary
Scelec, Miss		Upper Canada	M.E. Indian Missions teacher
Scott, Amey	b. ca. 1805 m. 1826	Vermont, U.S.	M.E. accompanied husband/exhorted

Sealy, Miss		Upper Canada	M.E. Indian Missions teacher
Sellicks(Sillick), Eliza		Upper Canada	M.E. Indian Missions teacher
Sexton, Lydia		United States	U.B. licensed preacher
Shaw, Anna Howard	b. 1847, England d. 1919	United States	M.E./M.P./U. preacher
Shipman, (Mrs. M.F. Shipman)	b. [England]	England/New England states	P.M. preacher
Smith, (Mrs. Isaac H. Smith)		United States	M.E. Indian Missions teacher
Smith, (Mrs. Aaron Choat)	m. 1839	Upper Canada	M.E./W.M. Indian Missions teacher
St. John, Eugenia F.		United States	M.E./M.P. ordained preacher
Stephenson, (Mrs. Stephenson)		Upper Canada	P.M.-husband assisted her
Stockton, Miss		Upper Canada	M.E. Indian Missions teacher
Stovold, Ruth (Mrs. Wm. Woodger)	b. 1818, Hampshire, England m. 1851 d. 22 Jan. 1889	England/ Upper Canada	B.C./P.M. preacher
Stubbs, Harriet		United States	M.E. Indian Missions teacher
Suddard, (Mrs. Suddard)		New England states	P.M. preacher
Sutton, Sister		New York State	P.M. preacher
Swales, Ann		Ontario	P.M. preacher
Thompson, (Mrs. Thompson)		United States	M.E. preacher
Towle, Nancy		United States	Holiness preacher
Towler, Mary Ann 1. (Mrs. Thos. Proctor) 2. (Mrs. Wm. Towler)	b. [England] m. June, 1830	United States/ Upper Canada	P.M. preacher

Trick, Elizabeth (Mrs. Charles Henwood)	b. 27 Apr. 1801, Devon, Eng. m. 2 Jan. 1822 d. 8 Jan. 1872	England/ Upper Canada	B.C. preacher
Trueman, Elizabeth (Mrs. Hoskin)	b. ca. 1807, [England] d. 26 Feb. 1882	England/ Upper Canada	B.C. preacher
Verplanck, Sister		Upper Canada	M.E. Indian Missions teacher
Vickery, Ann (Mrs. Paul Robins)	b. 1800, [England] m. 1831 or 1832 d. 18 Sept. 1853	England/ Upper Canada	B.C. preacher
Watkins, (Mrs. Nathaniel Watkins)	b. [England]	[England]/ Upper Canada	P.M. preacher
Watkins, Ruth	b. 1802, [England]	England/New England states	P.M. preacher
Watson, Caroline	b. [Canada]	[Canada]/ United States	P.M./M.E. preacher
Way, Amanda	b. 1824 d. 1914	United States	Q./Methodist preacher
Wearing, Ann	b. [Devon, England]	England/New England states	W.M./P.M. preacher
Wilkins, Ann (Mrs. Wilkins)	b. 1806, New England states d. 13 Nov. 1857	from U.S. to Liberia	missionary
Wood, (Mrs. Wm. Wood)		New England states	P.M. preacher
Woodill, Jane (Mrs. Isaac Wilson)	b. 20 Feb. 1824, York m. 27 Dec. 1849 d. 17 July 1893	Upper Canada	P.M. preacher
Worrall, Phoebe (Mrs. Walter Palmer)	b. 18 Dec. 1807, New York m. 28 Sept. 1827 d. 2 Nov. 1874	United States/ Ontario/ Great Britain	M.E./Holiness preacher
Yeomans, S.		Upper Canada	M.E. Indian Missions teacher

Abbreviations:

A.M.	African Methodist Episcopal		Q.	Quaker
B.C.	Bible Christian		U.	Unitarian
M.C.	Methodist Church		U.B.	United Brethren
M.E.	Methodist Episcopal		W.M.	Wesleyan Methodist
M.P.	Methodist Protestant			
P.M.	Primitive Methodist			

[1] Only one of Elizabeth Rolph or Emma Rolph worked on the Indian Missions.

APPENDIX B

The Methodist Church in Canada

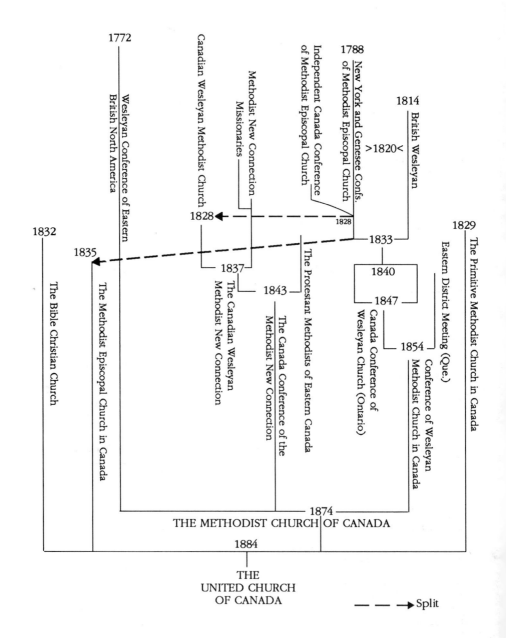

APPENDIX C

Selected Methodist Terms

African Methodist Episcopal Church: an autonomous black Methodist denomination that began officially in 1816 in the United States.

band: part of the Methodist church structure; made up of about four people, segregated by sex and marital status. The band was organized for prayer and spiritual growth.

Bible Christian Church: a Methodist movement that seceded from mainstream Wesleyan Methodism in England in 1815.

camp-meeting: a religious revival service held outdoors, lasting over a period of several days.

circuit: two or more local churches or societies joined together for pastoral supervision, served by an itinerant preacher and usually local preachers.

class: part of the Methodist church structure, made up of about six or seven members with a designated leader. The class met regularly to check up on the morality and spiritual progress of its members.

communion: a Christian worship practice based on the last supper Jesus ate with his disciples.

conference: the annual legislative and administrative assembly of a Methodist denomination.

connexion: generally referred to the entire organization of a Methodist denomination.

elder: a senior church overseer or minister.

evangelist: generally one who preaches the gospel; sometimes understood as a preacher who travels from place to place to hold revivals; a term used in Methodist churches in the late nineteenth century.

exhortation: a form of sermon or religious speech, usually given after the main sermon, to urge people to do their duty.

exhorter: a man or woman who exhorts or gives an exhortation; a special kind of preacher.

field-meeting: a religious service held outdoors, in a field.

Free Methodist Church: one of the Methodist denominations that began in the mid-nineteenth century in North America, an off-shoot of mainstream Methodism.

itinerant: a preacher or minister who travelled from place to place on a circuit to preach, generally on foot in Great Britain and generally on horseback in America.

local preacher: a lay preacher or minister, authorized to preach on his or her own circuit, often substituting for an itinerant and sometimes in training to become an itinerant.

love-feast: a fellowship meal in which the early Christians joined to commemorate Jesus' last supper. The meal was restored by the Methodists and other religious movements.

Methodism: an evangelistic religious movement that traces its origin to John Wesley (1703-1791) in Great Britain. The movement was initially characterized by field-preaching, lay preaching, religious zeal, strict discipline, and emphasized behaviour rather than doctrine. An ordained minister in the Church of England, John Wesley never intended to form a new church, but Methodism officially became a separate denomination in America in 1784 and in Great Britain soon after his death.

Methodist Episcopal Church: 1) the largest Methodist Church in America, which began officially in 1784 as a result of missionary activity from England. 2) a Methodist denomination that continued in Canada after the union of the Methodist Episcopal Church and the British Wesleyan Methodists in 1833.

Methodist Protestant Church: organized in 1830, one of the Methodist denominations in America, an off-shoot of mainstream Methodism.

mission: a society dependent on and overseen by the parent body.

missionary: traditionally, a man or woman sent by his or her religious body to convert others.

on trial: a qualifying period required for Methodists who believed they were called to be preachers.

penitent: one who repents of one's sins.

perfection: a state in which one is filled with perfect love and therefore is incapable of wilful or intentional sin.

plan: official circuit schedule for preachers, listing the chapels or other stations where they were to preach, generally drawn up quarterly.

preaching: the proclamation of the gospel in the form of a religious discourse or sermon.

Primitive Methodist Church: a Methodist movement that seceded from mainstream Wesleyan Methodism in England in 1811.

protracted service: a religious revival service held indoors that continued over several hours or days.

quarterly-meeting: the traditional Methodist business and governing body in a local area.

revival: a reawakening of religious fervour.

sanctification: a state of religious perfection or perfect love in which one is incapable of wilful or intentional sin.

society: a religious community of men and women in a local area.

station: a single church or preaching place supplied by a pastor.

ticket: a small card given to members of societies, listing their name, a scripture passage, and date.

Wesleyan Methodism: 1) the mainstream Methodist tradition in Great Britain; 2) in Canada, the Methodist Episcopal Church united with the Wesleyan Methodists in 1833, forming the Wesleyan Methodist Church in Canada; 3) the Wesleyan Methodist Church was one of the Methodist denominations that formed in the United States in the nineteenth century.

NOTES

Chapter I Introduction

1. The *Cyclopedia of Methodism*, ed. Matthew Simpson, defines exhorting as a form of preaching, a "sort of probation to the ministry." At the end of the sermon, an exhorter aroused the people to their "sense of duty."
2. Marian Fowler, *The Embroidered Tent* (Toronto: House of Anansi Press, 1982), 10.
3. Harley Parker, "Art and Pollution: A Proposal," *Arts-canada*, April 1970, as quoted in John Robert Colombo, ed., *Colombo's Canadian Quotations* (Edmonton: Hurtig Publishers, 1974), 463. It is generally believed that the quotation originated with Marshall McLuhan.
4. Charles W. Flint, *Charles Wesley and His Colleagues* (Washington, D.C.: Public Affairs Press, 1957), 63. V.H.H. Green, *John Wesley* (London: Nelson and Sons Ltd., 1964), 94.
5. Gerda Lerner, *The Majority Finds Its Past* (New York: Oxford University Press, 1979), passim, esp. 145ff. Elisabeth Schüssler Fiorenza, *In Memory of Her* (New York: Crossroads Publishing Company, 1983), passim, esp. xxff. The latter develops a "hermeneutics of suspicion" for her reconstruction of the history of women in the early church and calls for an increase in "historical imagination."

Chapter II The Evolution of Women Preachers

1. George J. Stevenson, *City Road Chapel London and its Associations* (London: George J. Stevenson, 1872), 33ff. W.W. Stamp, *The Orphan-House of Wesley* (London: John Mason, 1863), 63. Part of the Methodist church structure, the Select Society was made up of class leaders and met regularly.
2. Stevenson, *City Road Chapel*, 607.
3. J.B. Wakeley, *Lost Chapters From the Early History of Methodism* (New York: Carlton and Porter, 1858), 69-73. Twenty-five of the contributors cannot be identified as to sex. *Twenty-Fifth Canada Sunday School Union Annual Report*, p.21. Carroll Smith-Rosenberg, *Disorderly Conduct* (New York: A.A. Knopf, 1985), 148.
4. Stamp, The Orphan-House, 33. L.F. Church, *More About the Early Methodist People* (London: Epworth Press, 1949), 180ff.
5. Stamp, *The Orphan-House*, 28f. Nathan Bangs, *The Methodist Episcopal Church* Vol. 1 (New York: Carlton and Phillips, 1856), 291.
6. Stevenson, *City Road Chapel*, 29ff.

7. *Methodist Conference Minutes,* London: 1770, Question #69; 1780, Question #67; 1786, Question #22.

8. *Methodist Magazine* 1803, p.34, undated letter.

9. Bangs, *The Methodist Episcopal Church,* 205. J.E. Sanderson, *The First Century of Methodism in Canada,* Vol. 2 (Toronto: William Briggs, 1908), 213. *The Doctrines and Discipline of the Wesleyan Methodist Church in Canada,* (Toronto: Matthew Lang, 1836), 76.

10. *The Doctrines of the Wesleyan Methodist Church,* 36. John Wesley, *Letters,* to Mrs. Elizabeth Bennis: 1 Apr. 1773; 18 Jan. 1774; to Miss Furly: 2 Aug.1776, Oct. 1776. C.H. Crookshank, *Memorable Women of Irish Methodism in the Last Century,* Vol. 2 (London: Wesleyan Methodist Book Room, 1882), 20: Evidently Eliza Bennis heeded John Wesley's advice, for on her death in the United States in 1802, it was noted that she "had called people to repentance."

11. Stevenson, *City Road Chapel,* 33ff.

12. Wesley, *Letters,* 14 Feb. 1761; 18 Mar. 1769.

13. Wesley, *Letters,* 13 June 1771; 13 Nov. 1778.

14. Church, *More About,* 140ff. Robert Wearmouth, *Methodism and The Common People of the Eighteenth Century* (London: Epworth Press, 1945), 228. C.H. Crookshank, *History of Methodism in Ireland,* Vol. 2, (Belfast: R.S. Allen, 1886), 30ff. Zechariah Taft, *Biographical Sketches of the Lives and Public Ministry of Various Holy Women* (London: Mr. Kershaw, 1825), 91, 49ff., 291.

15. Church, *More About,* chap. 4, esp.145, 151ff. Other details of the preaching careers of the three women can be found in Taft, *Biographical Sketches,* 19ff., 269f., Crookshank, *History,* passim; and Crookshank, *Memorable Women,* 191. Letter from Wesley to Sarah Crosby, 2 Dec. 1777, in George Smith, *History of Wesleyan Methodism* Vol. 2 (London: Longmans, Brown, Green, Longmans and Roberts, 1862), 420f.

16. Church, *More About,* 39, 159ff., 169f. Crookshank, *Memorable Women,* 193, 353f., 400. Crookshank, *History,* Vol. I, 410. Taft, *Biographical Sketches,* 145, 326. John Taylor, *The Apostles of Flyde Methodism* (London: T. Woolmer, 1885), 59.

17. Legh Richmond, *The Annals of the Poor and The Dairyman's Daughter* (London: F. Warne and Co., n.d.), passim.

18. Wesley, *Letters,* 29 Mar. 1766. Leonard Sweet, *The Minister's Wife: Her Role in Nineteenth-Century Evangelicalism* (Philadelphia: Temple University Press, 1983), 89.

19. *Methodist Minutes,* London, 1753-1789, pp.564-5. John Kent, *Jabez Bunting, The Last Wesleyan* (London: The Epworth Press, 1955), 39f.

20. Earl Kent Brown, "Women in Church History: Stereotypes, Archetypes and Operational Modalities," in *Methodist History* 18 (January 1980), 130. Gerald R. Cragg, *The Church and The Age of Reason 1648-1789, The Pelican History of The Church,* Vol. 4 (Harmondsworth, Eng.: Penguin Books, 1960), 152.

H.F. Mathews, *Methodism and The Education of the People 1791-1851* (London: The Epworth Press, 1949), 36f. W.J. Townsend, H.B. Workman, George Eayrs eds., *A New History of Methodism*, Vol.1 (n.p.: Hodder and Stoughton, 1909), 413.

21. Stamp, *The Orphan-House*, 43ff. Abel Stevens, *The History of the Religious Movement in the Eighteenth Century Called Methodism*, Vol. 1 (London: Wesleyan Conference Office, 1878), 208f.

22. Church, *More About*, 49. Wesley, *Letters*, undated letter. Mathews, *Methodism and The Education*, 183. Valentine Ward, *A Miniature of Methodism; or a Brief Account of the History, Doctrines, Discipline and Character of the Methodists* (London: John Mason, 1834), 149. *The Doctrines and Disciplines of the Wesleyan Church in Canada*, 54. Richard M. Cameron ed., *The Rise of Methodism: A Source Book* (New York: Philosophical Library, 1954), 29.

23. Stevenson, *City Road Chapel*, 190f. *Sermons to Young Women* 4th ed. (London: 1767) and John Bennett, *Letters to a Young Lady . . . Calculated to Improve the Heart, to Form the Manners, and to Enlighten the Understanding* (Warrington: 1789), as quoted in Fowler, *The Embroidered Tent*, 18f.

24. Taft, *Biographical Sketches*, 175. Church, *More About*, 145, 161.

25. Crookshank, *History*, Vol. 2, 30ff. Crookshank, *Memorable Women*, 191ff. Church, *More About*, 155ff. Deborah M. Valenze, *Prophetic Sons and Daughters: Female Preaching and Popular Religion in Industrial England* (Princeton: Princeton University Press, 1985), 52ff. Taft, *Biographical Sketches*, 301ff.

26. Church, *More About*, 163ff. Valenze, *Prophetic Sons and Daughters*, 56ff.

27. William Smith, *History of Methodism in Ireland* (n.p.: ca.1828), 85. *Methodist Minutes*, (London: 1803): Q.#19.

28. Church, *More About*, 146. Taft, *Biographical Sketches*, 84ff., 145ff., 168n. Valenze, *Prophetic Sons and Daughters*, 71ff.

29. Crookshank, *History*, passim. Wm. Smith, *History of Methodism*, 85f. Lorenzo Dow, *The Dealings of God, Man And The Devil; as Exemplified in the Life, Experience and Travels of Lorenzo Dow* (New York: Cornish, Lamport and Co., 1851), 52.

30. Church, *More About*, 156. Julia Stewart Werner, *The Primitive Methodist Connexion Its Background and Early History* (Madison, Wisconsin: University of Toronto Press, 1984), 144.

31. Church, *More About*, 156f. Valenze, *Prophetic Sons and Daughters*, 64, 144.

32. Church, *More About*, 137. *Methodist Minutes* London, 1835. Taft, *Biographical Sketches*, 172ff. Werner, *The Primitive Methodist Connexion*, 27. Stamp, *The Orphan-House*, 296: The actual net profit was £1,784.11.3. Valenze, *Prophetic Sons and Daughters*, 187ff.

33. Stevenson, *City Road Chapel*, 309ff., 607.

34. Stevenson, *City Road Chapel*, 28ff.

35. Taft, *Biographical Sketches*, 26ff. Abel Stevens, *The Women of Methodism* (New York: Carlton and Lanahan, 1869), 12f. 56. Gabriel P. Disosway, *Our*

Excellent Women of the Methodist Church in England and America (New York: J.C. Buttre, 1861), 45ff. Church, *More About*, 147. Matthew Simpson, ed., *Cyclopedia of Methodism*.

36. Taft, *Biographical Sketches*, 13ff., 267.
37. For a detailed analysis of the shift from sect to church see: John S. Moir, "Sectarian Tradition in Canada," in John Webster Grant, ed., *The Churches and The Canadian Experience* (Toronto: The Ryerson Press, 1963), 119-132; S.D. Clark, *Church and Sect in Canada* (Toronto: University of Toronto Press, 1949), passim; Ernst Troeltsch, *The Social Teaching of the Christian Churches*, Vol. 1, tr. Olive Wyon (London: George Allen & Unwin Ltd., 1931), esp. 330ff.
38. C.B. Sissons, *Egerton Ryerson - His Life and Letters* Vol. 1 (Toronto: Clarke and Irwin and Co. Ltd., 1937), 141.
39. Mary Wollstonecraft, *A Vindication of the Rights of Woman*, ed. M.B. Kramnick (Harmondsworth, England: Penguin Books, 1975), 17. Judy Chicago, *The Dinner Party, A Symbol of Our Heritage* (New York: Anchor Books, 1979), 177ff.
40. Werner, *The Primitive Methodist Connexion*, 4ff.
41. Alec R. Vidler, *The Church in an Age of Revolution, The Pelican History of the Church*, Vol. 5 (Harmondsworth, England: 1961), 34ff.
42. Valenze, *Prophetic Sons and Daughters*, 19ff. Werner, *The Primitive Methodist Connexion*, 4ff.
43. Egerton Ryerson, *The Story of My Life* (Toronto: William Briggs, 1883), p.273. Werner, *The Primitive Methodist Connexion*, 7ff. Church, *More About*, 250ff. Kent, *Jabez Bunting*, 30ff.
44. As quoted in Valenze, *Prophetic Sons and Daughters*, p.7 (1833).
45. Sissons, *Egerton Ryerson*, Vol. 1, 130-40, 162-4.
46. *Wesleyan Protestant Methodist Magazine* 1832, 75ff. *Minutes of the London Conference* 1835, 589.
47. Hugh Bourne, *History of the Primitive Methodists* (London: J. Bourne, 1823), passim. *Christian Journal*, 18 Aug. 1860, p.1, c.2. Valenze, *Prophetic Sons and Daughters*, 95ff.
48. Dorothy Graham, *Chosen By God* (Cheshire, England: Bankhead Press, 1989), 29. Lorenzo Dow, *The Dealings of God,* 171. Werner, *The Primitive Methodist Connexion*, 81f. Townsend, *A New History*, 575. "Sarah Kirkland," in *Encyclopedia of World Methodism* ed. Nolan B. Harmon.
49. Valenze, *Prophetic Sons and Daughters*, 7.
50. *Primitive Methodist Magazine* 1821, p.161; 1824, p.3f.
51. *Primitive Methodist Magazine* 1824, p.37.
52. *Primitive Methodist Magazine*, 1820, p.233ff.; 1834-1836. Werner, *The Primitive Methodist Connexion*, 141. Valenze, *Prophetic Sons and Daughters*, p.112f. Smith-Rosenberg, *Disorderly Conduct*, 149.
53. Graham, *Chosen By God* , 21. *Primitive Methodist Magazine* 1837, p.181.
54 *Primitive Methodist Magazine* 1837, p.218f.

55. Thomas Russell, *Record of Events in Primitive Methodism* (London: William Lister, 1869), passim esp. 86, 88, 123. Dow, *The Dealings of God*, 171.
56. Russell, *Record of Events*, 28f.
57. Townsend, *A New History*, Vol.1, 586f. Valenze, *Prophetic Sons and Daughters*, 274ff.
58. *Wesleyan Methodist Minutes*, London, 1791, 246. F.W. Bourne, *The Bible Christians*, 1ff.
59. F.W. Bourne, *The Bible Christians*, 32ff., 80ff. *Observer*, 9 May 1883, p.1, c.1f. Taft, *Biographical Sketches*, 275ff. *Primitive Methodist Magazine*, 1821, p.162ff.
60. *Observer*, 25 April 1883, p.1, c.2ff.; 2 May 1883, p.4, c.3ff.; 1 Aug 1883, p.4, c.3ff.
61. *Observer*, 9 May 1883, p.1, c.1f. F.W. Bourne, *The Bible Christians: Their Origin and History*, (n.p.: Bible Christian Book Room, 1905), 81.
62. *Observer*, 9 May 1883, p.4, c.4f. *Primitive Methodist Magazine* 1821, pp.190ff. Valenze, *Prophetic Sons and Daughters*, 150ff.
63. *Bible Christian Conference Minutes* (England), 1820, p.7.
64. F.W. Bourne, *The Bible Christians*, passim esp. 85, 104ff., 161.
65. F.W. Bourne, *The Bible Christians*, 135, 139ff., 165. Bible Christian Conference *Minutes* 1819-1851.
66. F.W. Bourne, *The Bible Christians*, 81, 181, 244, 293.
67. *Minutes of the Bible Christian Conference* 1820, 6. *Bible Christian Magazine* 1853, memorial tribute by Paul Robins. F.W. Bourne, *The Bible Christians*, 241.
68. Bible Christian Annual Conference *Minutes* 1830-1853, esp. 1830, p.13; 1832, p.9.

Chapter III Partners in Ministry

1. *Observer*, 28 March 1883, p.1, c.1ff. The *Observer* editor spells her name "Elisabeth."
2. *Bible Christian Magazine*, June 1865, p.384.
3. Sweet, *The Minister's Wife*, 3ff.
4. *Observer*, 28 March 1883, p.1, c.2f.; 18 April 1883, p.4, c.4; 25 April 1883, p.1, c.3; 2 May 1883, p.4, c.3; 9 May 1883, p.4, c.5.
5. *Observer*, 28 March 1883, p.1, c.3.
6. *Observer*, 28 March 1883, p.1, c.4; 4 April 1883, p.4, c.3ff.
7. *Observer*, 11 April 1883, p.4, c.4f.
8. *Observer*, 18 April 1883, p.4, c.3ff.; 23 May 1883, p.4, c.3. *Works of Wesley*, letter to Lady Maxwell, London, 8 Aug. 1788.
9. F.W. Bourne, *The Bible Christians*, 22, 54. *Observer*, 25 April 1883, p.1, c.1ff.
10. A "love-feast" is a fellowship meal or representation of a meal which

originated as part of the early Christian eucharist or communion service, but became separated from it. The love-feast was introduced into early Methodism after a practice of the Moravians. F.W. Bourne, *The Bible Christians*, passim, esp. 41f. *Observer*, 2 May 1883, p.4, c.3ff.; 9 May 1883, p.4, c.4f.; 23 May 1883, p.4, c.3f.; 30 May 1883, p.5, c.1f.; 25 July 1883, p.4, c.3f.; 1 Aug. 1883, p.4, c.3ff. Wesley believed that sanctification or perfection was possible in this life, although he was aware of few people who had reached that level of spirituality. In that state, the believer wilfully committed no sin.

11. Jas B. Fairbairn, *History and Reminiscences of Bowmanville* (Bowmanville: Bowmanville Newsprint, 1906), 42. F.W. Bourne, *The Bible Christians*, 346. *Bible Christian Magazine*, 1833, p.218ff. her letter dated 3 May 1833. D. McTavish, *Religious Romance and Reminiscences: An Interesting History of James Street Church, Exeter* (n.p.: n.d.) Ontario Archives, 6. *Observer*, 11 April 1883, p.5, c. 4, letter from Mary Greene.

12. *Cobourg Star*, 3 July 1833, p.196. F.W. Bourne, *The Bible Christians*, 175. *Bible Christian Magazine* 1833, pp.349f. John's Journal, passim, and letter from Quebec, 19 June 1833; 1834, pp.26ff., 67ff.

13. Francis Metherall Biographical File, United Church Archives. F.W. Bourne, *The Bible Christians*, 210. *Bible Christian Magazine*, April 1834, p.214.

14. *Christian Guardian*, 6 April 1904, p.6. John's picture is on the front page. *Bible Christian Magazine*, 1833, p.218.

15. *Bible Christian Magazine*, 1833, p.218f.; 1834, pp.27ff., 67ff., 108ff., 215ff., letters from Elizabeth and John, and John's diary.

16. *Bible Christian Magazine*, 1834, pp.26ff., 71. Catherine Parr Traill, *The Backwoods of Canada* (Toronto: McClelland and Stewart Ltd., 1966), 25ff. Clara Thomas, *Ryerson of Upper Canada* (Toronto: The Ryerson Press, 1969), 50f.

17. P. Baskerville, "The Entrepreneur and The Metropolitan Impulse: James Grey Bethune and Cobourg, 1825-1836", in *Victorian Cobourg*, ed. J. Petryshyn (Belleville: Mika Publishing Co., 1976), 57ff., 109. *Cobourg Star*, 2 July 1833, p.214; 7 Aug. 1833, p.239; 16 Oct. 1833; 4 Dec. 1833, p.2 c.5; 18 Dec. 1833, p.3 c 5; 8 Jan. 1834, p.239. Traill, *The Backwoods*, 32f. Edwin C. Guillet, *Cobourg 1798-1948* (Oshawa: Goodfellow Printing Co. Ltd., 1948), 18. Edwin C. Guillet, *Pioneer Days in Upper Canada* (Toronto: University of Toronto Press, 1933), 172.

18. See Smith-Rosenberg, *Disorderly Conduct*, esp. ch.3; also Smith-Rosenberg, "Women and Religious Revivals: Anti-Ritualism, Liminality, and the Emergence of the American Bourgeoisie" in Leonard I. Sweet, ed., *The Evangelical Tradition in America* (Macon, Georgia: Mercer University Press, 1984), passim, for details of the proposed connection between social and economic disruption and anti-ritualistic religion.

19. *Bible Christian Magazine*, 1834, p.74, letter from John Eynon. Traill, *The Backwoods*, 105, 48ff. Baskerville, "The Entrepreneur," 58.

20. F.W. Bourne, *The Bible Christians*, 216. *Bible Christian Magazine*, 1834, pp.110ff. Elizabeth Muir, "Elizabeth Dart (Eynon)," in *Dictionary of Canadian*

Biography 8, gen. ed. F.G. Halpenny (Toronto: University of Toronto Press, 1985).

21. F.W. Bourne, *The Bible Christians*, 310f. *Bible Christian Magazine*, 1834, John's journal; 1835, pp.50f.; May 1856, p.201, letter from J. Tapp. Protracted meetings were emotionally charged religious services similar to camp meetings but which were held indoors and lasted for lengthy periods of time from a few days to a couple of weeks.

22. F.W. Bourne, *The Bible Christians*, 302. *Christian Guardian*, 6 April 1904, pp.2, 6. *Bible Christian Magazine*, 1834, p.111, letter from Elizabeth; 1848, p.241, letter from Henry Ebbot, 1 Jan. 1848.

23. *Minutes of Elders' Meetings*, Cobourg, 28 April 1852, 18 Oct. 1855, 24 Jan. 1855. *Bible Christian Magazine*, March 1857, p.244.

24. Cemetery visited by author.

25. Bible Christian Church (Canada) *Year Book*, 1857, p.2. *Canadian Statesman*, 22 Jan. 1857, p.2, c.2; 11 April 1888, p.8, c.1. *West Durham News*, 20 April 1888, p.1. Methodist Conference, *Minutes* (London:1888). *Christian Guardian*, 6 April 1904, pp.1,6. William Luke, T*he Bible Christians, Their Origin, Constitution, Doctrine and History* (London: Bible Christian Book Room, 1878), passim.

26. *Centennial of Canadian Methodism*, (Toronto: Wm. Briggs, 1891), 210. Sanderson, *The First Century*, Vol.2, 427. F.W. Bourne, *The Bible Christians*, passim.

27. Sanderson, *The First Century*, 427. *Bible Christian Magazine*, 1848, p.123, letter from Paul Robins, 2 Dec. 1847.

28. *Bible Christian Magazine*, 1853, p.474f., memorial tribute by Paul Robins.

29. *Bible Christian Magazine*, May 1847, p.200, letter from John Eynon of 3 Dec. 1846; Oct. 1847, pp.399, 403, journal of Paul Robins; 1853, p.475, memorial by Paul Robins. F.W. Bourne, *The Bible Christians*, 520. *Minutes of Elders' Meetings*, Cobourg, 28 Jan. 1852, 21 Feb. 1852. Bible Christian Conference *Minutes*, England, 1832-1852.

30. *Minutes of Elders' Meetings*, Cobourg, 1851-1860 esp. 12 Apr. 1860. *Minutes of the Canadian Bible Christian Conference* (1872), 8f. *Bible Christian Magazine*, 1841, p.237. *Observer*, 27 October 1869, p.2, c.5, letter to the editor.

31. *Observer*, 15 March 1882, p.3, c.4f.

32. Elizabeth Peters and William Peters, *The Diaries of William and Elizabeth Peters Recounting the Voyage to the New World on the Good Brig Friends in 1830*, ed. Howard H. Finley (Berwyn, Illinois: Howard H. Finley, 1942), passim.

33. Bible Christian preachers' plans, United Church Archives. Trick-Henwood Papers, private collection of Howard Harris: Two of Elizabeth's children died in infancy. Newspaper clippings from 1928 describe Elizabeth as a "regularly ordained Local Preacher in the Wesleyan Church."

34. *Bible Christian Magazine*, 1848, p.321ff. Biographical file of John Williams, United Church Archives.

35. *Bible Christian Magazine*, Jan. 1847, pp. 39; Feb. 1847, 80ff; Jan. 1859, p.43. John Harris, *The Life of the Rev. Francis Metherall and The History of the Bible Christian Church in Prince Edward Island* (London: Bible Christian Book Room, 1883), 34. Albert Burnside, "The Bible Christians in Canada 1832-1884," D.Th diss., Toronto Graduate School of Theological Studies, 1969, 64. *Christian Guardian*, 24 April 1889, obituary of Ruth Woodger. Biographical file of Thomas Green, United Church Archives.

36. *Bible Christian Magazine*, Jan. 1857, p.42f. Andrew Cory had drowned in 1833, leaving his widow and one child: *Bible Christian Magazine*, 1834, p.29; Bible Christian Conference *Minutes*, 1834, England, p.5.

37. Harris, *The Life of the Rev. Francis Metherall*, 32ff., 49f., 64, 75. *Bible Christian Magazine*, Canadian Missionary Reports: 1845, Missionary Chronicles, letter from Richard Cotton; 1847, passim; 1848, pp.400f., passim; 1858, passim; May 1860, p.201ff. Biographical file of William Harris, United Church Archives.

38. Annie R. Gordon, "Whither Thou Goest - Ann Copp, A Devon Maid," United Church Archives, 1,16.

39. Gordon, "Whither Thou Goest," 9, 14.

40. Gordon, "Whither Thou Goest," 15f. Sweet, *The Minister's Wife*, 41.

41. *New Outlook*, 9 Sept. 1931, p.867. *Bible Christian Magazine*, January 1859, pp.79, 202. Gordon, "Whither Thou Goest," 14, 18f., 39ff.

42. Gordon, "Whither Thou Goest," 48, 51. Sweet, *The Minister's Wife*, 205: Sweet noted that it was more acceptable for women to engage in public speaking which was "topical" than preaching which was "exegetical." In Ann's case, the reverse appears to be true, indicating the complexity of the resistance to women speaking and preaching.

43. Gordon, "Whither Thou Goest," 35, 39, 59f. For Elizabeth Dart Eynon's dreams, see *Observer*, 9 May 1883, p.4, 5; 30 May 1883, p.5, c.1.

44. Gordon, "Whither Thou Goest," 39, 61. *Christian Guardian*, 4 Dec. 1830, p.10, c.4.

45. Andrew Gordon Biographical File, United Church Archives.

46. *Observer*, 19 Sept. 1883, p.6, c.4; 16 Jan. 1884, p.4, c.2; 18 June 1884, p.1, c.5.

Chapter IV From Itinerant to Guest Preacher

1. Jane Agar Hopper, *Old-Time Primitive Methodism in Canada 1829-1884* (Toronto: William Briggs, 1904), 74, 255. W.J. Townsend, *A New History of Methodism*, 585.

2. Edith Firth, "William Lawson," in *Dictionary of Canadian Biography* 10. Hopper, *Old-Time Primitive Methodism*, 20f., 32. Perkins Bull papers, United Church Archives, n.p.

3. John Petty, *The History of the Primitive Methodist Connexion From Its Origin to the Conference of 1860, The First Jubilee Year of the Connexion* (London: John

Dickenson, 1880), 312. *Primitive Methodist Magazine*, 1831, letter from N. Watkins, York Town, 27 Oct. 1830, pp.94f. Letters from Wm. Lawson et al. at York to Hugh Bourne, 1 Oct. 1830 and to Wm. Summersides, 2 Dec. 1830, United Church Archives.

4. Letters from Ruth Watkins ca. 1835 and William Summersides ca. 1837. The John H. Rylands University Library of Manchester, England.

5. W.F. Clarke and R.L. Tucker, *A Mother in Israel, or some Memorials of The Late Mrs. M.A. Lyle* (Toronto: W.C. Chewett & Co., Printers, 1862), 4f. *Christian Journal*, 1 Jan. 1874, p.2, c.4.

6. *Christian Journal*, 1 Jan. 1874, p.2, c.4; 23 Jan. 1874, p.2, c.5; 30 Jan. 1874, p.2, c.5. Preachers' Plans, United Church Archives and John Rylands University Library of Manchester. Letter from William Summersides, ca. 1837, John Rylands University Library of Manchester. *Minutes* of the 21st Annual Conference of the Primitive Methodist Church in Canada, 1874.

7. *The Doctrines and Disciplines of the British Primitive Methodist Connexion* [Canada] (York: W.J. Coates, 1833), passim.

8. *Primitive Methodist Magazine* 1845, p.274, letter of John Towler; 1846, p.426, Journal of M. Nichols. *Christian Journal*, 16 May 1862, p.2, c.l; 1 Jan. 1874, p.2, c.4; 30 Jan. 1874, p.2, c.4. W.F. Clarke and R.L. Tucker, *A Mother in Israel*, 4f. Hopper, *Old-Time Primitive Methodism*, 29.

9. *Evangelist*, January 1848, p.14; July 1848, p.95; October 1848, pp.134, 138; December 1851, p.191. John A. Acornley, *A History of the Primitive Methodist Church in the United States of America* (Fall River, Mass: R.R. Acornley & Co., 1909), 48f.

10. Perkins Bull Papers, United Church Archives, n.p. Perkins Bull Papers, Ontario Archives, letter from Hannah Elizabeth Thomas. Preachers' Plans, United Church Archives. *Christian Guardian*, 13 Jan. 1909, p.35, c.2. Fred Landon, "The Common Man In The Era of the Rebellion in Upper Canada," in F.H. Armstrong, H.A. Stevenson, and J.D. Wilson, *Aspects of Nineteenth-Century Ontario* (Toronto: University of Toronto Press, 1974), 158.

11. Perkins Bull papers, Ontario Archives, Thomas letter. Hopper, *Old-Time Primitive Methodism*, 52. Memorial to Jane Woodill Wilson, Betty Ward Papers. *Christian Guardian*, 13 Jan. 1909, p. 35, c.2, obituary of Isaac Wilson.

12. Hopper, *Old-Time Primitive Methodism*, 52f.

13. Hopper, *Old-Time Primitive Methodism*, 100. Perkins Bull Papers, Ontario Archives, letters from Beattie, Thomas, and Mary J. Rodwell. Their children were Mary Jane Rodwell, Hannah Elizabeth Thomas, Ellen Woodill Killam, Sarah Ann Beattie, and William Thomas Wilson. William later became a preacher.

14. Perkins Bull Papers, United Church Archives. Perkins Bull Papers, Ontario Archives, Beattie, Rodwell and Thomas letters. Beth Early, *Criteria For Preservation, Salem United Church* (n.p.: Caledon Heritage Committee, 1985),1f.

15. Hopper, *Old-Time Primitive Methodism*, 53, 122f., 177. Perkins Bull Papers,

United Church Archives, n.p.

16. Perkins Bull Papers, United Church Archives, n.p; Beattie and Thomas letters, Ontario Archives. George S. Tavender, *From This Year Hence - A History of the Township of Toronto Gore, 1818-1967* (Brampton: Charters Pub. Co., 1967), 94f.

17. Perkins Bull Papers, Ontario Archives.

18. *Primitive Methodist Magazine*, 1844, pp.225, 298. *Christian Guardian*, 24 Apr. 1889, obituary of R. Woodger. Hopper, *Old-Time Primitive Methodism*, 102, 210, 218. Preachers' Plans, United Church Archives.

19. *Primitive Methodist Magazine*, 1844, p.274. *Evangelist*, Sept. 1848, p.122; Jan.1851, p.15. Preachers' Plans, United Church Archives.

20. Hopper, *Old-Time Primitive Methodism*, 250. Perkins Bull Papers, United Church Archives, n.p.

21 *Christian Journal*, 14 July 1860, Ladies' Dept; 18 Aug. 1860, Ladies' Dept; 8 Sept. 1860, p.3; 6 Apr.1861, p.1.

22. Sweet, *The Minister's Wife*, 140.

23. W.F. Clarke and R.L. Tucker, *A Mother in Israel*, 6f., 14f.

24. *Christian Journal*, 26 Dec. 1873, p.1, c.3; 23 Jan. 1874, p.1, c.5.

25. H.B. Kendall, *History of the Primitive Methodist Connexion* (London: Joseph Toulson, [ca. 1888]), passim. Petty, *The History of the Primitive Methodist Connexion*, 279. Hopper, *Primitive Methodism*, passim, esp. 22.

Chapter V Women Settle Down

1. A.G. Dorland, *The Quakers in Canada: A History*, 2nd ed. (Toronto: Ryerson Press, 1968), 130f. Quaker women participated extensively in their denomination in Upper Canada. Quaker women were speaking in Upper Canada in the 1830s, and in 1837, a Quaker woman preached the funeral sermon for Joshua Doan, executed after the 1837 rebellion: 166f., 227, 278. In 1821 and 1822, two women and two men from England and United States led forty-five services and travelled twenty-two hundred miles in the province: Phoebe Roberts, "Phoebe Roberts' Diary of a Quaker Missionary Journey to Upper Canada," ed. Leslie R. Gray, *Ontario Historical Society* 42 (January 1950): passim. A Quaker woman debated with the Methodist itinerant Alvin Torrey: Alvin Torrey, *Autobiography of Alvin Torrey*, ed. Wm. Hosmer (Auburn: Wm. J. Moses, 1865), 40f.

2. John Carroll, *Case and His Cotemporaries; or The Canadian Itinerants' Memoiral* Vol. 1, (Toronto: Samuel Rose, 1867), 223f. Nathan Bangs Biographical File, United Church Archives. *Methodist Episcopal Church in Canada Minutes*, 1863. Abel Stevens, *Life and Times of Nathan Bangs* (New York: Carlton and Porter, 1863), 351. Sweet, *The Minister's Wife*, 117ff. Sanderson, *The First Century*, Vol. 1, 200. Sissons, *Egerton Ryerson*, 47f.: The

British Wesleyans under Henry Pope were particularly interfering and aggressive in the Niagara region, attracting Methodist Episcopal members to their denomination, and Gatchell may well have harboured resentment. Some sources spell Gatchell with only one *l*.

3. References to Abigail and Absalom are found in 1 Samuel 25:3, 2 Samuel 14:25. George F. Playter, *The History of Methodism in Canada* (Toronto: Anson Green, 1862), 55f., 100f. Carroll, *Case and His Cotemporaries*, Vol. 1, 19f, 174ff. Sanderson, *The First Century*, Vol. 1, 59f. Thomas, *Ryerson*, 26. *Methodist Magazine* 1811, p.475, letter from Samuel 11 Dec. 1810. *Christian Guardian*, letter of 25 Aug. 1858 from Ann: 25 May 1859, p.81, c.7.

4. *Christian Guardian*, 13 April 1859, p.1, memorial to Margaret Taylor. W.G. Ormsby, "John George Bowes" in *Dictionary of Canadian Biography* 9. W. H. Pearson, *Recollections and Records of Toronto of Old* (Toronto: Wm. Briggs, 1914), 288. Sissons, *Egerton Ryerson*, Vol. 2, 5.

5. Carroll, *Case and His Cotemporaries*, Vol. 3, 169.

6. *Christian Guardian*, 11 May 1887, p.299, c.3, obituary. *Christian Advocate*, 24 Aug. 1827, p.201, c.4, report from W. Case; 4 Jan. 1828, p.70, c.2, report from W. Case; 9 May 1828, p.141, c.2, report from J. Davis. Information from the United Methodist Church Archives Biographical Files indicates that Rev. Dan Barnes (1784-1840), who may have been a relative of Eliza Barnes, was working with the Oneida Indians in New York state sometime between 1810 and 1835. A Rev. Barnes contributed to one of her fundraising campaigns: *Christian Advocate*, 24 June 1831, p.169, c.4f. *Methodist Episcopal Missionary Society Report, Canada Conference*, 1827, p.22.

7. Carroll, *Case and His Cotemporaries*, Vol. 3, 219, 279. Sanderson, *The First Century*, Vol. 1, 220. Peter Jones, *Life and Journals of Kah-Ke-Wa-Quo-Na-By* (Toronto: Anson Green, 1860), 205, 216, 263. *Christian Advocate*, 6 Mar. 1829, p.106, c.2, report from W. Case; 15 May 1829, p.145, c.2. *Christian Guardian*, 12 Dec. 1829, p.27, c.3.

8. Jones, *Life and Journals*, 278f. Carroll, *Case and His Cotemporaries*, Vol. 3, 286. *Christian Guardian*, 28 May 1831, p.114. *Christian Advocate*, 10 Feb. 1832, p.95, c.3,4. James Youngs, *History of the Rise and Progress of Methodism in England and America* (New Haven, Conn.: H. Daggett and Co., 1830), 417. In addition to Rev. Barnes, Dr. Hubbard of Lowell, Mass. contributed to Barnes' fundraising campaigns. He may have been a relative of Hetty Ann Hubbard: *Christian Advocate*, 14 Sept. 1832, p.12, c.5. Dorcas is mentioned in Acts 9:36.

9. Carroll, *Case and His Cotemporaries*, Vol. 3, 177, 184, 220f., 227. Playter, *The History*, 342. Jones, *Life and Journals*, 139f., 157, 216. Elizabeth Muir, "The Bark Schoolhouse: Methodist Episcopal Missionary Women in Upper Canada, 1827-1833," chap. in *Canadian Protestant and Catholic Missions, 1820s-1960s*, eds. John S. Moir and C.T. McIntire (New York: Peter Lang Pub. Inc., 1988), 24f. John Webster Grant, *Moon of Wintertime* (Toronto: University of Toronto Press, 1984), 75f.

10. Letitia Creighton Youmans, *Campaign Echoes* (Toronto: Wm. Briggs, 1893), 64f.

11. Youmans, *Campaign Echoes*, 65. Carroll, *Case and His Cotemporaries*, Vol. 3, 169; Vol. 4, 268. Sanderson, *The First Century*, Vol. 2, 86. *Christian Guardian*, 15 Oct. 1834, p.195, c.5; 9 Sept. 1835, p.175, c.3; 11 May 1887, p.299, c.3, obituary.

12. Playter, *The History*, 342. *Christian Advocate*, 15 May 1829, p.145, c.2; 24 Oct. 1828, p.30, c.1. Carroll, *Case and His Cotemporaries*, Vol. 3, 171, 202, 228, 233. Jones, *Life and Journals*, 139f., 217, 269. William Case Biographical File, United Church Archives.

13. Muir, "The Bark Schoolhouse," 23.

14. *Christian Guardian*, 29 Oct. 1873, p.351, c.2, obituary; Jones, *Life and Journals*, 229, 289. Muir, "The Bark Schoolhouse," 25.

15. Youngs, *History*, 417: It is likely that there was only one fire, and that Youngs is mistaken in referring to a second fire. Solomon Waldron, "A Sketch of the Life, Travels and Labors of Solomon Waldron, A Wesleyan Methodist Preacher," United Church Archives. *Christian Guardian*, 14 Aug. 1833, p.158, c.3; 3 Dec. 1890, p.779, c.2. *Christian Advocate*, 19 Sept. 1828. p.10, c.3; 1 March 1833, p.106, c.3; 12 July 1833, p.182, c.4; 13 Dec. 1833, p.62, c.3. Muir, "The Bark Schoolhouse," 25f.

16. Waldron, "A Sketch," 32. *Christian Advocate*, 24 Oct. 1828, p.30, c.1; 3 July 1829, p.173, c.5; 26 Mar. 1830, p.118, c.2. *Christian Guardian*, 21 Nov. 1829, p.28, c.1f., obituary. Egerton Ryerson Papers, United Church Archives, letter from George Ryerson to Egerton Ryerson, London, England, 29 Mar. 1832. Muir, "The Bark Schoolhouse," 26f. Sweet, *The Minister's Wife*, 60.

17. *Orillia Times*, 15 Oct. 1891, Pioneer Families. Peter Jones Letters, United Church Archives, letter to Eliza Field, 10 July 1834. *Christian Advocate*, 24 Oct. 1828, p.30, c.1; 13 April 1832, p.130, c.3; 1 Mar. 1833, p.106, c.3. *Christian Guardian*, 13 Feb. 1830, p.98, c.3; p.99, c.1f. Muir, "The Bark Schoolhouse," 27.

18. Waldron, "A Sketch," 21. *Christian Advocate*, 12 May 1827, p.141, c.4. Muir, "The Bark Schoolhouse," 27f.

19. Nathan Bangs, *The Methodist Episcopal Church*, Vol. 1, 238. Peter Jones, *Life and Journals*, 151. *Christian Guardian*, 21 Nov. 1829, p.8, c.1f., obituary of Sarah Ryerson; 19 Dec. 1849, p.240, obituary of Sophia Cook. Eliza Barnes' *Diary* excerpt, United Church Archives. Muir, "The Bark Schoolhouse," 28.

20. *Christian Advocate*, 17 Oct. 1828, p.26, c.1; 26 Mar. 1830, p.118, c.2. *Christian Guardian*, 12 Dec. 1829, p.12, c.1f. Jones, *Life and Journals*, 284. Grant, *Moon*, passim. Muir, "The Bark Schoolhouse," 28f.

21. *Christian Guardian*, 5 Nov. 1831, p.208, c.2. *London Conference Methodist Minutes*, 1780. Muir, "The Bark Schoolhouse," 29.

22. Waldron, "A Sketch," 13ff. Muir, "The Bark Schoolhouse," 29.

23. *Christian Advocate*, 1 Mar. 1833, p.106, c.3. Muir, "The Bark Schoolhouse," 29f. Playter, *The History*, 358.

24. *Christian Guardian,* 5 Dec. 1829, p.21, c.2; 12 Dec. 1829, p.29, c.1f. *Christian Advocate,* 15 May 1829, p.145, c.2; 1 Apr. 1831, p.122, c.5: The article does not specify which Ryerson spoke, but it was likely Egerton. Carroll, *Case and His Contemporaries,* Vol. 3, 169. Muir, "The Bark Schoolhouse," 32.

25. *Christian Guardian,* 27 Nov. 1830, p.6, c.3; 18 Sept. 1833, Missionary Reports; 29 Oct. 1873, p.351, c.2. *Canada Conference Missionary Society Report,* 1829. Muir, "The Bark Schoolhouse," 32f.

26. *Christian Guardian,* 21 Nov. 1829, p.5, c.2; 5 June 1830, p.230, c.3; 4 Dec. 1830, p.10, c.4. Muir, "The Bark Schoolhouse," 33.

27. *Christian Advocate,* 9 Sept. 1826, p.4, c.4. *Christian Guardian,* 28 Nov. 1829, p.13, c.4; 12 Dec. 1829, p.28, c.3. Muir, "The Bark Schoolhouse," 33f. *Colonial Advocate,* 12 July 1827, p.1, c.5.

28. *Christian Guardian,* 21 Nov. 1829, p.5, c.1. Muir, "The Bark Schoolhouse," 34.

29. *Christian Advocate,* 21 Mar. 1834, p.119, c.1. *Christian Guardian,* 7 Nov. 1833, p.208. Muir, "The Bark Schoolhouse," 34f.

30. *Christian Guardian,* 9 July 1831, p.139 c.5; 19 Mar. 1831, p.75, c.5. Alison Prentice, "The Feminization of Teaching" in S.M. Trofimenkoff and A. Prentice, *The Neglected Majority* (Toronto: McLelland and Stewart, 1977), 49-65, and A. Prentice, *The School Promoters* (Toronto: McLelland and Stewart, 1977; 2nd ed., 1984), passim. Muir, "The Bark Schoolhouse," 35. J. Donald Wilson, "The Teacher in Early Ontario" in F.H. Armstrong et al., *Aspects,* 223.

31. Prentice, "The Feminization," 60f. *Missionary Society Reports,* 1825-1832, 1847-1851. Muir, "The Bark Schoolhouse," 35f.

32. *Christian Guardian,* 12 June 1830, p.236, c.2. Muir, "The Bark Schoolhouse," 37.

33. Sweet, *The Minister's Wife,* 8.

34. *Primitive Methodist Disciplines,* 40. Prentice, "The Feminization," 60. *Missionary Society Reports,* passim. Muir, "The Bark Schoolhouse," 36f. John Howison, *Sketches of Upper Canada* (Edinburgh: Oliver & Boyd, 1821), Reprinted (Toronto: Coles Pub. Co., 1980), 235. J. Donald Wilson, "The Teacher," in *Aspects,* 222: Some teachers were evidently paid as little as £4 per annum. William Cattermole, *Emigration. The Advantages of Emigration to Canada* (London: Simpkin and Marshall, 1831), Reprinted (Toronto: Coles Pub. Co., 1970), 13, 20, 85, 94, 98, 205. Traill, *The Backwoods,* 13. Anna Jameson, *Winter Studies and Summer Rambles in Canada,* Vol. 1 (London: Saunders and Otley, 1838), Reprinted (Toronto: Coles Pub. Co., 1970), 269, 312f. Kenneth Barker, *From Indian Mission to City Church* (Orillia: Dyment-Stubley, 1980), 4: claims that Mercy Miner Manwaring was paid £35 in 1833.

35. J.D. Wilson, "The Teacher," 222

36. *Christian Advocate,* 18 Nov. 1826, p.41, c.5. Muir, "The Bark Schoolhouse," 40.

37. Edwin Guillet, *Pioneer Days,* 184. *Missionary Society Report,* 1827, 1. *Chris-*

tian Advocate, 8 Aug. 1828, p.195, c.3; 6 Mar. 1829, p.106, c.2; 3 April 1829, p.122, c.5. Muir, "The Bark Schoolhouse," 40.

38. *Christian Guardian*, 24 Oct.1832, p.199, c.3. Muir, "The Bark Schoolhouse," 38.

39. *Christian Guardian*, 14 Apr. 1830, p.309, c.2. Muir, "The Bark Schoolhouse," 38.

40. *Orillia Times*, 15 Oct. 1891, Pioneer Families. *Christian Guardian*, 7 Aug. 1830, p.298, Ladies' Dept.

41. Jane Errington, *The Lion, the Eagle and Upper Canada, A Developing Colonial Ideology* (Kingston and Montreal: McGill-Queen's University Press, 1987), 52.

42. *Northwestern Christian Advocate*, 6 Aug. 1873, p.254, c.1.

43. Clark, *Church and Sect*, 409. The 1877 *Minutes of the Montreal Conference of the Methodist Church* note that James A. Gordon's "widow" was paid as a temporary supply on the Ottawa East Circuit after his death, but they fail to mention her by name. Marilyn F. Whiteley, "Modest, Unaffected and Fully Consecrated - Lady Evangelists in Canadian Methodism, 1884-1900," in *Canadian Methodist Historical Society Proceedings* (1987), passim: At least twenty-five women were involved in evangelistic meetings between the beginning of 1885 and 1900, taking part in at least three hundred revival campaigns in the Methodist Church. They disappeared when evangelism became institutionalized at the beginning of the twentieth century. Weir may have had these women in mind.

44. *Christian Guardian*, 11 May 1887, p.299, c.3; 3 Dec. 1890, p.779, c.2. Mrs. F.C. Stephenson, *One Hundred Years of Canadian Methodist Missions 1824-1924* (Toronto: The Missionary Society of the Methodist Church, 1925), 70f.

45. A Spectator of the Scenes, *Past and Present or a Description of Persons and Events Connected With Canadian Methodism For the Last Forty Years* (Toronto: Alfred Dredge, 1860), 49.

Chapter VI Inching Towards Ordination

1. Jameson, *Winter Studies*, Vol. 2, 153.

2. *Christian Advocate*, 21 March 1834, p.119, c.1; 11 April 1834, p.129, c.2.

3. James Porter, *A Compendium of Methodism* (New York: Carlton and Porter, 1851), 487ff.

4. Barbara Brown Zikmund, "The Struggle For the Right to Preach," in R.R. Ruether and R.S. Keller, *Women and Religion in America: Volume I The Nineteenth Century A Documentary History* (San Francisco: Harper and Row, 1981), 208.

5. Zechariah Taft, *Biographical Sketches*, 205ff. Dorothy Ripley, *The Bank of Faith and Works United*, 2d ed. (Whitby: G. Clark, 1822), passim. John T.

Wilkinson, "Dorothy Ripley" in Nolan B. Harmon, *Encyclopedia of World Methodism* (Nashville: United Methodist Pub. House, 1974). *Christian Advocate*, 10 Feb. 1832, p.95, c.4f.

6. Lorenzo Dow, *The Dealings of God*, 150, 189. Ripley, *The Bank of Faith*, 253, 279, 303. Sweet, *The Minister's Wife*, 45.

7. Taft, *Biographical Sketches*, 205ff. Ripley, *The Bank of Faith*, passim, esp. 180. Wilkinson, "Dorothy Ripley" in Harmon. Elaine Magolis, *Conduct Becoming To a Woman* (n.p.: The United Methodist Church, 1977), 108; and Leonard Sweet, *The Minister's Wife*, 129f.: Another woman, Harriet Livermore, preached in the United States Congress in 1824, 1832, 1838 and 1843, and in the Hall of Representatives in 1827. Livermore belonged successively to the Congregationalists, Quakers, Free-Will Baptists, and Methodists.

8. Whitney R. Cross, *The Burned-Over District* (Ithaca, New York: Cornell University Press, 1950), 37f., 263. Nancy A. Hardesty, *Great Women of Faith* (Nashville: Abingdon, 1982), 68f. *Free Baptist Cyclopedia*, 668f. Sweet, *The Minister's Wife*, 127.

9. Cross, *The Burned-Over District*, 37f., 177. George Coles, *Heroines of Methodism or Pen and Ink Sketches of the Mothers and Daughters of the Church* (New York: Carlton and Porter, 1857), 181. M.T. Blauvelt, "Women and Revivalism," in Ruether, *Women and Religion*, Vol. 1, 1ff. Bangs, *The Methodist Episcopal Church*, Vol. 2, 31.

10. Sweet, *The Minister's Wife*, 103, 117ff.

11. Coles, *Heroines of Methodism*, preface, 94ff., 105ff., 194ff., 266ff., 288ff. It is particularly difficult to tell from Coles' accounts of Methodist women which are American and which are British. Many more of the women he mentions in leadership roles may have been American. Gabriel Disosway, *Our Excellent Women*, 45ff., 85ff., 145f., 261ff., 276f. John Wesley's letters to Mrs. Jane Barton 13 Nov.1778; to Elizabeth Bennis 18 Jan. 1774. C.H. Crookshank, *Memorable Women*, 20. Letter from Wesley to Sarah Crosby, 2 Dec. 1777, in George Smith, *History of Wesleyan Methodism*, 420f.

12. Coles, *Heroines of Methodism,* 13.

13. James B. Finley, *Sketches of Western Methodism* (Cincinnati: R.P. Thompson, 1854), 531ff.

14. Disosway, *Our Excellent Women*, iv. Coles, *Heroines of Methodism*, 14. 75.

15. George Brown, *Recollections of Itinerant Life: Including Early Reminiscences* (Cincinnati: R.W. Carroll & Co., 1868), 183ff. William T. Noll, "Women as Clergy and Laity in the 19th Century Methodist Protestant Church," in *Methodist History* 15 (1977), 110. Sweet, *The Minister's Wife*, 142.

16. Sweet, *The Minister's Wife*, 128, 139ff. According to George Rawlyk, Queen's University, Nancy Towle also preached in Nova Scotia and New Brunswick from 1827 to 1829.

17. F.A. Norwood, "Expanding Horizons" in Richard L. Greaves ed., *Triumph Over Silence: Women in Protestant History* (Westport, Conn.: Greenwood Press, 1985), 166. Abel Stevens, *Life and Times of Nathan Bangs*, 350ff.

Hardesty, *Great Women*, 87ff.

18. *Christian Guardian*, 21 Nov. 1829, p.3, c.2. R. Pierce Beaver, *American Protestant Women in World Mission* (Grand Rapids, Mich.: Wm. B. Eerdmans Pub. Co., 1986), 75ff., 60: In 1820, the United Foreign Mission Society sent six single women to the Osages west of the Mississippi. Disosway, *Our Excellent Women*, 241, 155. Abel Stevens, *The Women*, 275; Sarah Hale, *Woman's Record; or Sketches of all Distinguished Women from The Creation to A.D. 1868* (New York: Harper and Brothers, 1874), 917.

19. Sweet, *The Minister's Wife*, 140ff.

20. Janet S. Everhart, "Maggie Newton Van Cott: The Methodist Episcopal Church Considers the Question of Women Clergy," in R.S. Keller, L.L. Queen and H.F. Thomas, *Women in New Worlds*, Vol. 2, 303ff. Greaves, *Triumph*, 9. W.T. Noll, "Women and Clergy," 110ff. W.G. McLoughlin, *Modern Revivalism* (New York: The Ronald Press, 1959), 158. Sweet, *The Minister's Wife*, 117, 226.

21. *Primitive Methodist Magazine* 1829, p.322f., letter from William Clowes, 19 June 1829, p.381ff., letter from Ruth Watkins, 10 Aug. 1829, p.279ff., Ruth Watkins Journal, Oct. 1830-Feb. 1831; 1831, pp.184ff., Journal of Ann Wearing, 1830.

22. According to Acornley, *A History*, 19, the books were confiscated, but this is contradicted by Knowles' letter. Letter from Samson, 19 Jan. 1836, Philadelphia, to Mr. John Flesher; letter from Ruth Watkins to William Clowes and John Flesher, 35 March 1835 from New York City, John Rylands University Library of Manchester. *Primitive Methodist Magazine* 1829, p.378f., letter from Knowles, New York, 15 Aug. 1829; p.322f. letter from William Clowes to James Bourne, Liverpool, 19 June 1829.

23. Ruth Watkins, letter to William Clowes; Samson, 6 Nov. 1835 from Philadelphia, John Rylands University Library of Manchester.

24. Acornley, *A History*, 59. *Primitive Methodist Magazine*, June 1831, p.207, Ann Wearing's Journal, 5 Aug. 1830; 1829, p.384, Ruth Watkins Journal, 10 Aug.1829.

25. *Primitive Methodist Magazine* 1831, p.279ff., Ruth Watkins Journal, Oct. 1830 to Feb. 1831.

26. *Primitive Methodist Magazine* 1831, p.184ff., p.206ff., Ann Wearing's Journal, Mar. to May and July to Dec.1830; p.95f., letter of Wm. Summersides from Philadelphia 10 Nov. 1830.

27. Letter from Ruth Watkins, John Rylands University Library of Manchester. Acornley, *A History*, 22. Hopper, *Old-Time Primitive Methodism*, 22. Letter from Wm. Summersides, Toronto to Hull Circuit Committee, 1 July 1835, mentions that Sister Watkins was a local preacher at Newark, but the alienation in her 1835 letter makes this unlikely.

28. *Primitive Methodist Magazine* 1831, p.95f., letter of Wm. Summersides, Philadelphia, 10 Nov. 1830. Acornley, *A History*, 24f., 30, 101, 262, 361.

29. Broadsheet, John Rylands University Library of Manchester. *Primitive Meth-*

odist Magazine 1829, p.378ff., letter from Wm. Knowles, New York, 15 Aug. 1829; 1831, Knowles' 1831 Journal; 1832, Knowles' 1830 Journal.

30. *Primitive Methodist Magazine* 1829, p.378ff., letter from Wm. Knowles, New York, 15 Aug. 1829; 1831, p.168ff., Knowles' Journal, 14 Dec. 1830; 1832, p.135ff., Knowles' 1831 Journal.

31. Acornley, *A History*, 40ff.

32. Acornley, *A History*, 58f.

33. Acornley, *A History*, 53, 120, 151f., 198, 207, 255, 329, 351, 356, 363. There is both a Catherine Watson and a Caroline Watson, but it appears to be the same person.

34. Acornley, *A History*, 278, 284. Letters from Ruth Watkins, March 1835, and William Samson, 3 Nov. 1835, John Rylands University Library of Manchester.

35. George Brown, *The Lady Preacher or the Life and Labors of Mrs. Hannah Reeves* (Philadelphia: Daughaday and Becker, 1870), passim. Reeves had three children, but all three died in early childhood.

36. Noll, "Women and Clergy," 110ff. Anna Howard Shaw had been licensed to preach in the Methodist Episcopal church in 1872. In 1880, however, women's licences were withdrawn in that denomination.

37. Sweet, *The Minister's Wife*, 136ff. Jualynne Dodson, "Nineteenth Century A.M.E. Preaching Women," in Thomas and Skinner, *Women in New Worlds*, 279.

38. Hardesty, *Women Called*, 96f. Norwood, "Expanding Horizons," in Greaves, *Triumph*, 167.

39. Hardesty, *Women Called*, 98. Norwood, "Expanding Horizons," in Greaves, *Triumph*, 167.

Chapter VII The Legend of Barbara Heck

1. Eula C. Lapp, *To Their Heirs Forever* (Belleville: Mika Pub. Co., 1977), passim esp. 301. *Christian Guardian*, 26 Dec. 1866, p.206, c.7.

2. *Methodist Magazine*, October 1823, pp.384ff., 427ff., 461ff.

3. Francis Asbury, *The Journals and Letters of Francis Asbury*, Vol. 2, ed. E.T. Clark (Nashville: Abingdon, 1958), 678. *Christian Guardian*, 15 July 1846, p.154, c.5 - p.155, c.1. *Methodist Magazine* 1825, 247.

4. *Christian Guardian*, 25 May 1859, p.1, c.2ff., p.81, c.1, p.82, c.1. Bangs, *The Methodist Episcopal*, Vol. 1, 546ff.; William Smith, *A Consecutive History of the Rise, Progress and Present State of Wesleyan Methodism* (Dublin: T.W. Doolittle, 1830), 351; James Dixon, *Methodism in America* (London: James Dixon, 1849), 158f.

5. *Christian Guardian*, 25 May 1859, p.1, c.1-7, p.81, c.1, p.82, c.1; 27 July 1859, p. 118, c.4f.; 10 Aug. 1859, p.126, c.3; 2 Apr. 1862, p.53, c.2f.; 30 Dec. 1863, p.2, c.6; 11 Apr. 1866, p.58, c.7; 25 Apr. 1866, p.67, c.2; 9 May 1866, p.74, c.7.

6. *Christian Guardian*, 30 Oct. 1839, p.2, c.225; May 1859, p.1, c.1-7, p.81, c.1, p.82, c.1. Abel Stevens, *The Women*, 175ff.

7. *Christian Advocate*, 7 Nov. 1866, p.1, c.6. Wm. Crook, *Ireland and the Centenary of American Methodism* (London: Hamilton, Adams & Co., 1866), 94.

8. Stevens, *The Women*, 175ff. W.H. Withrow, *Makers of Methodism* (Toronto: Wm. Briggs, 1898), 179f. W.H. Withrow, *Barbara Heck, A Tale of Early Methodism* (Toronto: Wm. Briggs, n.d.), passim. Mrs. J.R. Hill, "Early Canadian Heroines," in *Women's Canadian Historical Society of Ottawa* 10 (1928), passim. *Prescott Journal*, 16 Aug. 1934, p.1,4.

9. Sweet, *The Minister's Wife*, 30.

10. Ann Douglas, *The Feminization of American Culture* (New York: Alfred A. Knopf, 1977), 6. *Methodist Magazine* 1875, p.26f.

11. Egerton Ryerson, *The Story*, 412. Egerton Ryerson, *Canadian Methodism: Its Epochs and Characteristics* (Toronto: William Briggs, 1882), 35.

12. Nathan Bangs, *The Methodist Episcopal*, Vol. 1, 300ff.

13. Finley, *Sketches*, 531ff.

14. George Brown, *The Lady*, 63. Sweet, *The Minister's Wife*, 177.

15. Bangs, *History of the Methodist Episcopal*, Vol. 2, 319. James Rogers, *The Experience and Spiritual Letters of Mrs. Hester Ann Rogers: With a Sermon, Preached on the Occasion of Her Death by the Rev. Thomas Coke* (London: Methodist Book Room, n.d.), 197f., 210. Disosway, *Our Excellent Women*, 85ff. Stevens, *The Women*, 98ff. Robert F. Wearmouth, *Methodism*, 228. Townsend, *A New History*, 322.

16. *Christian Guardian*, 11 May 1887, p.299, c.3. Stephenson, *One Hundred Years*, 71. A Spectator, *Past and Present*, 49.

Chapter VIII The Devolution

1. Douglas, *The Feminization*, 5. Alison Prentice et al., *Canadian Women A History* (Toronto: Harcourt Brace Jovanovitch, 1988), 92, 99. Lerner, *The Majority*, 16ff.

2. Lerner, *The Majority*, 18ff.

3. Sanderson, *The First Century*, Vol. 2, 102, 104, 113. Playter, *The History*, 378f.

4. Jameson, *Winter Studies*, Vol. 2, 337. John Webster Grant, *A Profusion of Spires: Religion in Nineteenth Century Ontario* (Toronto: University of Toronto Press, 1988), 168.

5. Playter, *The History*, 37. *Christian Guardian*, 4 Dec. 1830, p.10, c.4. Ryerson, *The Story*, 214.

6. Troeltsch, *The Social Teaching*, 330ff. Grant, *Profusion*, Chapter 4 passim.

7. Fiorenza, *In Memory*, 60, 85. Lerner, *The Majority*, 149. A Spectator of the Scenes, *Past and Present*, 49.

8. *Cobourg Reformer*, 23 Oct. 1834, p.28. Prentice, *Canadian Women*, 174ff. Nancy Hardesty, *Women Called To Witness* (Nashville: Abingdon, 1982), 18. Sissons, *Egerton Ryerson*, Vol. 2, 252.

9. Mary McCoy Bradley, *A Narrative of the Life and Christian Experience of Mrs. Mary Bradley of Saint John, New Brunswick* (Boston: Strong and Brodhead, 1849), passim esp. 150, 163.

10. Porter, *A Compendium*, 487ff.

11. Porter, *A Compendium*, 487ff. John R. Rice, *Bobbed Hair, Bossy Wives and Women Preachers* (Wheaton, Illinois: Sword of the Lord Publishers, 1941). Geoffrey Chaucer, "The Canterbury Tales" III in *The Poetical Works of Chaucer*, ed. F.N. Robinson (Boston: Houghton Mifflin Co., 1933), 165. *Christian Guardian*, 12 Dec. 1829, p.28, Ladies' Department; 3 May 1837, p.1, c.3. Taylor, *The Apostles*, 59. Sweet, *The Minister's Wife*, 140.

12. Smith-Rosenberg, *Disorderly Conduct*, Ch.3 and "Women and Religious Revivals," passim.

13. *Plain-Speaker*, 14 Aug. 1838, p.40, "Women." Anne Langton, *A Gentlewoman in Upper Canada, The Journals of Anne Langton*, ed. H.H. Langton (Toronto: Clarke, Irwin and Co. Ltd., 1950), 99.

14. John S. Moir, *The Church in The British Era*, Vol. 2 of *A History of the Christian Church in Canada*, gen. ed., John Webster Grant (Toronto: McGraw-Hill Ryerson Ltd., 1972), 88f.

15. Gerald M. Craig, *Upper Canada, The Formative Years 1784-1841* (Toronto: McClelland and Stewart, 1963), 165f. J.M. Bliss, ed. *Canadian History in Documents 1763-1966* (Toronto: The Ryerson Press, 1966), 34f.

16. *The Patriot*, 19 Feb. 1839 as quoted in Craig, *Upper Canada*, n.24, 296, 114, 166.

17. Howison, *Sketches*, 135, 296, 309. Cattermole, *Emigration*, 185. Jameson, *Winter Studies*, Vol. 2, 218. Traill, *The Backwoods*, 99.

18. Landon, "The Common Man," in Armstrong, *Aspects*, 160.

19. *Patriot*, 6 Sept. 1833: letter from York signed "A British Methodist," as quoted in Edith Firth, *The Town of York 1815-1834* (Toronto: University of Toronto Press, 1966), 180.

20. Craig, *Upper Canada*, 172ff. Errington, *The Lion*, 187. Sissons, *Egerton Ryerson*, Vol. 1, 20ff., 244ff. Playter, *The History*, 272f.

21. *Colonial Advocate*, 11 May 1826, p.18ff. The course consisted of "Divinity, Logic, Ecclesiastical History, Grammar, Geography" as essential subjects, and "Natural Philosophy, Ancient and Modern History, Poetry, Biography, and Chronology" as optional, with five hours each morning to be spent in reading. John S. Moir, *The Church*, 116ff. Sissons, *Egerton Ryerson*, Vol. 1, 20ff. Playter, *The History*, 260.

22. Craig, *Upper Canada*, 172ff. Sissons, *Egerton Ryerson*, Vol. 1, 20ff. Moir, *The Church*, 113 ff.

23. Ryerson, *Canadian Methodism*, 86, 304. Playter, *The History*, 285, 336ff. Sissons, *Egerton Ryerson* Vol. 1, 54ff. *Colonial Advocate*, 2 Mar. 1826, p.1,

c.3. Grant, *Moon*, 77, 83: The Methodists themselves were not entirely innocent. Some of their actions were designed to gain Indian converts from Church of England Missions.

24. Craig, *Upper Canada*, 56, 175. Sissons, *Egerton Ryerson*, Vol. 1, 77ff. Letter from Lawson et al. from York to Hugh Bourne, 1 Oct. 1830, United Church Archives.

25. Sissons, *Egerton Ryerson* Vol. 1, 138f: Letter dated Aug. 6, 1831.

26. Sissons, *Egerton Ryerson* Vol. 1, 43, 154, 190. Letter from John to Egerton 15 Nov. 1833: 211; Vol 2, 60. O. E. Tiffany, *The Canadian Rebellion of 1837-38* (Buffalo, New York: Buffalo Historical Society, 1905) reprinted (Toronto: Coles Pub. Co.), 18, and Craig, *Upper Canada*, 247: Rolph was considered to be devious, clever, subtle-minded, sagacious and accused of playing a double role, working both for the government and for the reformers.

27. P. E. Shaw, *The Catholic Apostolic Church Called Irvingite* (New York: King's Crown Press, 1946), 117ff. Sissons, *Egerton Ryerson*, Vol. 1, 36, 271. Letter of Mary Ryerson to James Lewis, 8 Dec. 1835. Letter from Wm. Summersides, John Rylands University Library of Manchester.

28. Sissons, *Egerton Ryerson*, Vol. 1, 39, 168, 170, 260. Shaw, *The Catholic Apostolic Church*, 119. Clark, *Church and Sect*, 209: By the 1830s, fences were used to separate men and women at camp-meetings. Sanderson, *The First Century*, Vol. 1, 324.

29. William Lyon MacKenzie, "Seventh Report on Grievances, 1835" in Bliss, *Canadian History*, 38. Letter from Summersides, 20 March 1833, from York to Hull Circuit, United Church Archives.

30. Sissons, *Egerton Ryerson*, Vol. 1, 58, 171, 155, 260, 381, 535.

31. Ryerson, *The Story*, 99. Sissons, *Egerton Ryerson*, Vol. 1, 575; Vol. 2, 23, 147, 161, 343. Goldwyn French, *Parsons and Politics* (Toronto: The Ryerson Press, 1962), 152. Ryerson, *Canadian Methodism*, 138.

32. Sissons, *Egerton Ryerson*, Vol. 1, 3ff., 15; Vol. 2, 81, 85. Ryerson, *The Story*, 44.

33. Sissons, *Egerton Ryerson*, Vol. 1, 404; Vol. 2, 123, 126, 287ff., 371. Although legislated, compulsory attendance at class meetings was not being enforced.

BIBLIOGRAPHY

Primary Source Material

The Works of John Wesley.

Encyclopedias and Dictionaries

The Canadian Biographical Dictionary.

The Canadian Men and Women of the Time, ed. H.J. Morgan.

Cyclopaedia of Methodism, ed. Matthew Simpson.

Cyclopedia of Methodism in Canada 2 Vols., ed. G.H. Cornish.

Dictionary of Canadian Biography.

The Encyclopedia of World Methodism 2 Vols., gen. ed. Nolan B. Harmon.

Free Baptist Cyclopaedia.

Newspapers and Periodicals

Bible Christian Magazine.

Canada Protestant Herald.

Canada Temperance Advocate.

Canadian Emigrant and Western District Advertiser.

Canadian Methodist Magazine.

Canadian Statesman.

Christian Advocate.

Christian Guardian.

Christian Journal. (Primitive Methodist)

Cobourg Star and Newcastle Commercial and General Advertiser.

Colonial Advocate.

Evangelist. (Primitive Methodist)

Methodist Magazine.

Morning Herald. (New York)

New Outlook.

Northwestern Christian Advocate.

Observer. (Bible Christian)

Orillia Times.

Plain-Speaker.

Prescott Journal.

Primitive Methodist Magazine.

Protestant Magazine.

Reformer.

Templar.

Weekly Herald. (New York)

Wesleyan Protestant Magazine.

West Durham News.

Winnipeg Tribune.

Minutes, Annual Reports

Bible Christian Conference, Canada, *Minutes.*

Bible Christian Conference, England, *Minutes.*

Bible Christian Conference, *Missionary Society Reports.*

Canada Sunday School Union, *Annual Reports.*

Canada Conference Missionary Society of the Methodist Episcopal Church, *Reports.*

Canada Primitive Methodist Missions, Toronto District, *Treasurer's Report.*

Elders' Meetings, Bible Christian Church, Cobourg, 1849-1881, *Minutes.*

Erskine Sabbath School Society (Montreal), *Minutes.*

Methodist Church of Canada, Montreal Conference, *Minutes.*

Methodist Conference, London, *Minutes.*

Methodist Episcopal Church in Canada, Ontario Conference, *Minutes.*

Methodist Episcopal Church in Canada, Canada Conference, *Minutes.*

Missionary Society of the Wesleyan Church in Canada, *Annual Reports.*

Montreal Auxiliary Bible Society, *Annual Report.*

Montreal Temperance *Pledge Book.*

Primitive Methodist Church, Canada, *Minutes.*

Primitive Methodist Connexion, England, *Minutes*.

Wesleyan Methodist Church in Canada Annual Conference, *Minutes*.

Doctrines and Disciplines

The Doctrines and Discipline of the British Primitive Methodist Connexion [Canada]. York: W.J.Coates, 1833.

The Doctrines and Discipline of the Wesleyan Methodist Church in Canada. Toronto: Matthew Lang, 1836.

Autobiographies, Biographies, Diaries, Journals

Asbury, Francis. *The Journals and Letters of Francis Asbury*, ed. E.T. Clark. Nashville: Abingdon, 1958.

Barnes, Eliza. *Diary* Excerpts, 1833. United Church Archives.

Barrass, E. Vol. I, *A Gallery of Deceased Ministers*. London: T. Holliday, 1853.

Beaven, James. *Recreations of a Long Vacation; or a Visit to Indian Missions in Upper Canada*. London: James Burns, 1846.

Bradley, Mary McCoy. *A Narrative of the Life and Christian Experience of Mrs. Mary Bradley of St. John, New Brunswick*. Boston: Strong and Brodhead, 1849.

Brown, George. *The Lady Preacher or The Life and Labors of Mrs. Hannah Reeves*. Philadelphia: Daughaday and Becker, 1870.

_____. *Recollections of Itinerant Life: Including Early Reminiscences*. Cincinnati: R.W. Carroll & Co., 1868.

Burwash, Nathaniel. *Memorials of Edward and Lydia A. Jackson*, Toronto: Methodist Book Room, 1876.

Cattermole, William. *Emigration. The Advantages of Emigration to Canada.* London: Simpkin and Marshall, 1831. Reprinted Toronto: Coles Pub. Co., 1970.

Clarke, Wm. F. and R. L. Tucker. *A Mother In Israel; or Some Memorials of The Late Mrs. M. A. Lyle.* Toronto: W.C. Chewett & Co., 1862.

Coles, George. *Heroines of Methodism or Pen and Ink Sketches of the Mothers and Daughters of the Church.* New York: Carlton and Porter, 1857.

Cooke, Sarah A. *The Handmaiden of the Lord or Wayside Sketches.* Chicago: T.B. Arnold, Pub., 1896.

Crookshank, C.H. *Memorable Women of Irish Methodism in the Last Century.* London: Wesleyan Methodist Book Room, 1882.

Disosway, Gabriel P. *Our Excellent Women of the Methodist Church in England and America.* New York: J.C. Buttre, 1861.

Dow, Lorenzo. *The Dealings of God, Man, And The Devil; as Exemplified in the Life, Experience, and Travels of Lorenzo Dow,* 2 Vols. New York: Cornish, Lamport and Co., 1851.

Gordon, Annie R. "Whither Thou Goest - Ann Copp, A Devon Maid." United Church Archives.

Hale, Sarah. *Woman's Record; or Sketches of all Distinguished Women from the Creation to A.D. 1868.* New York: Harper and Brothers, 1874.

Harris, John. *The Life of the Rev. Francis Metherall and The History of the Bible Christian Church in Prince Edward Island.* London: Bible Christian Book Room, 1883.

Hill, Mrs. J. R. "Early Canadian Heroines." *Women's Canadian Historical Society of Ottawa* 10 (1928): 98-109.

Howison, John. *Sketches of Upper Canada.* Edinburgh: Oliver & Boyd, 1821. Reprinted Toronto: Coles Pub. Co., 1980.

Hume, Blanche. *Barbara Heck.* Toronto: The Ryerson Press, 1930.

Jacobs, P. *Journal of the Rev. Peter Jacobs - Indian Wesleyan Missionary.* New York: 1858.

Jameson, Anna. *Winter Studies and Summer Rambles in Canada,* 3 Vols. London: Saunders and Otley, 1838. Reprinted Toronto: Coles Pub. Co., 1970-72.

Jones, Peter. *Life and Journals of Kah-Ke-Wa-Quo-Na-By.* Toronto: Anson Green, 1860.

Langton, Anne. *A Gentlewoman In Upper Canada,* The Journals of Anne Langton, ed. H.H. Langton. Toronto: Clarke, Irwin and Co. Ltd., 1950.

Paddock, Z. *Memoir of Rev. B.G. Paddock.* New York: Nelson and Phillips, 1875.

Peters, Elizabeth and William Peters. *The Diaries of William and Elizabeth Peters Recounting the Voyage to the New World on the Good Brig Friends in 1830,* ed. Howard H. Finley. Berwyn, Illinois: Howard H. Finley, 1942.

Richmond, Legh. *The Annals of the Poor and The Dairyman's Daughter.* London: F. Warne and Co., n.d.

Ripley, Dorothy. *The Bank of Faith and Works United.* 2d ed. Whitby: G. Clark, 1822.

Roberts, Phoebe. "Phoebe Roberts' Diary of a Quaker Missionary Journey to Upper Canada," ed. Leslie R. Gray. *Ontario Historical Society* 42 (January 1950): 7-46.

Rogers, James. *The Experience and Spiritual Letters of Mrs. Hester Ann Rogers: With a Sermon, Preached on the Occasion of Her Death by the Rev. Thomas Coke.* London: Methodist Book Room, n.d.

Russell, Thomas. *Record of Events in Primitive Methodism.* London: William Lister, 1869.

Ryerson, Egerton. *The Story of My Life*. Toronto: William Briggs, 1883.

Sissons, C.B. *Egerton Ryerson - His Life and Letters*, 2 Vols. Toronto: Clarke and Irwin and Co. Ltd., 1937-47.

Stevens, Abel. *The Women of Methodism*. New York: Carlton and Lanahan, 1869.

Taft, Zechariah. *Biographical Sketches of the Lives and Public Ministry of Various Holy Women*. London: Mr. Kershaw, 1825.

Taylor, John. *The Apostles of Flyde Methodism*. London: T. Woolmer, 1885.

Traill, Catherine Parr. *The Canadian Settlers' Guide*. Toronto: The Old Countryman Office, 1855. Reprinted Toronto: McClelland and Stewart Ltd., 1969.

_____. *The Backwoods of Canada*. Toronto: McClelland and Stewart Ltd., 1966.

Waldron, Solomon. "A Sketch of the Life, Travels and Labors of Solomon Waldron, A Wesleyan Methodist Preacher." United Church Archives.

Withrow, W. H. *Makers of Methodism*. Toronto: Wm. Briggs, 1898.

_____. *Barbara Heck, A Tale of Early Methodism*. Toronto: Wm. Briggs, n.d.

Early Histories

Acornley, John A. *A History of the Primitive Methodist Church in the United States of America*. Fall River, Mass.: R.R. Acornley and Co., 1909.

Bangs, Nathan. *An Authentic History of the Missions Under the Care of The Missionary Society of The Methodist Episcopal Church*, 4 Vols. New York: J. Emory and B. Waugh, 1832.

_____. The *Methodist Episcopal Church*, 4 Vols. New York: Carlton and Phillips, 1856.

Bourne, Frederick William. *The Bible Christians, Their Origin and History*. n.p.: Bible Christian Book Room, 1905.

Bourne, Hugh. *History of the Primitive Methodists*. London: J.Bourne, 1823.

Cade, Robert. "Primitive Methodism in Canada." *Canadian Historical Society* (December 1906).

Canuck, a. *Pen Pictures of Early Pioneer Life in Upper Canada*. Toronto: William Briggs, 1905.

Carroll, John. *Case and His Cotemporaries or the Canadian Itinerants Memorial*, 5 Vols. Toronto: Samuel Rose, 1867-77.

_____. *Past and Present*. Toronto: 1860.

Centennial of Canadian Methodism. Toronto: Wm. Briggs, 1891.

Crook, William. *Ireland and the Centenary of American Methodism*. London: Hamilton, Adams and Co., 1866.

Crookshank, C.H. *History of Methodism in Ireland*, 3 Vols. Belfast: R.S. Allen, 1885-86.

Cummings, A.W. *The Early Schools of Methodism*. New York: 1886.

Dixon, James. *Methodism in America*. London: James Dixon, 1849.

Fairbairn, Jas B. *History and Reminiscences of Bowmanville*, Bowmanville: Bowmanville Newsprint, 1906.

Finley, James B. *Sketches of Western Methodism*. Cincinnati: R.P. Thompson, 1854.

Hopper, Jane Agar. *Primitive Methodism in Canada 1829-1884*. Toronto: William Briggs, 1904.

Johnson, D.W. *History of Methodism in Eastern British America.* n.p.: Sackville Tribune Printing, [1925].

Kendall, H.B. *History of the Primitive Methodist Connexion.* London: Joseph Toulson, [ca. 1888].

Luke, William. *The Bible Christians, Their Origin, Constitution, Doctrine and History.* London: Bible Christian Book Room, 1878.

Montgomery, Helen Barrett. *An Outline Study of Fifty Years of Woman's Work in Foreign Missions.* New York: The MacMillan Co., 1911.

_____. *Western Women in Eastern Lands.* New York: The MacMillan Co., 1911.

Pearson, W.H. *Recollections and Records of Toronto of Old.* Toronto: Wm. Briggs, 1914.

Petty, John. *The History of the Primitive Methodist Connexion From Its Origin to the Conference of 1860, The First Jubilee Year of the Connexion.* London: John Dickenson, 1880.

Playter, George F. *The History of Methodism in Canada.* Toronto: Anson Green, 1862.

Porter, James. *A Compendium of Methodism.* New York: Carlton and Porter, 1851.

Ryerson, Egerton. *Canadian Methodism: Its Epochs and Characteristics.* Toronto: William Briggs, 1882.

Sanderson, J.E. *The First Century of Methodism in Canada,* 2 Vols. Toronto: William Briggs, 1909-10.

Schoolcraft, Henry R. *The Indian in His Wigwam or Characteristics of the Red Race of America.* New York: Dewitt and Davenport, 1848.

Slight, Benjamin. *Indian Researches; or Facts Concerning the North American Indians.* Montreal: J.E.L. Miller, 1844.

Smith, George. *History of Wesleyan Methodism.* 4 Vols. London: Longmans, Brown, Green, Longman and Roberts, 1862.

Smith, William. *A Consecutive History of the Rise, Progress and Present State of Wesleyan Methodism.* Dublin: T.W. Doolittle, 1830.

_____. *History of Methodism in Ireland.* n.p.: ca.1828.

Spectator of the Scenes, a. *Past and Present or a Description of Persons and Events Connected With Canadian Methodism For the Last Forty Years.* Toronto: Alfred Dredge, 1860.

Stamp, W.W. *The Orphan-House of Wesley.* London: John Mason, 1863.

Stephenson, Mrs. Frederick C. *One Hundred Years of Canadian Methodist Missions 1824-1924.* Toronto: The Missionary Society of the Methodist Church, 1925.

Stevens, Abel. *History of Methodism,* 4 Vols. New York: Carlton and Porter, 1867.

_____. The *History of the Religious Movement in the Eighteenth Century Called Methodism,* 3 Vols. London: Wesleyan Conference Office, 1878.

_____. *Life and Times of Nathan Bangs.* New York: Carlton and Porter, 1863.

Stevenson, George J. *City Road Chapel London and its Associations.* London: George J. Stevenson, 1872.

Telford, John. *Two West-End Chapels or Sketches of London Methodism From Wesley's Day 1740-1886.* London: Wesleyan Methodist Book Room, 1886.

Tiffany, Orrin Edward. *The Canadian Rebellion of 1837-38.* Buffalo, New York: Buffalo Historical Society, 1905. Reprinted Toronto: Coles Pub. Co. Ltd, 1980.

253

Townsend, W.J., H.B. Workman and George Eayrs, eds. *A New History of Methodism*, 2 Vols. n.p.: Hodder and Stoughton, 1909.

Wakeley, J.B. *Lost Chapters Recovered From the Early History of American Methodism*. New York: Carlton and Porter, 1858.

Ward, Valentine. *A Miniature of Methodism; or a Brief Account of the History, Doctrines, Discipline and Character of the Methodists*. London: John Mason, 1834.

Webster, Thomas. *History of the Methodist Episcopal Church in Canada*. Hamilton: Canada Christian Advocate Office, 1870.

Youmans, Letitia Creighton. *Campaign Echoes*. Toronto: Wm. Briggs, 1893.

Youngs, James. *History of the Rise and Progress of Methodism in England and America*. New Haven, Connecticut: H. Daggett and Co., 1830.

Church Histories

Barker, Kenneth. *From Indian Mission to City Church*. Orillia: Dyment-Stubley, 1980.

Early, Beth. *Criteria For Preservation: Salem United Church*. Caledon Heritage Committee, 1985.

Caledon East United Church. *Caledon East United Church*.

McTavish, D. *Religious Romance and Reminiscences: An Interesting History of James Street Church, Exeter*. n.p.: n.d. (Ontario Archives).

Salem United Church. *125th Anniversary*.

St. Paul's United Church, Orillia. *125 Years After*.

Collections of Documents

Bliss, J.M., ed. *Canadian History in Documents, 1763-1966.* Toronto: The Ryerson Press, 1966.

Cameron, Richard M., ed. *The Rise of Methodism: A Source Book.* New York: Philosophical Library, 1954.

Firth, Edith G. *The Town of York, 1815-1834.* Toronto: University of Toronto Press, 1966.

Moir, John S., ed. *Church and State in Canada 1627-1867,* Basic Documents. Toronto: McClelland and Stewart, 1967.

Miscellaneous

Antliffe, Wm. *Woman: Her Position and Mission, A Lecture.* London: T. King, 1856.

Bible Christian Preachers' Plans. United Church Archives.

Biographical and Church Files. United Church Archives.

Chadwick, Edward Marion. *Ontarian Families.* Lambertville, New Jersey: Hunterdon House, 1970.

Correspondence of the Primitive Methodist Mission in Philadelphia and Upper Canada 1830-37. The John H. Rylands University Library of Manchester, England.

Correspondence of the Primitive Methodist Mission in Upper Canada 1830-1837. United Church Archives.

Documents relating to the Hecks, Emburys and Other Clans. United Church Archives.

"The Duties Etc. of Wives." 1816. United Church Archives.

Egerton Ryerson Papers. United Church Archives.

Graham, Dorothy E. *Chosen By God - A List of the Female Travelling Preachers of Early Primitive Methodism.* Cheshire, England: Wesley Historical Society Publishing Office, 1989.

Mackenzie-Lindsey clippings. Ontario Archives.

McKenzie, Donald A. *Death Notices From The Christian Guardian 1836-1850.* Lambertville, New Jersey: Hunterdon House, 1982.

_____. *Death Notices From The Christian Guardian 1851-1860.* Lambertville, New Jersey: Hunterdon House, 1984.

_____. *More Notices From Methodist Papers 1830-1857.* Lambertville, New Jersey: Hunterdon House, 1986.

Perkins Bull Papers. Ontario Archives.

Perkins Bull Papers. United Church Archives.

Primitive Methodist Preachers' Plans. The John H. Rylands University Library of Manchester, England.

Primitive Methodist Preachers' Plans. United Church Archives.

Reid, William D. *Death Notices of Ontario.* Lambertville, New Jersey: Hunterdon House, 1980.

_____. *Marriage Notices of Ontario.* Lambertville, New Jersey: Hunterdon House, 1980.

Tombstone inscriptions. Bethesda Cemetery, Bowmanville.

Trick-Henwood Papers. Private Collection of Howard Harris.

Wilson, Thomas B. *Marriage Bonds of Ontario 1803-1834.* Lambertville, New Jersey: Hunterdon House, 1985.

_____. *Ontario Marriage Notices.* Lambertville, New Jersey: Hunterdon House, 1982.

Woodill-Wilson Papers. Private collection of Betty Ward.

Secondary Source Material

Armstrong, F.H., H.A. Stevenson, and J.D. Wilson. *Aspects of Nineteenth-Century Ontario*. Toronto: University of Toronto Press, 1974.

Beaver, R. Pierce. *American Protestant Women in World Mission*. Grand Rapids, Michigan: Wm. B. Eerdmans Pub. Co., 1986.

Brown, Earl Kent. "Women in Church History: Stereotypes, Archetypes and Operational Modalities." *Methodist History* 18 (January 1980): 109-32.

Brown, George W. "The Early Methodist Church and the Canadian Point of View." *The Canadian Historical Association Proceedings* (1938): 79-96.

Burnside, A. "The Bible Christians in Canada 1832-1884." D.Th. diss., Toronto Graduate School of Theological Studies. 1969.

Brunger, Ronald A. "The Ladies Aid Society in Michigan Methodism." *Methodist History* 5 (Jan. 1967): 31-48.

Chicago, Judy. *The Dinner Party, A Symbol of Our Heritage*. New York: Anchor Books, 1979.

Church, L.F. *The Early Methodist People*. London: Epworth Press, 1948.

_____. *More About the Early Methodist People*. London: Epworth Press, 1949.

Clark, S.D. *Church and Sect in Canada*. Toronto: University of Toronto Press, 1949.

_____. *Movements of Political Protest in Canada* 1640-1840. Toronto: University of Toronto Press, 1959.

Craig, Gerald M. *Upper Canada, The Formative Years 1784-1841*. Toronto: McClelland and Stewart, 1963.

Cragg, Gerald R. *The Church and The Age of Reason 1648-1789*, The Pelican History of the Church, Vol. 4. Harmondsworth, England: Penguin Books, 1960.

Cross, Whitney R. *The Burned-Over District.* Ithaca, New York: Cornell University Press, 1950.

Dorland, A.G. *The Quakers in Canada: A History.* 2nd ed. Toronto: Ryerson Press, 1968.

Douglas, Ann. *The Feminization of American Culture.* New York: Alfred A. Knopf, 1977.

Elgee, Wm. H. *The Social Teachings of the Canadian Churches.* Toronto: The Ryerson Press, 1964.

Errington, Jane. *The Lion, the Eagle and Upper Canada, A Developing Colonial Ideology.* Kingston and Montreal: McGill-Queen's University Press, 1987.

Fiorenza, Elisabeth Schüssler. *In Memory of Her.* New York: The Crossroad Publishing Company, 1983.

Flint, Charles Wesley. *Charles Wesley and His Colleagues.* Washington, D.C.: Public Affairs Press, 1957.

Fowler, Marian. *The Embroidered Tent - Five Gentlewomen in Early Canada.* Toronto: House of Anansi Press Limited, 1982.

French, Goldwyn. *Parsons and Politics.* Toronto: The Ryerson Press, 1962.

Green, V.H.H. *John Wesley.* London: Thomas Nelson and Sons, 1964.

Grant, John Webster. *The Church in the Canadian Era.* Toronto: McGraw-Hill Ryerson Ltd., 1972.

_____. ed. *The Churches and the Canadian Experience.* Toronto: The Ryerson Press, 1963.

_____. *Moon of Wintertime*. Toronto: University of Toronto Press, 1984.

_____. *A Profusion of Spires: Religion in Nineteenth Century Ontario*. Toronto: University of Toronto Press, 1988.

Greaves, Richard L., ed. *Triumph Over Silence: Women in Protestant History*. Westport, Connecticut: Greenwood Press, 1985.

Guillet, Edwin C. *Cobourg 1798-1984*. Oshawa: Goodfellow Printing Co. Ltd., 1948.

_____. *Pioneer Days in Upper Canada*. Toronto: University of Toronto Press, 1933.

Hardesty, Nancy A. *Great Women of Faith*. Nashville: Abingdon, 1982.

_____. *Women Called to Witness*. Nashville: Abingdon, 1984.

Headon, C. "Women and Organized Religion in Mid and Late 19th Century Canada." *Journal of the Canadian Historical Society* 20 (1978): 3-18.

Hoover, John Douglas. "The Primitive Methodist Church in Canada 1829-1884." M.A. diss., University of Western Ontario. 1970.

Houston, Susan E. and Alison Prentice. *Schooling and Scholars in Nineteenth-Century Ontario*. Toronto: University of Toronto Press, 1988.

James, Janet Wilson, ed. *Women in American Religion*. Philadelphia: University of Pennsylvania Press, 1976.

Keller, R.S., L.L. Queen, and H.F. Thomas. *Women in New Worlds*. 2 Vols. Nashville: Abingdon, 1981-82.

Kent, John. *Jabez Bunting, The Last Wesleyan*. London: The Epworth Press, 1955.

Lapp, Eula C. *To Their Heirs Forever*. Belleville: Mika Publishing Co., 1977.

Lelliott, Cynthia. "Pre-1930 Cobourg Schools." *Cobourg and District Historical Society Review* 1980-1982: 33-40.

Lerner, Gerda. *The Majority Finds Its Past.* Oxford: Oxford University Press, 1979.

Magolis, Elaine. *Conduct Becoming To a Woman.* n.p.: The United Methodist Church, 1977.

Mathews, H.F. *Methodism and the Education of the People 1791-1851.* London: The Epworth Press, 1949.

McLoughlin, William G. *Modern Revivalism.* New York: The Ronald Press Company, 1959.

Miller, Perry. *Nature's Nation.* Cambridge, Mass.: Harvard University Press, 1967.

Mitchell, Norma Taylor. "From Social to Radical Feminism: A Survey of Emerging Diversity in Methodist Women's Organizations, 1867-1974." *Methodist History* 13 (April 1975): 21-44.

Moir, John S. *Church and State in Canada West.* Toronto: University of Toronto Press, 1959.

_____. *The Church in The British Era,* Vol. 2 of A History of the Christian Church in Canada, gen. ed. John Webster Grant. Toronto: McGraw-Hill Ryerson Ltd, 1972.

_____. "Relations Between Church and State in Canada West 1841-1867," chap. in *Religion in Canadian Society,* eds. Stewart Crysdale and Les Wheatcroft. Toronto: The Macmillan Co. of Canada, 1976.

_____. "Methodism and Higher Education." *Ontario History* 44 (1952): 109-28.

Muir, Elizabeth. "The Bark Schoolhouse: Methodist Episcopal Missionary Women in Upper Canada, 1827-1833," chap. in *Canadian Protestant and Catholic Missions, 1820s-1960s,* eds. John S. Moir and C.T. McIntire. New York: Peter Lang Pub. Inc., 1988.

_____. "Elizabeth Dart (Eynon)," in *Dictionary of Canadian Biography* 8, gen. ed. F.G. Halpenny. Toronto: University of Toronto Press, 1985.

_____. "Methodist Women Preachers: An Overview." *Canadian Methodist Historical Society Proceedings* (1987): 46-57.

_____. "Three Early Canadian Methodist Women." *Canadian Society of Church History Proceedings* (1984): 26-49.

_____. "Woman as Preacher: Early 19th Century Canadians." *Women: Images, Role-Models*, CRIAW Conference Proceedings (1984): 195-201.

Noll, William T. "Women and Clergy and Laity in the 19th Century Methodist Protestant Church." *Methodist History* 15 (1977): 107-21.

Norwood, Frederick A. "Report on Seminar: Women in Methodism." *Methodist History* 10 (October 1971): 56-7.

Petryshyn, J., ed. *Victorian Cobourg*. Belleville: Mika Pub. Co., 1976.

Prentice, Alison et al. *Canadian Women A History*. Toronto: Harcourt Brace Jovanovich, 1988.

_____. *The School Promoters*. 2d ed. Toronto: McClelland and Stewart, 1948.

Propst, Neil Brown. "Voice From the Frontier." *Methodist History* (January 1982): 51-9.

Reeve, Harold. *The History of the Township of Hope*. Cobourg: Cobourg Sentinel-Star, 1967.

Ruether, R.R. and R.S. Keller, gen. eds. *Women and Religion in America: Volume I The Nineteenth Century A Documentary History*. San Francisco: Harper and Row, 1981.

Shaw, P.E. *The Catholic Apostolic Church Called Irvingite*. New York: King's Crown Press, 1946.

Smith, Donald B. *Sacred Feathers*. Toronto: University of Toronto Press, 1987.

Smith-Rosenberg, Carroll. *Disorderly Conduct*. New York: A.A. Knopf, 1985.

Stanger, F.B. "The Reopening of John Wesley's City Road Chapel, A Call For Methodist Renewal." *Methodist History* (April 1978): 178-99.

Stewart, Gordon and George Rawlyk. *A People Highly Favoured of God - The Nova Scotia Yankees and the American Revolution*. Toronto: Macmillan, 1972.

Sweet, Leonard I. *The Evangelical Tradition in America*. Macon, Georgia: Mercer University Press, 1984.

_____. *The Minister's Wife: Her Role in Nineteenth-Century Evangelicalism*. Philadelphia: Temple University Press, 1983.

Tavender, George S. *From This Year Hence - A History of the Township of Toronto Gore, 1818-1967*. Brampton: Charters Pub. Co., 1967.

Thomas, Clara. *Ryerson of Upper Canada*. Toronto: The Ryerson Press, 1969.

Trofimenkoff, Susan Mann and Alison Prentice, eds. *The Neglected Majority*. Toronto: McLelland and Stewart, 1977.

Troeltsch, Ernst. *The Social Teaching of the Christian Churches*. 2 Vols. trans. Olive Wyon. London: George Allen & Unwin Ltd., 1949.

Valenze, Deborah M. *Prophetic Sons and Daughters: Female Preaching and Popular Religion in Industrial England*. Princeton: Princeton University Press, 1985.

Vidler, Alec R. *The Church in an Age of Revolution*, The Pelican History of the Church, Vol. 5. Harmondsworth, England: 1961.

Walsh, H.H. *The Christian Church in Canada*. Toronto: The Ryerson Press, 1956.

262

Wearmouth, Robert F. *Methodism and the Common People of the Eighteenth Century.* London: Epworth Press, 1945.

Werner, Julia Stewart. *The Primitive Methodist Connexion Its Background and Early History.* Madison, Wisconsin: University of Wisconsin Press, 1984.

White, Randall. *Ontario 1610-1985, A Political and Economic History.* Toronto: Dundurn Press, 1985.

Whiteley, Marilyn F. "Modest, Unaffected and Fully Consecrated - Lady Evangelists in Canadian Methodism, 1884-1900." *Canadian Methodist Historical Society Proceedings* (1987): 18-31.

Wilson, Douglas J. *The Church Grows in Canada.* Toronto: The Ryerson Press, 1966.

Bibliographies

Rowe, Kenneth Earl. *The Struggle For Lay and Clergy Rights in the Methodist Tradition, a Bibliography.* Madison, New Jersey: Drew University, 1975.

INDEX

THE CIRCLE
Brescia College
1285 Western Road
London, ON   N6G 1H2

Printed in Canada

910476